A Sociological Yearbook of Religion in Britain · 6

J. H. Turner
1975.

A Sociological Yearbook of Religion in Britain · 6

Edited by Michael Hill

SCM PRESS LTD

334 01580 4

First published 1973
by SCM Press Ltd
56 Bloomsbury Street London
© *SCM Press Ltd 1973*

Printed in Great Britain by
Northumberland Press Ltd, Gateshead

CONTENTS

THE CONTRIBUTORS

AUDREY CHAMBERLAIN   Research Student, University of Leeds

ROBERT W. COLES   Lecturer in Sociology, University of York

MARK COZIN   Graduate Student, University College, London

DOUGLAS J. DAVIES   Theological Student, St John's College, Durham

MICHAEL HILL   Lecturer in Sociology, London School of Economics and Political Science

RONALD IPHOFEN   Graduate Student, Department of Sociology, University of York

HUGH MCLEOD   Lecturer in the Department of History, University of Warwick

JOHN MOORE   Roman Catholic Priest and Postgraduate Student, London School of Economics and Political Science

ROBERT MOORE   Senior Lecturer in Sociology, King's College, Aberdeen

KENNETH J. PANTON   Lecturer in Geography, City of London Polytechnic

ROBERT TOWLER   Lecturer in Sociology, University of Leeds

ROY WALLIS   Lecturer in Sociology, University of Stirling

STEPHEN YEO   Lecturer in History, School of Social Sciences, University of Sussex

PREFACE

In this issue of the Yearbook there is, as in previous years, a broad selection of articles. One feature which characterizes this selection is the contemporary or historical focus of contributions, since there is a fairly clear balance between articles concerned with new religious movements or approaches to religion and those with a historical emphasis. Perhaps this historical aspect provides an interesting comment on the way in which the sociology of religion has developed in Britain, in contrast to both the United States and the rest of Europe. It ultimately concerns the way in which research is funded in these countries. In the States there would appear to be better facilities and finance for large-scale empirical research, typified by the studies of Lenski, Demerath and Glock and Stark, and so one finds that a historical study – such as that of Protestantism and capitalism – is remodelled as a search for 'the religious factor'. In Europe there has been a much more consistent policy on the part of ecclesiastical bodies for the development of socio-religious research institutes, and thus there have been a series of important contemporary studies which fall broadly within the tradition of *sociologie religieuse*. Interestingly, the only attempt by the Catholic hierarchy in Britain to establish something of this sort – the Newman Survey – very rapidly evolved into a private undertaking run by an enterprising and energetic individual. Also interesting is the fact that the only two recent large-scale empirical studies of religion in Britain were funded by commercial television companies. Thus in Britain, the sociology of religion has been characterized by a number of small-scale, in-depth contemporary studies and by a series of historical researches. History has often provided the British sociologist with his research laboratory, and in this sense the historical balance of the Yearbook is representative of the sociological study of religion as a whole in this country.

The first paper is an important and in many respects pioneering study of 'common religion', which its authors define as the set of super-empirical beliefs lying between church-orientated religion and the inclusive definition of religion proposed by sociologists such as Luckmann that need not refer to the supernatural at all. Research into this type of religion cannot adopt church-based criteria of religiosity, nor can it make the *a priori* assumption that such beliefs will be logically coherent and systematic. By means of a series of probe questions at the end of a questionnaire concerned with attitudes to high fertility, Towler and Chamberlain have opened up an entirely new area in the sociology of religion.

McLeod's paper analyses in great depth the regional variations of religious participation in the latter part of the nineteenth century. He shows that the crude distinction between rural and urban areas, as well as between middle and working class, is insufficient if we are to understand the place of religion in nineteenth-century England. This contribution, and the later one by Panton, represent a field of growing interest in this country, namely the social geography of religion.

The study by John Moore on the Catholic Pentecostal movement provides a valuable insight on a new and as yet fairly unpredictable upsurge within Catholicism. It gives an account of the history of the movement and suggests a number of sociological models which might be useful in understanding it. The following article, on Methodism as a religious order, also looks at the applicability of a sociological model for the analysis of another type of radical movement within a church type of institution, in this case early Methodism.

Cozin's article on the history and contemporary position of the Unified Family will probably be the first encounter for a number of readers with the Korean millennial movement described by Lofland in *Doomsday Cult* and now transplanted to suburban England. There is an interesting account of the 'charismatic education' of the group's new members which leads them to accept the authority of its founder, Mr Moon. Another kind of millennium and another kind of transplant is outlined by Davies in his study of Mormon eschatology. He shows that the initial teaching of the Latter Day Saints which encouraged emigration to Salt Lake City as the Zion to which the Lord would return was gradually changed so that Zion was defined as 'the pure in heart' and not as a geographical location. This made possible the strengthening of Mormon churches in countries such as Britain.

Scientology has often been seen as a rather esoteric cult with an amalgam of religious and quasi-scientific ideas. In recent years, however, its activities have reportedly become more exclusive and aggressive. This, as Wallis suggests in his paper, means that Scientology may be analysed in relation to its explicitly sectarian features.

One of the most interesting attempts to link religious and political beliefs and activity was the study made by Halévy of the extent to which the Methodist and Evangelical revivals can be seen as preventing a revolution in eigtheenth- and nineteenth-century England. Robert Moore adopts Halévy's hypothesis, shows that it was not intended to apply to the mass of the proletariat, and examines some of its implications in the Durham mining villages of the nineteenth century.

Panton's study of the social geography of religion in Alloa raises some interesting questions. Why is it, he argues, that 'peaks' of church adherence appear on the boundaries of status groups. Tentatively, he interprets this as a form of overconformity to the norms of the higher social group on the part of those who are socially mobile. Yeo is also interested in a contextual view of religious organization, and his paper examines the place of religion in the whole social framework of Reading in the late nineteenth century. He is particularly interested in the function of churches as 'clubs for the clubbable classes' and of the immensely important weight of religious bricks and mortar.

Finally, Bob Coles has provided another appendix to the list of publications and research in the sociology of religion in Britain. As in previous years, we would very much appreciate our readers' help in keeping this section as complete and as up-to-date as possible, and we also welcome general comments on editorial policy.

1 Common Religion

Robert Towler and Audrey Chamberlain

The importance for the sociology of religion of the beliefs held by the man in the street, as opposed to the man in the pew, is widely recognized. Despite this recognition, however, such phenomena as secularization, for example, continue to be assessed either by reference to how the churches are or are not flourishing as organizations, or else in terms of how frequently the man in the street says that he subscribes to beliefs which the churches once upon a time prescribed. Neither method of assessment is claimed as satisfactory, and so the absence of any preferable alternative suggests that the problem is methodological. Perhaps no alternative approach to the problem exists. Sociologists of religion, unwilling to grant such a pessimistic conclusion and yet unable to devise an adequate method, commonly turn to related philosophical or psychological considerations, or else opt for a different subdiscipline within sociology. At any rate the problem remains unsolved.

The beliefs held by the common man are, nonetheless, of special importance for the study of contemporary religion, and failing some attempt at their systematic investigation the sociology of religion is in danger of becoming a mere appendage to the propaganda of religionists or anti-religionists. Some writers indeed argue that this has already happened to an alarming degree.[1]

Theoretical Problems

Two theoretical assumptions frequently found in the sociology of religion stand in the way as obstacles to the study of common religion (the usefulness of the term 'common religion' will be argued below). First there is the assumption that the religiousness of a society and the religious commitment of individual actors must be assessed by reference to traditional canons of religiosity; in practice these almost invariably prove to be those laid down not just by church members, but by church theologians. The second assumption is that a set of beliefs, regardless of what they are, will hang together as a coherent whole: this too, it will be argued, is a legacy from the theologians.

That there are as many ways of being religious as there are societies is acknowledged by students of religion. The religiousness of the Welsh and the religiousness of the Andaman Islanders may be different but each is of equal validity in their respective societies.[2] Within a single society, however, the limits of tolerance are more firmly fixed. State agencies recognize the alternatives presented by certain religious groupings such as, in England, Church of England, Roman Catholic and Nonconformist, or in the United States, Protestant, Catholic or Jew. Something will be said below of the important implications of the fixed choices which these alternatives represent, but for our present point they are less important than the range of variation for which allowance is made by social scientific theories. In recent years a number of writers have proposed various multi-dimensional models of religious commitment.[3] Most of these models are intended to embrace 'all the possible distinctions in what religiousness can mean'[4] but on closer examination it is generally found that the various dimensions on which religiousness is assessed comprise only the several manifestations of religious devotion which are envisaged by the dominant religious organizations. In western societies this usually means the Christian churches. Hunt, from an examination of the items on the religious interest scale of the Allport-Vernon-Lindzey Study of Values, similarly found that a scale which was intended to measure religiousness in its most generalized form in fact takes into account only those traits which would indicate commitment to a conventional religious organization.[5] It would seem that the most that sociological and psychological measures of religiousness succeed in doing is to measure religiousness without reference to particular denominational allegiance: they tap only organized or church-orientated religion.

Writers who have attempted to estimate the degree of secularization in various societies, which involves the special case of decline of religion, have similarly restricted their attention to religion of an organizational kind. For example, Wilson[6] and MacIntyre[7] have distinguished between beliefs, practices and institutions, and estimated the decline of each of these separate aspects, without stressing that all three, as they use them, are aspects of organizational religion. It may be argued that such authors have restricted themselves to the only forms of religion which are amenable to empirical study, but that would be a weak defence. Nor is it maintained that organized religion is the only kind worthy of serious study. The fault is simply one of failing to go beyond religion as practised and defined by the churches.

This same point was made by Luckmann[8] in his blistering attack on research which limits itself to what he has termed 'church-orientated religion', but it is a point which few appear to have taken. The distinction which Luckmann draws is between 'church-orientated' religion and religion conceived more generally as an invariable factor in the 'anthropological condition', and this is something of which more will be said below. At this juncture it is necessary to observe how sweeping is Luckmann's distinction. Having distinguished religion which is specifically church-related he contrasts it with 'natural religion' which need not necessarily contain any element of belief in the supernatural. Berger[9] has argued that this distinction is altogether too sweeping, and indeed it does run counter to the tendency prevalent among sociologists and anthropologists to prefer exclusive definitions of religion to inclusive ones.[10] Since we are concerned here specifically with religion which is not completely under the domination of church organizations we need only to note that Luckmann's distinction is so wide that it leaves out of account those other beliefs which, while not being church-orientated, nevertheless are still predominantly supernatural – or, more accurately, super-empirical[11] – in their content. So while Luckmann undoubtedly made a valuable point when he emphasized that not all religion need be church orientated, it seems that he went too far in contrasting church-orientated religion with natural religion so starkly, thus leaving no area in between for important super-empirical beliefs which are not under the domination of religious organizations.

The existence of an important area of belief which falls between the two extremes treated by Luckmann has been underlined in a recent paper by Abercrombie and others.[12] That paper presented findings from an investigation of 'beliefs that might loosely be described as superstitious', and showed that any empirical analysis of secularization needs to take due account of the persistence of belief in such things as astrology, lucky numbers, fate and luck.

To point to the existence of beliefs which cannot with accuracy be described as either church-orientated or as a form of 'natural religion' is an empirical way of demonstrating the shortcomings of the dichotomy, although it does little to clarify the general categories of religious belief which may not be subsumed under either of these two headings.

In his discussion of secularization, Pratt[13] has drawn the useful distinction between intellectual and social aspects of the process, and for an adequate analysis of secularization this distinction is crucial. But leaving aside the decline in popularity of church-related activities and the eclipse of the churches as organizations integral to society, it is still useful to distinguish between the beliefs and thinking which are an institutionalized part of the religion enshrined in the churches on the one hand, and on the other hand beliefs of a more or less heterodox nature. Of these latter, many will be thought of as 'mere' superstition, which have nothing at all to do with the churches, or when there is some association they will be regarded as corruptions and pagan accretions. At any rate they are not susceptible to the controlling and organizing influence of official church authorities. Just as it can be shown that the social aspect of secularization does not always entail secularization in the intellectual sphere,[14] so the decline in church-related religious beliefs should by no means be taken as evidence of the decline of all super-empirical beliefs.

In order to bring out this contrast more clearly we propose to distinguish here between *official* religion and *common* religion. By official religion we mean those beliefs and practices (ignoring, for the sake of simplicity, specifically organizational factors) which are prescribed, regulated and socialized by organized and institutionalized churches or sects; by common religion we mean those beliefs and practices of an overtly religious nature which are not subject to continued control by the churches and whose significance and importance will not usually be recognized by the churches.[15]

Official religion is an unambiguous expression and we use it here in precisely the same way that Luckmann has employed it.[16] Common religion, however, is a more problematic phrase. The principal objection to its use is that it has been employed by Williams already to signify a 'common set of ideas, rituals and symbols' which is able to 'supply an overarching sense of unity even in a society riddled with conflicts'.[17] A very similar meaning, though a more precise one, is contained in the notion of 'civil religion'.[18] We use the expression common religion here to mean not so much the religion common to a people as the religion of common people. The distinction we wish to draw is nearer to that made by Mensching between universal and folk religions,[19] but it is not the same. Official and common religion are not styles of religiousness, nor stages in religious evolution, nor separate traditions within a single religion.[20] They are two relatively independent patterns of religious belief, either or both of which may be embraced by any member of a society. The one is an organized, coherent and relatively static religion, while the other comprises an unorganized, heterogeneous and more changeable set of beliefs and customs. Some writers have remarked on the need for a thorough examination of common religion and have been aware of the distortions which enter into the study of religion when this element is omitted. Thus Ling maintains that

> ... the sociology of religion has in a sense helped to perpetuate this view of religion as fundamentally organisational; at least, it has so far done little to suggest another perspective ... Had there been any serious comparative or cross-cultural sociology of religion the much needed corrective might have been discovered, for example, from the study of Indian religion, which does not exhibit anything like so prominent an ecclesiastical or organisational character even after its centuries of contact with, and response to, the West.[21]

He recognizes, furthermore, the influence which Christian theology has had on the general study of religion, and comments that

> Much attention is paid in theological studies to the structure of the *institutional* belief systems. What is needed ... is investigation into the structure of the *popular* belief system, that part of the sacred cosmos which lies outside the official dogmas.

The contrast can exist, it should be noted, only where a religious institution has become clearly differentiated in the first place, since only then will an official religion emerge, leaving as a residue of common religion all that is not incorporated into the official system.

Although modern western societies are the obvious examples of such institutional differentiation, examples may also be found in more primitive societies. Thus Radin found it necessary to distinguish between 'formulated religion' and the 'magical substratum' in his treatment of primitive religion.[22] The point we wish to make is that it is the 'official' definition of what shall count as religion which has often been adopted by social scientists – albeit unconsciously – and discussions and analyses of religion have consequently ignored part, if not the major part, of the phenomenon defined as the actors themselves define it.

Perhaps the clearest example of common religion is to be found in the sixteenth- and seventeenth-century European beliefs in witchcraft and magic, which is the more instructive since it was often the occasion of conflict between official religion and common religion. This subject has only recently received the full attention of historians who have broken through the official definitions of what is worthy of study. As a historian recently said: 'The presentation of witches is, to some, a disgusting subject, below the dignity of history. But it is also a historical fact ...'[23] The work of Thomas[24] and the more detailed study by Macfarlane[25] have added immeasurably to our understanding of English religion of the period by examining contemporary common religion with the aid of sociological methods and insights which sociologists themselves have so far failed to utilize. The main point to emerge from such studies is that beside the official religion of the church there existed another set of beliefs and practices which are usually treated – or dismissed – under the heading of magic. None but the most committed churchmen saw any need to make a choice; for the majority of lay people, and also for a good proportion of clergy, the official and the common religions were complementary. At some periods the two religions co-existed and indeed gave each other mutual support. At other periods common religion was vigorously repressed by those who saw in it a serious threat to 'true' religion. But it is abundantly clear that the official beliefs and practices sanctioned by the church did not exhaustively account for all the religion of the time.

If Luckmann's distinction between church-orientated religion and 'natural religion' went too far in its attack on the assumption that official religion is what sociologists should study, thus ignoring the important intermediate areas of common religion, in another way he has not gone far enough. When arguing that religion in modern society has been freed from the domination of an institution, Luckmann introduces the important notion of religious themes:

> The sacred cosmos is mediated neither through a specialised domain of religious institutions nor through other primary public institutions. It

is the direct accessibility of the sacred cosmos, *more precisely, of an assort-*
ment of religious themes, which makes religion today essentially a
phenomenon of the 'private sphere'.[26]

Unfortunately, this notion of religious themes is not developed.
It has been argued elsewhere that social scientists erroneously
assume people's religious ideas to be coherent and systematic.[27]
Luckmann's virtue is in his positive characterization of religion as
thematic; his fault is in his failure to point out that 'invisible
religion' is not unique in being thematic. If we are to investigate
common religion it is imperative that this assumption of systematic
coherence, which is proper to official religion but inapplicable in
general, should be lifted. Valuable evidence is available from recent
work which suggests that the beliefs of children are thoroughly
thematic.[28] We would suggest that the beliefs of children are not
so much underdeveloped in religious terms as common religion
which is as yet unaffected by the systematizing influence of official
religion.[29] Moreover, just as the beliefs which make up common
religion are influenced by official religion, so too have the models of
belief employed by social scientists been tainted, albeit unwittingly,
by the systematic and intellectualistic schemes of the theologians.

In fact the influence exerted by the theological formulations of
official religion upon the models of belief used by social scientists
is very partial. Modern biblical scholarship, far from preserving the
massive structures erected by the schoolmen, has emphasized the
fragmentary nature of early Christian belief. The canon of New
Testament scripture bears the marks of an earlier oral tradition
which was highly thematic, and enshrines a multitude of 'credal
tags' which had preceded the systematic doctrinal formulations of
a later generation of Christians. The popular theological impression
remains, however, that religion is a logical and coherent set of
detailed beliefs and practices, and it is this model of official religion
which remains the paradigm both for the public and also for the
general run of social scientists.

We aim to provide some evidence for the existence of a common
religion, consisting of a profusion of varied and unrelated beliefs
and opinions which relate to a super-empirical sphere. It may be
that early folk religions as well as primitive Christianity, witch-
beliefs and beliefs handed down in children's lore, to mention just
a few elements, constitute a real continuity of common religion
despite substantive variation from century to century and from

social class to social class. Upon such a tradition of common religion has been superimposed, with greater or lesser success, the systematic credal formulations of an official religion. If this is so, then any discussion of contemporary religion and any assessment of the secularization of modern society must avoid the exclusive study of official religion which, together with its institutional structure, may decline without the concomitant decline of common religion. This is an empirical question which demands an empirical study. To make possible such a study it is necessary that we do not assume either official religion or its popularly conceived systematic structure to be normative.

Methodological Problems[30]

The work conducted by Glock and Stark at the Survey Research Center at Berkeley, California, provides an excellent illustration of the approach which we wish to avoid.[31] Valuable and sophisticated though such studies are for the investigation of official religion, they set in advance the terms in which the findings will be couched. And yet any empirical study which does not rely entirely on data obtained from indirect sources is bound to rely on questions which have been framed by the researcher. The central problem is that of asking questions which are as near as possible to being neutral in tone and empty of prior meaning. This, however, is to ask for the impossible. The very word 'religion', for the average Englishman at least, may have overtones of fanaticism, respectability, dishonesty, unpleasant controversy or insincerity, to name but a few. The mention of the word by an interviewer may trigger off any one of these diverse associations depending on the person and the circumstances. In the research reported below greater tension and embarrassment was frequently caused by the mention of religion than by probing questions which sought detailed information about the methods of contraception used by respondents. If the mention of religion elicits such varied reactions in the first place, then how much more unreliable will be the answers to specific questions?

The problem is two-fold. In the first place the subject of religion is for many people a highly emotive one. In the second place it is impossible to know in advance anything about the likely substance of a respondent's beliefs. The first problem is only soluble by adopting indirect methods of observation. By using such a strategy the researcher can be assured that any emotive content found is inherent in the data, and does not derive from a research situation. If one adopts a direct method of investigation the problem is unavoidable, and the best one can hope for is to minimize it as far as possible. The most obvious way of minimizing the emotive content of a question about religion and of freeing it of extraneous implications is by placing it in a context where it will be as unobtrusive as possible. This is to say that, when investigating common religion, interviews which relate solely and specifically to religion should be avoided. Instead, simple questions, open to as wide an interpretation as possible, should be incorporated into interviews primarily concerned with other subjects, and inserted at a point when the interview is far enough advanced for the questions to appear as being of a strictly subsidiary nature.

The second problem is less intractable but more complex. Without doubt respondents will usually answer questions put to them as though they find them meaningful regardless of whether or not this is the case. Only rarely will a working-class respondent in particular complain that a question is meaningless. Furthermore, respondents may have a positive disinclination to formulate and articulate beliefs in general terms. Richard Hoggart has remarked that

> Most people in the working-classes appear ... not merely unfanatic but unidealistic; they have their principles but are disinclined to reveal them in their pure state. For the most part their approach is empirical; they are confirmed pragmatists.[32]

To ask such respondents to state or explain their beliefs in abstract terms is therefore to invite them to perform verbally in ways which they feel are expected of them: it is not to elicit natural responses. Thus it is imperative that questions should be susceptible of interpretation on several levels. Even the permissively open-ended method of enquiry which has been employed to such effect by Gorer[33] incorporates highly specific questions which admit of only one interpretation and which thus prompt replies rather than eliciting responses. Questions should also be phrased so that a respondent does not feel constrained to reply. It should be clearly implied that the respondent may well have no opinion on a question, or that it touches on a topic which has never exercised him, and that these responses would be perfectly acceptable. Obviously such response categories as these are not the same as 'don't know' or 'no response' – they are vitally important negative responses. Where the questions have involved some form of prompting – and this is often bound to be the case – then it must be borne in mind in interpreting the data. The comments by Piaget on interpreting the replies of children to questions which in substance or in phrasing may be foreign to their own conceptions are very instructive:

> We readily agree that children have never or hardly ever reflected on the matters on which they were questioned. The experiments aimed, therefore, not at examining ideas the children had already thought out, but at seeing how their ideas are formed in response to certain questions and principally in what direction their spontaneous attitude of mind tends to lead them.
> In such circumstances the results can only be negative and not positive. That is to say the explanation a child gives in answer to one of our questions must not be taken as an example of 'a child's idea', but serves simply to show that the child did not seek the solution in the same direction as we should have, but presupposed certain implicit postulates different from those we should suppose.[34]

Beyond these elementary points there is little which can be said about the method of investigating common religion. If such strategies are adopted the final success of a study then becomes dependent on the skills, ability and sensitivity of the researcher.

The Sample and the Method

The data reported below were obtained in the course of a study into a somewhat distant subject: attitudes associated with high fertility. The incorporation of questions on religion was originally prompted not so much by a concern for research into religion *per se* as by the references to the place of religion in patterns of fertility in sections of the demographic literature.[35] We shall restrict ourselves here, however, to the implications which the data contain for the general study of religion, leaving the implications for demography to be reported elsewhere. It hardly needs stating that the population from which the sample was drawn was highly atypical of the general population. It consisted of a 50% random sample (N=100; response rate, 81%) of women living in a northern city who in the first seven months of 1967 had had their sixth or subsequent live-born child. Were the study of common religion not so chronically under-developed we should not presume to present findings from such an atypical group in society. As it is, however, the paucity of material would seem to justify the publication of any additional evidence, no matter how specialized the source from which it derives, and we aim only to illustrate the kind of results which the approach here advocated can yield. In fact, the group is much less unusual in terms of educational attainment and social class than might be thought; whether high fertility is a crucial correlate of patterns of belief cannot be adjudged without comparable evidence from a sample with a normal fertility pattern. Some such evidence is available from Gorer, who cross-tabulates replies to the questions, 'Do your children go to Sunday School?' and, 'How many children have you?', showing that children of large families are very much more likely to be sent to Sunday School than are the children of small families.[36] Grave doubt is thrown on the validity of the reported sending of children to Sunday School as an indicator of religiousness, however, since it does not correlate with other indicators such as church attendance and the reported practice of saying prayers privately.[37] A more indubitable source of exaggeration in the data is the exclusively female constitution of the sample, but in this case the degree of bias is to some extent known from the findings of most empirical studies which have shown women to be more religiously inclined than men on almost all indicators.

All the interviews were conducted by the junior author in the homes of the respondents. The circumstances surrounding the interviews, such as the presence of other people, varied widely and the length of time taken also varied, all but two interviews requiring more than one session. Verbatim records of responses, as well as checking of factual items, were made during interviews and after the end of each interview session the verbatim notes were merely re-written in legible form by the interviewer. Such a method is very far from faultless. The use of a tape recorder is always to be preferred, but a trial run proved that it was totally unacceptable within this research design and so unavoidably heavy demands were made on the abilities of the interviewer.

At the end of each interview items 100 and 101 were as follows:

100 (*a*) Do you have any religion?
    (*b*) How much would you say it meant to you?
    (*c*) Why do you say that?

101 (*a*) And does your husband have any religion?
    (*b*) How much would you say religion meant to him?
    (*c*) Why do you think this is so with him?

The data reported below are drawn from the responses to these items and also from a few incidental remarks about religion which were made in response to questions earlier in the interviews. The written records of the responses were sorted, grouped and assigned general categories by the authors independently and then in collaboration. While we reached substantial agreement over both categories and also appropriate categorization, the disagreements all involved difficulties in interpretation which will be discussed below.

Findings and Discussion

1. What denomination?

As is to be expected, the first question of both items invariably elicited the denomination of official religion, if any, to which the respondent felt an affiliation. Yet it is precisely at this point that the problematic nature of religious affiliation first becomes clear. If you provide respondents with a check-list of denominations the findings are readily presentable in the categories provided, plus 'don't know' and 'no response', but the difficulties which were encountered in categorizing responses to the question, 'Do you have any religion?' make it plain that such simplicity is totally misleading. Three problems exist for establishing a respondent's denomination. In the first place, is a respondent properly assigned to a denomination, regardless of whether or not he attends a church, if he has so defined himself? Are these respondents correctly assessed as belonging to the denomination which they mention?

> Church of England but I don't go ... It's not important.

> Used to be a Catholic, but I stopped going to church before I was married ... I have no time for religion really.

> I used to be a Methodist and went three times a day ... It don't mean much to me ... I don't think about it much. It's there if you want to go.

> Catholic but not practising ... In some ways it means a lot. In others nothing at all.

For these respondents themselves the question is obviously problematic, and arbitrarily to assign them to a category is to beg the question. But in the second place responses may be more or less self-contradictory:

> I'm a Catholic. I wonder if there's a God ... It doesn't mean anything to me.

> No I don't have any religion ... I believe in God, but ...

> Church of England ... I don't believe, I'm an atheist.

Presumably the respondent's self-definition must be allowed to stand, but what does it stand for? And is it not trivializing the idea of religious affiliation to lump together all those who utter the words, 'Church of England'? In the third place there are the comparatively simple problems of deciding which denomination counts when a number are mentioned in one way or another.

> Church of England, I was christened. I used to go to the Methodist church.

> No religion really. Tend to go to Catholic because my husband is, but mother's Protestant and father's Jewish. I was brought up in Jewish religion.

> I was christened and married in a Church of England but the children are Methodist.

> Church of England, but really I'm a Jehovah's Witness.... I think it's lovely, but he won't let me have it.

These examples are far from uncommon among the 81 respondents, but they illustrate the difficulty of assigning a denominational label, or even a denominational preference, to many of them. Although it is of obviously dubious significance, the distribution of religious denominational allegiance was as follows: Respondents: Church of England 42%, Roman Catholic 31%, other 11%, none 16%; Respondents' husbands: Church of England 30%, Roman Catholic 33%, other 6%, none 31%. For the purposes of this distribution, non-practising adherents of a denomination were counted with those who were apparently more devout (although no explicit question was asked about attendance), whereas those respondents who said that they had been adherents, using the past tense, were counted as having no religious affiliation. Other contradictions were resolved by accepting the category to which the respondents had seemed to give priority.

Respondents appeared to feel quite commonly that they were under some obligation to give a reply in denominational terms although the wording of the question avoided any such direct implication. There was a definite sense of having to fit oneself into some category.

I suppose I would be Church of England. I'd put myself down as that.

I don't know (*lengthy pause*) Church of England.

This attitude might arise in at least two ways. It could be a habit which respondents had developed as a result of being asked what their denomination was by people who required to know it. For example, hospitals usually enquire about a patient's religious affiliation as a part of the admission procedure. As the members of the sample had all been into hospital on a number of occasions the enquiry in the interviews might have sounded similar to the routine of factual questions to which they were accustomed in a hospital context – age, sex, marital status, nationality, religion, occupation etc. – and thus it might seem to require a definite answer. On the other hand the slightly official aura which inevitably surrounds a person who conducts interviews might have evoked what respondents felt to be a 'respectable' reply. If it was indeed felt by the respondents to be somehow less respectable not to 'have a religion' this would explain not only the need to supply an 'appropriate' reply but also the note of apology which, as we shall see below, accompanied an admission that the respondent did not practise her religion, and the tone almost of defiance with which other respondents declared themselves or their spouses atheists.[38]

2. *'You don't have to go to church to believe'*

The general comments which were volunteered by respondents varied greatly in length and detail as well as in substance. As we have suggested above, the brevity of some other replies must be understood to have occurred within a distinctly tense and embarrassed atmosphere. A number of suggestions have been made to help account for this unease, but regardless of the cause its importance as a constraining factor cannot be emphasized strongly enough. We can only hope that greater experience of careful interviewing on the subject of common religion will facilitate the development of techniques to reduce strain further. But other reactions were also encountered. Some respondents were plainly bored by the questions, which they appeared to find trivial. Others were simply tired by a long interview session and seemed anxious to dispose of the questions with as little trouble as possible. Doubtless such reactions were encouraged by the apparent irrelevance to some respondents of two questions concerning religion at the end of an interview devoted to topics related to fertility, but irrespective of their origins these reactions are important.

In giving the percentage of respondents who made comments of specific kinds and on various themes we have worked from a base of 162 in every instance, since in theory each respondent was answering for her spouse as well as for herself when the husband was not actually present – which he was for only nine interviews. The frequencies which are given will be on the low side, therefore, since because of the very nature of the subject wives can answer for their husbands only very inadequately, and since a response was not generally counted twice even when it seemed true for both husband and wife, but only when explicitly mentioned for each of them separately. We report only those themes which were mentioned on at least 5% of the theoretically possible occasions.

The comment most frequently made (18%) was that 'believing' and 'going to church' are not necessarily the same thing. In touching on this theme respondents were almost invariably asserting that they counted themselves as religious, and that this was something of importance to them, but at the same time denying the importance of the churches.

> No [I have no religion]. I believe in the church but I have my own way of praying.

> I don't practise it a great deal. I feel quite a strong faith ... I have been brought up to think it doesn't matter about going to church, but I'd like them [the children] to get the feel of it.

> Religion itself doesn't mean a lot. Just what I believe myself. You don't have to go to church to believe.

> I don't go to church but I believe in my religion. I believe I can pray much better at home than going on Sundays.

> It means summat! You don't have to go to church every week to convince yourself you believe in God. I won't have it rammed down my throat.

> I don't go to church ... I pray every night, I have to. It's funny, isn't it?

> You can be good without going to church.

While there is doubtless an element of self-criticism in this theme which occasionally becomes explicit, as in

> I don't keep my religion as I should – with church and that

and as will be mentioned in 4(i) below, we would generally interpret this theme as representing a straight assertion by the actors them-

selves of the importance of non-official, common religion. Just what
the religion, the belief and the praying which the respondents mention consists of is of course another matter. It is quite possible that
the respondents would have been unable to explain further even
if they had been pressed. It is possible that the comments have no
deeper or more detailed meaning, and that they are themselves
religious statements or cognitive assertions. In any case this is
immaterial. The frequency with which this theme occurs is itself
sufficient to substantiate our argument for the need of further investigation of non-official religion.

3. *Some themes of belief*

   (i) From what we have said above about the possible equation of
religion with respectability, it is to be expected that some respondents should refer to an *ethical code* as at least a component in
religion. We have noted that MacIntyre comments on it, but
Hoggart, writing about working-class people in precisely the area
of England from which these data are drawn, has been unequivocal
in his interpretation. Because his work is so relevant it will be
worth quoting him at some length.

> In so far as they think of Christianity, they think of it as a system of
> ethics; their concern is with morals, not metaphysics ... round the sense
> of religion as a guide to our duty towards others, as the repository of good
> rules for communal life, the old phrases cluster. Ask any half-dozen
> working-class people what they understand by religion, and very easily,
> but not meaninglessly, they will be likely to answer with one of these
> phrases:
>
> 'doing good'
> 'common decency'
> 'helping lame dogs'
> 'being kind'
> 'doing unto others as y'would be done unto'
> 'we're 'ere to 'elp one another'
> ''elping y'neighbour'
> 'learning to know right from wrong'
> 'decent living'.[39]

There is some slight doubt about whether we should expect to find
a conception of religion completely dominated by ethics, since
Hoggart footnotes a dissenting comment: 'Professor Asa Briggs,
whose background is in many ways similar to mine, thinks I may
be generalizing from too limited an experience here.'[40] It is a
theme which we found to occur on only 6% of the possible occasions.

I believe in God. I know what's right and wrong.

I've always believed in Him. It helps to keep you steady. Church teaches kids that bit more than parents could. It's kept me out of trouble.

Should have it [religion]. It keeps you straight ...

Since the question which we used was just about as open-ended as that recommended by Hoggart these data are a reasonable test of his judgment, which is found wanting by our results. The connotations of religion have not, it seems, become exclusively ethical. Religion still means, for these people, a form of training which has the function of providing a practical ethic, rather than having been reduced to an ethic as Hoggart had suggested.

(ii) The idea of the *efficacy of prayer or belief*, mentioned by 14% of respondents, was the theme second only to the distinction between believing and church attendance in its frequency of occurence. This theme, together with 4(ii) below, is perhaps the most clearly and consciously super-empirical in its substance, for it presupposes the possibility of some kind of supernatural power. It is reminiscent of the primitive power ascribed to the prayers of Moses in the Book of Exodus in the relatively simple cause and effect relationship which is postulated.

When I'm confined: I always say my prayers that I'll come through.

When Nigel was poorly I prayed for him every night. I should believe in a life after death but I don't. People go their own way.

I prayed to God to help me [when I was ill] and I was alright ... I think if you ask for something and need it, it'll come eventually because you pray for it long enough. If ever you want help he'll come to you.

I pray to God. I think a lot depends on having faith in things ... Come to think a lot of it regarding death.

I like to think that if I need help, God will help.

Even when the statement is negative the very mention of supernatural intervention demonstrates that it is thought to be a force worth considering.

I don't believe God will provide ... It's up to man himself.

I think it was because I lost the kiddies. Up to then I did go to church and believe in God.

Religion can't help your circumstances: can't make them better. If I thought religion could make things better, I'd perhaps think of it.

I used to believe until my first husband died. He believed that because he believed he'd pull through, he would. He didn't. It's no good saying it's in God's hands. It's the surgeon that pulls you through.

Perhaps these disconfirmations count as even more important than the examples of positive belief in the power of prayer or belief. The total irrelevance of religious beliefs and their status as non-questions has been stressed recently as evidence of the secularization of consciousness.[41] Here, however, 14% of our respondents have made unsolicited reference to the efficacy of supernatural powers in everyday affairs. These data contain no mention of other beliefs, such as belief in ghosts, lucky numbers, horoscopes etc., which led Gorer to conclude that about a quarter of the population of England 'holds a view of the universe which can most properly be designated as magical',[42] but the remarks reported above indicate the prevalence of a similarly magical element in beliefs which are nearer to orthodoxy. This amounts to some evidence of the continuity of the common religion form of religious consciousness, despite the undoubted decline in official religion.

(iii) Ten per cent of the responses contained the clear implication that for them it was *natural to believe*, or that the fact of religious belief was taken for granted. This theme was found among churchgoers and others alike, and it would seem that the assumed necessity of belief is independent of the influence of official religion.

I'd say that everybody must have a belief, not as actual religion ...

Everybody must have a religion whether they are Jew or Protestant or Catholic. Must have a belief there is a God.

It means a great deal to me. Can't go through life without it.

[Church] learns you about God.

Such 'taken-for-granted' belief is the clearest example of unsecularized ways of thinking which still exist. Nor is this phenomenon at all similar to the 'faith in faith' to which recent writers have drawn attention,[43] and which is indeed as far from the genuine product as is 'falling in love with falling in love'. The faith with which we are concerned in this section is a simple and inarticulate belief which is unquestioningly assumed to be a necessary component of living.

(iv) A similar number of responses, 9%, included an explicit statement that the respondent had been *brought up to believe*.

I was taught when I was a kid.

Don't know why I feel it's important. I was always brought up to believe in God.

It's been my whole life – lived with God, in the mind. Way I've been brought up.

How I was brought up in Ireland.

This response might be interpreted as half-way between the religious consciousness and the secular consciousness. Belief is not assumed unreflectingly, but nor is it rejected or discounted. The popular American conception of belief as a voluntary choice is perhaps a New World equivalent of the Old World phenomenon of belief which is accepted as an inheritance, as a legacy to which people are resigned. The very consciousness of its having definite origins does, however, set this theme apart from the previous one. But again the awareness of religious belief as a product of up-bringing is common to those who participate in official religious institutions and those who do not. It is a true component of common religion.

The foregoing remarks do not apply to every respondent. There are some, usually those who have been exposed to more formal education, who are naturally inclined to reflect on both the source and also the cogency of all their beliefs and commitments. For these people there is little chance that their religious beliefs might be taken for granted. If they are aware that beliefs have been socialized and yet still adhere to them, it suggests that we are here dealing with a faith which is more sophisticated and perhaps more resilient in a changing modern society.

We shall return to the role of up-bringing in 4(iii) below.

(v) Another theme which has important implications is that of religion as a *source of meaning* for life, which was mentioned on 12% of the possible occasions. One of the main strands in the sociological theory of religion in the tradition of Weber has been the emphasis on religion's ability to give meaning to life. As Peter Berger has put it:

The religious enterprise of human history profoundly reveals the pressing urgency and intensity of man's quest for meaning. The gigantic projections of religious consciousness, whatever else they may be, constitute the historically most important effort of man to make reality humanly meaningful, at any price.[44]

The putative failure of religion in this respect, many have argued, is the most significant aspect of secularization. It is worth quoting Berger again:

> Probably for the first time in history, the religious legitimations of the world have lost their plausibility not only for a few intellectuals and other marginal individuals but for broad masses of entire societies ... In other words there has arisen a problem of 'meaningfulness' not only for such institutions as the state or the economy but for the ordinary routines of everyday life ... Most importantly the peculiar Christian theodicy of suffering lost its plausibility and thereby the way was opened for a variety of secularized soteriologies, most of which, however, proved quite incapable of legitimating the sorrows of individual life.[45]

Religion apparently still succeeds in making meaningful, or at least bearable, the suffering and perplexities which some respondents experience.

> Faith gives you the ability to face things.

> In times of stress it's been a help. You turn to it when you're upset and worried, you go to church ... if you're really unhappy, religion is soothing ... You need something to believe in, to face things that are big, to stabilize you.

> I've often felt if I didn't have any faith to believe in I'd be lost, be really depressed.

> A lot don't believe in God but I do – for the things that happen. David says he's only testing you when bad things come along. My sister got killed. I think there must be a reason.

On the other hand several of the references to this theme were of a negative kind, conscious of meaninglessness.

> Why does he let little children suffer?

> He used to go to church every week. He's just stopped going. When he were in pain, when he was ill, he said, 'Why should I suffer?' Since then he's never gone. He's got his opinion. He were going to be a priest.

> So many people suffer. If there was a God he wouldn't allow it. You hear of so many accidents.

The evidence suggests that Berger is correct in maintaining that a problem of 'meaningfulness' exists and these replies certainly indicate that some people at least still look for meanings rather than simply for rational explanations, as a more simplistic theory of secularization suggests. Most, but not all, of those who mentioned this theme when asked about religion found that it made their difficulties more meaningful. All the respondents shared one experience – that of having to cope with a large family – which calls for an explanation and has to be made meaningful. It may be useful to quote one or two remarks made in response to the question which was asked much earlier in the interviews (Question 60): 'What part would you say fate or luck plays in how many children you have?'

> It's what God gives you, so his mother used to say.

> It's up to Jesus Christ. If he says you're to have children you will. People who fall on with the pill, it's like him saying, 'You've not had your share.' I think when he says up there that you've had your share, you have. I know I'll have no more, I know I won't. I don't know why. Jesus Christ sets your fate.

> (*Husband*) It's not luck or fate. If you hit you hit, it's not your luck. (*Wife*) I'm not religious, but if you're to have them you'll have them.

> Don't know really. It's fate how many you'll have as far as I'm concerned. It's all planned what you're going to have. I kid myself I'm an atheist but I'm not.

> God sent Ann and Jenny. I didn't want them, but they were sent for a purpose ...

> It must be fate. I've said no more to Dave many times. God must have wanted me to have them. They have been sent to us. I can't make it out.

These five themes represent the most commonly mentioned topics of general belief to emerge from the data. They give some indication of ideas which are sparked off by a question about religion with little or no relevance to the religion of the churches.

4. *Unofficial views of official religion*

(i) A theme which occurred regularly (8%) in connection with church attendance was, '*I don't have time*', which is hardly surprising in view of their family commitments.

> I'd love to go if I had time.

> I wouldn't like to go without religion. I'll get more time as the children grow up.

> I stopped going – problems with cooking the dinner, and the kids won't sit still.

There are no obvious reasons to suppose that respondents like these are merely rationalizing a disinclination. The point worth noting is that church attendance is perceived as being a voluntary matter which takes its place beside or below other activities on a scale of priorities. We have noted a general tendency to feel obliged to 'have a religion' in order to be 'proper' and 'respectable': it should be noted that respectability does not now involve the need to go to church or to chapel as it did, at least for the bourgeoisie, two generations ago. Associated with this theme is the not uncommon remark (3%):

> I feel a lot better when I come out of chapel.

> It makes you feel good.

and also the practice of attending church occasionally (6%):

> I'd like to at Christmas.

> I like to go to Mass twice a year.

> I don't go as much as I should. I go on special occasions, Easter, Christmas and if the kiddies are doing anything.

But it should be emphasized again that no question was asked about church attendance, and that the comments were made in response to a very general question about 'religion'. Seen in the light of the frequent comment reported in section 2 above, and in contrast with the need to have some faith, these attitudes hang together as a coherent whole. Church attendance is nice as an extra, but it is not generally seen as necessary. And it is undesirable if taken to excess.

> It doesn't mean as much to me as it does to these fanatics who go to church every week: I don't go a lot.

> It's important for people to believe – but not too much.

> I wouldn't let it rule my life.

An understanding of the attitudes to churchgoing of which we have given a little evidence here seems to be important. Without such material, the bare statistics of attendance are only very superficially meaningful, whereas a thorough investigation of the significance church attendance has for people might demonstrate profound changes in attitudes as well as illuminate the statistical material which we already have available.

(ii) The efficacy ascribed to faith and prayers has been dealt with above, but related to that theme of belief is the idea, mentioned on 5% of the possible occasions, of the *necessity of rites of passage*.

> I was christened Church of England ... My beliefs are to take them to church to have them blessed. It's nice. It doesn't matter whether it's Church of England or Baptist.

> I've got no religion, but I like the kids to go to be christened.

> I've had them all christened. I'm strong on that. It's a lovely service and it gives a child a name.

> I don't go to church but I like the little one christened ... I've not been churched.

> I have them all christened. (*prompt:* Why?) Don't know. People have it done. It keeps them safe like wearing a St Christopher.

The effect of the prompt in the last quotation is particularly worthy of note, and indicates one of the possible lines of further research. The respondent comments spontaneously about christening, and when asked why she has the children christened immediately says she does not know; realizing that this is not an adequate reply, she follows it up with a remark which suggests that it is the natural and usual practice, and as such requires no further justification; still not satisfied with her answer, she then provides an account which makes her action seem purposive. The difficulties involved in interpreting a sequential response such as this are considerable and the advice given by Piaget which has been quoted already is obviously relevant. This example does, however, show that great care should be taken in moving from an approach which elicits near-spontaneous responses to one which probes in depth, for the increased complexity of interpretation which the move necessitates is very considerable. It should be observed that the questions which appear on most questionnaires are of this probing nature, while the very method itself precludes sensitive or subtle interpretations.

This theme of the necessity or efficacy of rites of passage did not occur as frequently as might have been anticipated. It was mentioned less than half as often as the necessity or efficacy of prayer and belief. This in itself is a significant finding since it has been suggested that, in the peculiar context of England, the demand for the occasional rites of the churches can be expected to persist for longer than other aspects of religiousness.[46] Our evidence suggests that rites such as baptism are not the first things people think of when one mentions religion, and that they are perceived as conventions rather than as efficacious rituals.

(iii) A further 7% of the replies included the statement about church attendance that the respondents had been *forced to go when children.* Just occasionally this was taken by the respondents as sufficient reason for subjecting their own children to the same traditional disciplines.

> Because I've been brought up strict. And that's how I'm bringing up mine.

More often the experience served as an effective source of immunity from further attendance.

> We were made to go as children and that put me off ...

> I don't go to church because as a child I had to go three times a day and it's put me off, because I had it drummed in.

> I believe in God but I think for myself ... my father made us go ... shouldn't force you to go.

This view is so well known that it needs no further comments. It remains to be seen whether the converse which is implied in these statements is true: whether a post-Spock generation will, in their maturity, flock to church.

Conclusions

In view of the very limited data which we have had at our disposal the substantive findings presented here could be no more than tentatively suggestive. The principal aim has been to demonstrate that a large grey area, which we have termed common religion, exists as an important part of the religious orientation of ordinary people. We have tried to demonstrate two properties which are characteristic of this common religion and which have tended to hide it from the view of empirical studies in the sociology of religion. Firstly, it bears little reference to the beliefs and practices of any recognized religious denomination. Since most research takes its model of religion from these 'official' sources the themes of common religion have tended to be overlooked. Secondly, it is highly thematic in form, and does not occur as a systematically elaborated set of codes and beliefs. The assumption that religion necessarily assumes a systematic form has been made both by the sociologists who have studied the decline of traditional religion and also by those who have looked for new and unfamiliar varieties of 'natural religion'.[47]

An adequate account of religion ought, we believe, to include this area of common religion, since it is an essential part of religious thinking. This view is not universally accepted, yet those who reject it demonstrate a certain inconsistency. Thus Wilson, for example, writes of secularization:

Religious *thinking* is perhaps the area which evidences most conspicuous change. Men act less and less in response to religious motivation: they assess the world in empirical and rational terms, and find themselves involved in rational organizations and rationally determined roles which allow small scope for such religious predilections as they might privately entertain.[48]

while maintaining at the same time that:

Sociology appropriately regards religion as primarily an institutional phenomenon. This is not to dismiss the discovery of beliefs and attitudes ... but rather to recognize that religious institutions, organizations, affiliations and practices, and institutionalized belief-systems, have been of more social consequence in all societies than are the contemporary private beliefs of individuals isolated by an interview-schedule.[49]

In this study we have followed the line described by Wilson in the first of the above quotations notwithstanding his implied dismissal of the same approach in the second one. We have tried to point to an important area in common religion, to suggest how it might be approached by research, and given a very preliminary example of the method and the kind of findings which it can produce.

NOTES

The data reported in this paper were collected by the junior author as part of a larger study which was made possible by the award of a research studentship by the SSRC, to whom she wishes to express her thanks. The paper has benefited from the comments of Professor Zygmunt Bauman, Professor Trevor Ling and the editor of this volume, to whom the authors are grateful.

1. Quite apart from the work of 'religious sociologists' proper, recent writings of Robert Bellah have come near to adopting a religious standpoint, as Nelson has argued, while David Martin on the other hand has warned that the notion of secularization may be a 'tool of counter-religious ideology' (Robert N. Bellah, 'Christianity and symbolic realism', *Journal for the Scientific Study of Religion*, vol. 9, 1970; Benjamin Nelson, 'Is the sociology of religion possible? A reply to Robert Bellah', loc. cit.; David A. Martin, 'Towards eliminating the concept of secularization' in *The Religious and the Secular*, Routledge & Kegan Paul 1969).

2. Although it remains a controversial view, such an opinion is at least seriously entertained now, even by theologians, as in Charles Davis, *Christ and the World Religions*, Hodder & Stoughton 1970.

3. Charles Y. Glock and Rodney Stark, *Religion and Society in Tension*, Rand McNally, Chicago 1965; Joseph E. Faulkner and Gordon F. DeJong, 'Religiosity in 5-D: an empirical analysis', *Social Forces*, vol. 45, 1966; Morton King, 'Measuring the religious variable: nine proposed dimensions', *Journal for the Scientific Study of Religion*, vol. 6, 1967; Andrew J. Weigert and Darwin L. Thomas, 'Religiosity in 5-D: a critical note', *Social Forces*,

vol. 48, 1969; Robert B. Tapp, 'Dimensions of religiosity in a post-traditional group', *Journal for the Scientific Study of Religion*, vol. 10, 1971.

4. Rodney Stark and Charles Y. Glock, *American Piety*, University of California Press 1968, p.13.

5. Richard A. Hunt, 'The interpretation of the religious scale of the Allport-Vernon-Lindzey Study of Values', *Journal for the Scientific Study of Religion*, vol. 7, 1968.

6. Bryan R. Wilson, *Religion in Secular Society*, Watts & Co. 1966.

7. Alasdair MacIntyre, *Secularization and Moral Change*, OUP 1967.

8. Thomas Luckmann, *Invisible Religion*, Collier-Macmillan 1967.

9. Peter L. Berger, *The Social Reality of Religion*, Faber & Faber 1969, Appendix I.

10. Robin Horton, 'A definition of religion and its uses', *Journal of the Royal Anthropological Institute*, vol. 90, 1960; Jack Goody, 'Religion and ritual: the definitional problem', *British Journal of Sociology*, vol. 12, 1961; Melford E. Spiro, 'Religion: problems of definition and explanation' in *Anthropological Approaches to the Study of Religion*, ed. Michael Banton, Tavistock Publications 1966; Roland Robertson, *The Sociological Interpretation of Religion*, Blackwells 1970, pp.34ff; the problem of establishing a satisfactory definition of religion is ultimately inescapable and it lurks beneath a good deal of the present discussion, but since it is an issue in its own right it deserves separate discussion beyond the scope of this paper.

11. Robertson, op. cit., pp.47ff.

12. Nicholas Abercrombie et al., 'Superstition and Religion: the God of the Gaps' in *A Sociological Yearbook of Religion in Britain* 3, ed. David Martin and Michael Hill, SCM Press 1970.

13. Vernon Pratt, *Religion and Secularization*, Macmillan 1970.

14. Ibid., p.8.

15. It will be apparent that we do not wish to distinguish between religion, magic, witchcraft, superstition, etc. as separate categories.

16. Luckmann, op. cit., pp.72ff.

17. Robin M. Williams Jr, *American Society: A Sociological Interpretation*, Alfred Knopf, NY 1951, p.312.

18. Robert N. Bellah, 'Civil religion in America' in *Beyond Belief*, Harper & Row, NY 1970.

19. Gustav Mensching, 'Folk and universal religion' trs. in *Religion, Culture and Society*, ed. Louis Schneider, Wiley, NY 1964; cf. E. Wilbur Bock, 'Symbols in conflict: official versus folk religion', *Journal for the Scientific Study of Religion*, vol. 5, 1966.

20. Robert Redfield's distinction between great tradition and little tradition is specific to peasant societies, whereas we are concerned primarily with industrial societies (Redfield, *Peasant Society and Culture*, University of Chicago Press 1956).

21. Trevor O. Ling, 'Anthropology and international understanding: the role of comparative religion', paper presented to the Indian Anthropological Society, November 1971; to appear in L. P. Vidyarthi (ed.), forthcoming.

22. Paul Radin, *Primitive Religion*, Hamish Hamilton 1938, pp.15-39 and 59-65; much the same distinction as we use here is employed by Leszek Kolakowski in a work not yet available in English, and it is also given eloquent expression in Norman Douglas' 1917 novel, *South Wind*, where the difference between vertical and horizontal gods is discussed by one character.

23. Hugh R. Trevor-Roper, *Religion, the Reformation and Social Change*, Macmillan 1967, p.xi.

24. Keith Thomas, *Religion and the Decline of Magic*, Weidenfeld & Nicolson 1971.

25. Alan Macfarlane, *Witchcraft in Tudor and Stuart England*, Routledge & Kegan Paul 1970.

26. Luckmann, op. cit., p.103 (our italics).

27. Peter Worsley, *The Trumpet Shall Sound*, MacGibbon & Kee, 2nd ed., 1968, pp.xxivf.

28. Iona Opie and Peter Opie, *The Lore and Language of Schoolchildren*, OUP 1959, pp.121-6; Gustav Jahoda, *The Psychology of Superstition*, Allen Lane The Penguin Press 1969, pp.105–10.

29. The beliefs in the nature of an after-life reported by Geoffrey Gorer seem to indicate that, at least in this area, doctrines of official religion are less important than the continuities from common religion learned in childhood (*Exploring English Character*, Cresset Press 1955, pp.254-62; *Death, Grief and Mourning in Contemporary Britain*, Cresset Press 1965, pp.161-8).

30. Some penetrating comments on the whole subject of investigating non-official religion have been made by Roland Robertson and Colin Campbell in 'Religion in Britain: the need for new research strategies', *Social Compass*, vol. 19, 1972.

31. E.g. Glock and Stark, op. cit.

32. Richard Hoggart, *The Uses of Literacy*, Penguin Books 1957, p.119.

33. Gorer, *Exploring English Character*.

34. Jean Piaget, *The Child's Conception of the World*, Routledge & Kegan Paul 1929, p.123.

35. See Ronald Freedman and P. K. Whelpton, 'Social and psychological factors affecting fertility: X. Fertility planning and fertility rates by religious interest denominations', *The Milbank Memorial Fund Quarterly*, vol. 33, 1950; Ronald Freedman, P. W. Whelpton and J. W. Smit, 'Socio-economic factors in religious differentials in fertility', *American Sociological Review*, vol. 26, 1961; Ru-Chi Chou and Susannah Brown, 'A comparison of the size of families in Roman Catholics and non-Roman Catholics in Great Britain', *Population Studies*, vol. 22, 1968; Ann Cartwright, *Parents and Family Planning Services*, Routledge & Kegan Paul 1970.

36. Gorer, *Exploring English Character*, p.246.

37. Ibid, pp.247f.

38. MacIntyre comments that working-class people in England share 'the concept of Christianity as it survives among Southern European peasants, where often the word "Christian" is almost an equivalent for "good man".' This is to interpret the usage only at its weakest, however, for it is used as a synonym for proper, right and respectable as well (MacIntyre, op. cit., p.18).

39. Hoggart, op. cit., pp.116ff.

40. Ibid., p.354.

41. Alasdair MacIntyre and Paul Ricoeur, *The Religious Significance of Atheism*, Columbia University Press 1969, p.37; Pratt, op. cit., pp.6f; see particularly the letter of Keynes.

42. Gorer, *Exploring English Character*, p.269.

43. Will Herberg, *Protestant-Catholic-Jew*, Anchor Books, NY, rev. ed. 1959, pp.89f and 265f; MacIntyre and Ricoeur, op. cit., passim.

44. Berger, op. cit., p.100.

45. Ibid., p.125.

46. Wilson, op. cit., pp.10-18.

47. The idea of themes of central meaning which give significance to the life situations of particular groups in society promises to be one which may again link the sociology of religion into the mainstream of sociological theory.

48. Wilson, op. cit., p.x.

49. Ibid., p.xviii.

2 Class, Community and Region: The Religious Geography of Nineteenth-Century England

Hugh McLeod

I

In France within recent years the proportion of practising Catholics in the population has varied from nearly 100% in some parts of Brittany or the Basque Country to little more than 0% in some of the 'dechristianized' rural areas such as those to the south-east of Paris or around Limoges.[1] Religious and political loyalties are closely linked, so that all the parties of the Right include among their supporters a majority who at least claim a Catholic allegiance, while even so moderate a party of the Left as the Radicals depends very largely on those who stay away from Mass.[2] If these differences are particularly well documented in France, they exist in comparable degree in many other European countries.[3]

In England, this is not the case. There are regional and class differences in religious attachment, and religious allegiances are still linked to political allegiances, but these differences and these links are not very significant by comparison with those in most other countries.[4] Except perhaps in sexual attitudes, religion does not form an important social dividing line. There are few issues on which the adherents of one religion separate themselves as a group from the adherents of another religion or of none at all. Yet a hundred years ago the reverse was true. Next to the division between the classes, there were no dividing lines more significant than those between believer and unbeliever, Catholic and Protestant, churchman and dissenter, evangelical and liberal; political parties existed above all on a religious basis, and to be a Primitive Methodist or a Unitarian, a Plymouth Brother or a Ritualist, was to declare a position not only in theology but in many other areas of life. The variations in religious allegiance between class and class and between county and county, though less extreme than in France, were still very considerable, as well as being more complex.

It is the purpose of this paper to determine where the religious divisions of later nineteenth-century England ran, and particularly those within and between the cities: to explain the contrasts between the 'immense and well-ordered cemetery'[5] that was Westminster and the City on a Sunday in 1858, and the 'fair-like' Sabbath a mile away in Bethnal Green which, according to the Rector, forced him to live outside his parish for the protection of his wife and children;[6] between the Braintree of the 1880s, described by F. H. Crittall, where 'social ostracism' awaited a member of his own class of large shopkeepers who failed to appear in the Congregational chapel at the correct times, and the 'wider, more tolerant life' that he found in Birmingham.[7] The basis of this study will be the statistical sources – chiefly the counts of church attendance organized on a national scale in 1851, and on a local scale by newspapers at various points in the later nineteenth and early twentieth century. These sources are both rich and so far very meagrely exploited. They provide only a necessary starting-point for an investigation that must largely depend on other types of evidence. They are necessary because they provide a sounder basis than the accumulation of subjective impressions for answering questions of chronology or concerning the numbers and social composition of those involved in particular activities at a given time. These sources are limited both because measurable indicators of religious allegiance, such as membership of churches or attendances at services, indicate so little, and because so few such indicators actually have been measured.[8] It is their religious meaning that is most obscure. It would, for instance, be foolish to use church attendance statistics as an index of assent to particular doctrines,[9] or of the 'religiosity' of social classes.[10] Individual belief was always much too complex and ambivalent to be measured in such a way. On the other hand, the formal act of attending services at a given church or chapel had immense social and political significance in nineteenth-century England, recognized not least by governments. Statistics of attendance are essential indices both of the force and nature of the social controls prevailing in any community, and of the boundaries between one cultural unit and another. The question of what people at various social levels believed, and why, about the sacred, about the purpose of life and about human relations is even more interesting and important, but it is also much more difficult, and it can only be answered by different sorts of evidence.

II

The national pattern of churchgoing closely resembled the Anglican pattern and likewise showed very wide variations between class and class and between county and county.[11] Since the Church of England was, besides being by far the largest of the religious denominations, the Establishment, one of the 'settled institutions' to the defence of which the Conservative Party was committed,[12] the map of Anglican strength can also be seen as a map of the acceptance, voluntary or forced of these institutions. Equally, non-churchgoing and religious Nonconformity were forms of social and political dissent, conscious or unconscious. They were most common where the controls exercised by the governing class were least effective – at the lower end of the social scale, and in the remoter rural areas. Church attendances were higher in the upper class than the middle class; higher, generally speaking, in country than in town, in lowland than in upland, in small villages than in large; they were highest of all in the closed village.[13] In the upper class enjoyment of a privileged position within the social order was associated with the recognition of an obligation to perform certain acts, among which churchgoing was one.[14] A similar sense of self-identification with the social order and its needs was felt by many in the upper middle class. The higher up the middle class you went, the smaller was the role of personal choice, the greater the social control exercised not only by servants – an even more compelling reason than children for observing the decencies[15] – but by the sense of what duty to society demanded. Members of the lower middle class, on the other hand, were less likely to accept that society had any such claim on their time; and members of the working class were apt to see the connection between Anglicanism and loyalism as a reason for staying away.[16]

As for the geography of Anglicanism, the areas of high attendance were in the South and East, where parishes were small and the rural population relatively concentrated.[17] The work of Dorothy Sylvester suggests that this particular religious division was well established by the thirteenth century. Using figures for 1811 – before the great sub-division of parishes in the nineteenth century – she identified a 'parish line' dividing the multi-township parishes of

Northern and North-Western England, the West Midlands, and North-East Wales from the rest of England and Wales, where most parishes included only one township and their average area was smaller. The multi-township parish was associated with upland, scattered settlement, and the Celtic church, but no one of these factors was sufficient to explain its distribution.[18] The distribution of Anglican church attendance has now changed: congregations are largest in relation to population in the remoter rural counties of the West and North-West, such as Hereford, Shropshire, Cornwall and Cumberland.[19] But in 1851 Anglican strength was still heavily concentrated to the south of the 'parish line' in the counties of nucleated villages and large arable farms, in such cities as Bristol and Portsmouth, or such small towns as Cambridge or Reading.

The strength of the established church was thus in the higher social classes and in the more productive and more accessible rural areas. These two factors, social and geographical, in the distribution of support for any institution provide a useful indication of its position within the social system. Thus, the Church of England in the nineteenth century was in a comparable position to the Church of Scotland at the same time – strongest in the rich farming counties of the East, where total church attendances were highest, weaker in the cities, and very weak in the Highlands, dominated by the Free Church.[20] But this pattern was rather different from that in contemporary England, or, for instance, in nineteenth- and twentieth-century France or in Eastern Europe since 1945. In France, too, the Catholic Church is strong in the higher social classes, but it is strongest of all in the remoter rural areas – the equivalent of those parts of England which often had no Anglican church before the later nineteenth century: in France, ever since the Revolution, it has been the nucleated village that has been synonymous with dechristianization, the isolated farm, preferably in mountainous country, that has signalled 'pays chrétien'.[21] In Czechoslovakia, at the present day, it is also in the remoter areas that religious beliefs are most widely held, but socially they are concentrated at the lower extreme of the scale – among peasants and urban workers;[22] while in nineteenth-century England those who received the best education also got the most indoctrination in Anglican beliefs, in communist Czechoslovakia they receive the most indoctrination in atheism – and the exercise seems to be equally effective.

In the mid-nineteenth century, therefore, the Anglican Church was secure in the loyalty of the dominant classes, and in most of the rural South it was not effectively challenged by Nonconformity, let alone by secularism. But there were still large sections of the rural population with which it had little contact. In the sixteenth and seventeenth centuries areas of moor, heath and forest were noted for their isolation from official religion.[23] In the nineteenth century, Anglican worshippers were outnumbered by Nonconformists in most of the northern counties, and in none of them did rural church attendances exceed the median for all English counties. In many parts of Northern England, and not only in industrial areas, the local religion was Methodist or none at all.[24] If the farm labourer of Southern England was often a rather irregular church-goer,[25] except where pressure could be applied from above, the small farmer of Cumberland or the West Riding seems to have taken advantage of his relative isolation and freedom from community pressures by staying at home on Sunday, often saving himself a long walk.

There was thus a marked social bias and an equally marked regional bias in Anglican strength. If Nonconformity and non-churchgoing represented alternative forms of dissent, both objectionable in the eyes of large sections of the gentry and of the Anglican clergy, the distribution of the two forms differed, and also had distinctive social and regional features. In so far as both could only flourish where control from above was weak, they were often found in the same places;[26] but while the pattern of religious abstention was simply the reverse of the pattern of Anglican church attendance, the Nonconformist pattern was more complex, and depended to a considerable degree on local factors. In social terms, non-churchgoers were most numerous at the bottom end of the hierarchy, Nonconformists around the middle; geographically, the former were most numerous in the three northern-most counties, in Middlesex and in the towns, while the latter were stronger in villages and small towns, in the East and in the South-West. The support for the various Nonconformist denominations was in fact as regionalized as that of the church: Congregationalists and Baptists being strongest in the areas where Puritanism flourished in the seventeenth century, and weak in the North and West, Methodism spreading fastest in 'the dark corners of the land',[27] but later filling in some of the gaps left by Old Dissent in the South and East.[28] In general, it was in the more isolated communities that religious dissent was strongest: on the one hand, official religion was often very late in reaching such places and, on the other, they might be insulated from the suspicion of organized religion, together with a certain intolerance of its adherents, which prevailed in the working class as a whole, and from which those living in large towns could scarcely escape. The fact that Nonconformists were found much more often around the middle than at the bottom of the social hierarchy can partly be explained in cultural terms, but partly also in terms of social status: those who had some status to lose were aware that there was something disreputable about a failure to attend some sort of church.[29] It was certainly not as bad as avowed atheism. As an Oxfordshire clergyman wrote in 1802: 'Though the inhabitants of this place are in some degree neglectful of their Christian duty – yet I know of none so depraved as to abstain from public worship *continually* or from principle';[30] or as an advanced thinker in one of Gissing's novels complained: 'most kinds of immorality are far more readily forgiven by people of the world than sincere heterodoxy on moral subjects'.[31] If those in the lower middle and upper working classes, from which the chapels drew most of their members, were less likely than their social superiors to attend church as a matter of duty, they were still sensitive to the issue of their own respectability, and the map of churchgoing thus reflected the varying strength of this pull. There was a relative respectability at every point of the social scale, so that Roman Catholic priests, for instance, whose congregations were still largely working-class, still found that it was the poorest who seldom went to Mass, and a priest in Fulham was able to distinguish between the 'rough poor' (mostly costers), who sent their children to Catholic schools but did not go to Mass themselves, and the 'respectable poor', who 'attend well to their religious duties'.[32]

But within the national social status system as a whole there was a clear line between the poorest clerk or shopkeeper and the most highly-paid, skilled and self-improving artisan, who none the less bore the stigmata of the manual worker – ingrained dirt, workman's clothes – and the contagion of a rough working environment.[33] This was one of the two basic social divides (the other being between the middle class and those who were gentlemen). The difference in identity between those on either side was not necessarily paralleled by a difference in life-style, though it frequently was.[34] But it did mean that the working man, conscious of an inferior status in the eyes of his social superiors, was far more likely than a clerk enjoying a similar standard of living to behave in ways condemned by these superiors, and far less likely to identify himself with the social system. Thus, a clerk of intellectual tastes and social reforming sympathies was likely to become a Liberal and a leading light of the debating society at his Congregational chapel, while an artisan whose style of life was very similar might join the SDF and the Secularists, a thoroughly disreputable body from the point of view of most of the middle class,[35] yet from an objective point of view thoroughly 'respectable', and sharply differentiated from large sections of the working class in the values adopted by most of its members.[36] If, therefore, Nonconformity often represented a middle-class rejection of the politics and cultural values of the gentry, working men frequently signalled their rejection of both upper class and middle class values by Secularism or by simple indifference.

These class and regional differences were more significant determinants of the national religious pattern than the urban/rural or industrial/agricultural distinctions that have fascinated so many scholars – whether they have seen something rather odd in the habits of city-dwellers generally, or merely in those habits which fail to tally with their own urban stereotype.[37] In 1851, the villager or small townsman was more likely to attend church than the city-dweller – the median percentage of total attendance to population was 64·8 in rural areas of English counties and 49·6 in large towns (or 52·4 if the London boroughs are treated as a single unit).[38] But the range was great in both cases – from 104·6 (Bedfordshire) to 37·3 (Cumberland) in the rural areas, and from 89·5 (Colchester) to 25·5 (Preston) in the large towns. This overall tendency for churches to be rather better attended in country than in city was due not to some generalized rural mentality, but to more specific factors that applied in some areas and not in others.

The most important of these was social control – the fact that certain sections of the rural population were subject to direct pressure from landowners, while those living in the town were only liable to the more subtle pressures of the public opinion in the milieu within which they moved.[39] Yet such pressures were felt only by some of the rural population, and not by country-dwellers as such. Indeed, David Thompson, in a recent study of 'The Churches in Nineteenth Century England. A Rural Perspective', indicated the close parallels between the position of the churches in the city and in the 'open' village with large numbers of small freeholders.[40] Another important factor was the social status of the population – the degree to which individuals possessed recognition that could be lost by deviant behaviour. It was of course because of their high prestige that the gentry were obliged to maintain very high levels of public decorum (including regular attendance at the parish church). But the same considerations affected the actions of the small property owner, and made him readier than the landless labourer to adopt orthodox and 'respectable' standards of behaviour. In an industrial town where a very large proportion of the population enjoyed very little social status, deviant behaviour on a large scale was the logical corollary.[41]

Another factor affecting Anglican (and Roman Catholic) strength in the city was the slowness of these churches in adapting to movements of population by creating new parishes – though the parish system was not always as efficient or effective in the countryside as its apologists tended to assume, and when, in the second half of the nineteenth century, both churches were establishing large numbers of new parishes in working-class districts, it was the nominal Catholics rather than the nominal Protestants who took advantage of the improved facilities.[42] Nevertheless, if churches were held together by the strength of personal ties, and if the slum parson won more converts through the schools, the choir or the boys' club than through the mission, it was in small communities, where the parson might reasonably be expected to know all his parishioners, that such ties were most easily formed. But the difference in this respect between town and country seems in practice to have been small. There was an association between small communities and very high or very low levels of churchgoing, but this was a function of their isolation rather than of involvement in any particular type of production, since the members of such communities might be fishermen or small farmers, or they might equally be miners or even mill-workers.

The 1851 census suggested that while large towns seldom had attendance rates above the national average, areas of industrial villages varied very considerably: some such areas (e.g. the Potteries) were near the bottom of the national scale, while others were above the national average, with one or other branch of Nonconformity particularly strong (e.g. West Cornwall, the Northamptonshire boot-making district, and parts of the Black Country and North-East Lancashire). Such communities might develop their own highly localized traditions[43] and remain, at least for a time, immune from the levelling out of opinions frequently associated with life in a large town, where everyone could listen to park orators and public lectures, where books, tracts and periodicals on a wide range of subjects were easily available,[44] and where even in the matter of something as universal as sermons there was a choice not open to the villager.[45]

The rather sharp contrast often drawn between the religiosity of the countryside and the secularism or religious apathy of the town[46] tends to be based on two assumptions, one of which – the cultural shock experienced by the new city-dweller – is interesting and deserves much more systematic research, but remains so far unproven, while the other – the deep hold of the Anglican Church over the rural population – is simply false. Though there are important differences between the religious situation in the nineteenth-century city and in some parts of the countryside, it is equally necessary to emphasize the elements of continuity. The most important reason for this continuity was that most migration was over a short – often over a very short – distance. This was established by Arthur Redford, using both literary evidence from the early nineteenth century and the statistical evidence provided by the 1851 census.[47] More recently, micro-studies have provided more detail: in a sample taken in Preston in 1851, 42% of those born outside the town had been born within 10 miles, a further 28% had been born within 30 miles, and 14% came from Ireland; of the non-Irish, only 2% had been born more than 100 miles away.[48] The sources of immigration to Winson Green, an industrial suburb of Birmingham growing rapidly in the 1850s and the '60s, were similar.[49]

To this rule only London provided a partial exception, long-distance migrants composing a far larger proportion of the population than in other cities, but natives of the South-East still being the largest element among them.[50] In London, most new immigrants would be unable to communicate except by letter with relatives and neighbours in the places from which they had come; in most other cities, however, the majority of migrants would be no more than a few hours walk from the village or town of their birth and could easily maintain contacts if they wished to do so. Moreover, the choice of a job or of a place to live on moving to the city frequently depended on the help of relatives or friends already settled there. Although we cannot know what proportion of new migrants to the town were able to depend on such help, it is clear both from the censuses[51] and from the experiences of some of those who happen to have written autobiographies[52] that the move to the town did not always mark such a complete hiatus as many have assumed. Some cases could provide perfect illustrations of 'before' and 'after': for instance, when George Howell migrated in turn from a Somerset village, to Weston, to Bristol, and finally – all alone – to London, where he moved around the city working on a series of building sites, Methodism occupied a progressively smaller place in his life, and he began to drink (in moderation).[53] But Howell was in few respects a representative figure. For many people, changes in life-style following the move to the town were less marked. Life and work were still localized;[54] relations between neighbours intimate, the force of tradition strong, the popular outlook parochial;[55] amusement, until the appearance of professional football in the '80s, still centred round the traditional pillars of cultural self-help – the church and the pub – together with pigeons, whippets, rabbits, dogs, cats and fishes.[56] The ancient forms of ritual expression of community disapproval seem also to have survived in some towns and industrial areas.[57] If the increasingly urban character of rural life is a significant feature of life in our own time, working-class life in the nineteenth-century city corresponds more closely to a rural than to an urban stereotype.

In the religious sphere the similarities were quite as significant as the differences. In both town and country a constant theme was the failure of the established church to make much contact with the labouring population, and the very erratic and partial character of the successes achieved by other religious groups. The Bethnal Green vicar who, in 1858, attributed the smallness of his congregation to 'Irreligion and Dissent, but Irreligion bears the palm'[58] was paralleled by the incumbent in a Leicestershire industrial village who concluded in 1881 'it is not easy to say which are more numerous, the dissenters or heathen'[59] or the vicar of the tiny Oxfordshire parish of Binsey (of Perch and Poplars fame), who in 1854 reported 'there is much godless apathy which no human means seem able to touch'.[60] Complaints of this sort came more often from urban parishes; but they were still common enough in a county with little industry, where parishes were often very small, and where church attendance was slightly above the rural average. Similarly, the Kentish Town parson who told Charles Booth 'I would die for the working man, but I do not really understand him; I cannot speak his language and I cannot think his thoughts'[61] was in no different case from the North Oxfordshire rector in the 1880s, described by Flora Thompson, who regularly visited his parishioners, but found, a few 'kindly enquiries' having made, that they had nothing more to say to one another.[62] The only difference was that the country parson's established status might blind him to his real isolation. Something of the same feeling of two worlds barely intersecting is conveyed in the memoirs of a more energetic rural incumbent, J. C. Atkinson, where he describes the difficulty with which he penetrated the world of fairies, witches and farming ritual, the details of which he was so anxious to record and interpret.[63]

If the absence from church services of most working men in the cities was often a continuation of habits learnt in the countryside, this was no less true of the quasi-religious customs that *did* survive the transition. In the urban parish, where no landowner could apply pressure and the parson, whose flock had multiplied by ten or twenty times, could exercise no personal supervision, marriage in church, churching of mothers and baptism of infants continued to be the rule, though urban life also found room for new rites – Watch Night, and Whit Walks.[64]

III

Continuity between town and surrounding countryside is an equally prominent feature of urban churchgoing statistics.

In 1851 there were two belts of very high churchgoing – in the East Midlands and in the South-West. Most of the counties in the South-East, the West Midlands and the North returned much lower figures. It will be apparent that whereas some of the older industrial centres lay in counties near to the top of the scale, the major centres of nineteenth-century industry lay without exception in the counties at the opposite end. Most discussions of the census have focused on this latter fact, and they have tended to see the relationship between industry and non-churchgoing as one of cause and effect.[65] However, the regions of low churchgoing include such thoroughly agricultural counties as Sussex, Hereford and Westmorland, and if the rural areas and small towns of each county are detached from the 'large towns' as defined by Horace Mann, the organizer of the census (most places of over 15,000 people, including such relatively minor centres as Colchester and Gravesend), it will be seen that the non-churchgoing counties remain the same, and that the gap between, for instance, Lancashire and Northamptonshire is little diminished. It would seem, therefore, that there are considerable regional differences in rural church attendance, a fact that comparisons between parishes of similar type in different counties confirms.[66] Comparison between 'large towns' shows that although part of the wide differences can probably be explained in terms of social composition, there were also significant regional contrasts.

The national differential between urban and rural attendance rates was exaggerated by the fact that the urban population was most heavily concentrated on the North and West, the rural population on the South and East. Urban, as well as rural rates were higher in East and South-West England (as well, of course, as in Wales) than elsewhere, and there seems to be a fairly consistent relationship between the figures for the countryside and those for 'large towns' within each county. At the top of the scale were cathedral cities and other county centres, with populations of 20,000-30,000 and large numbers of traders and professional men – for instance, Exeter, York, Chester, Worcester, Wakefield, Reading, Colchester, together with some towns with a large upper and upper-middle-class population – Bath, Brighton, Cheltenham. In such places, the ratio of attendances to population was always close to and generally above the rural average for the same county. At the opposite end were large centres of small-scale production, often with a long industrial history, and mostly in the Midlands or South – London, Birmingham, Coventry, Sheffield, Norwich, Northampton. It is here, though seldom in the textile towns of Lancashire and Yorkshire, that attendances are 30% lower than in the surrounding countryside.[67] (Of course, the rate for Northampton was still high by national, as opposed to local standards, while that for Sheffield was low by both.) Rates for ports are about 15—25% below those for the surrounding areas – Bristol, for instance, being fairly typical, with a rate of 56·7%, as against 69% for rural areas and small towns in Somerset and 69·7% for Gloucestershire.[68] On the other hand, Lancashire, the West Riding and the Black Country show quite a wide range within a small area, varying from a few towns, like Preston, far below the rural average to a few, such as Huddersfield and Dudley, rather above, with most towns between 10% and 25% below. Finally, in the North-East, where rates both for mining and for agricultural districts were low, there is scarcely any difference between the figures for 'large towns' and those for other areas (see Diagram 1).

There was thus a nation-wide tendency for church attendance to be lower in town than in country, and to rise with social status. But regional differences were still so marked that there was not a single national pattern of religious allegiance determined by these factors, but a number of local systems, sharing common characteristics. It is thus broadly true, but still a considerable over-simplification, to conclude with K. S. Inglis: 'Abstinence from religious worship, then, was most common where the largest number of working-class people lived – in London and in many of the towns where the industrial revolution was wrought': [69] industrial towns in the East Midlands differed so far in their religious pattern from those in the West Riding; mining villages in Cornwall from those in County Durham; cotton towns in South Lancashire from those in North-East Lancashire, that they cannot be regarded as a single category – and what about South Wales? [70] To lump together, as Harold Perkin does, all English and Welsh towns of a given size is positively misleading. By dividing all towns into four such groups and comparing the mean attendance rates, he concludes that 'the larger the town the smaller the proportion of the population attending any place of worship'. [71]

Before any such conclusions can be drawn, like must be compared with like; towns differing in the dimension under study must be similar in other crucial respects. Thus, if Manchester, instead of being compared with Colchester, is compared with other industrial towns in East Lancashire, it will be found to rank lower than Ashton and Rochdale, but higher than Oldham, and only marginally below Bolton; similarly, Leeds ranks below Huddersfield, but above Bradford and Halifax; Newcastle above Gateshead, but below South Shields; while the large towns of Leicester and Nottingham had higher rates than a district of mining and hosiery villages lying between them. [72] Birmingham, however, *does* rank lower than any of the towns immediately to the North-West, though so amorphous is the West Midlands industrial belt that 'Birmingham' is perhaps an artificial unit. [73] The rule would seem to be that

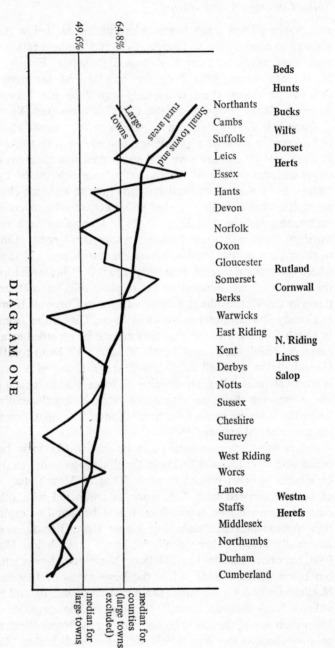

DIAGRAM ONE

Church Attendance in 1851: mean percentage of attendances to population in large towns and in small towns and rural areas within each county. Counties given in bold type are those with no large towns.

both the highest and the lowest figures are likely to be found in small towns, but that cities tend to be below rather than above the regional average.

IV

The pattern established in 1851 was largely confirmed by the minia-ture religious census of 1881, in which about eighty towns in England and forty in Scotland were the subjects of enquiries by local newspapers. The movement seems to have begun when the *Newcastle Daily Chronicle* decided to greet the delegates to the Church Congress then meeting in the city by counting attendances at morning service in the Tyneside boroughs. The *Liverpool Daily Post* decided to count both morning and evening congregations in its own city, and a nation-wide movement followed, in which the majority of the leading provincial centres were covered. Some of the counts were produced very carefully, others less so; but the results were probably in most cases more accurate than those of the 1851 census.[74] There was usually no stated reason for holding a census, beyond the obvious fact that many people might be interested in the results, and that the paper concerned could thus temporarily increase sales and gain some publicity for itself.[75] In most cases comparisons with 1851 were made, and there was an attempt to show whether attendances had risen or dropped in the intervening period, though the value of such comparisons was limited by boundary changes and by the fact that Sunday school children attending ordinary services as a group were counted in 1851 but not in 1881.[76]

When allowance for these factors is made, the figures suggest very little change since 1851, although it is clear that the period in which churchgoing was 'one of the recognized proprieties of life' was coming to an end, and those editors who expressed any opinions were agreed that there must have been a decline.[77] Whether or not the absolute numbers of churchgoers had changed, their distribu-tion remained very much the same. If the relative positions of nine-teen towns in 1851 and in 1881 (or, in the cases of London and Birmingham, in 1886 and 1892 respectively) are compared, a close correspondence between the ranking orders appears. There are only three major changes – the progress of Coventry and the retrogres-sion of Nottingham and Warrington – and three minor changes – the relatively high positions occupied in 1881 by Bristol, Hull

and Bolton. On the other hand, the main features are remarkably
consistent: the very high position of Bath and Ipswich; the placing
of Bristol, Hull, Wolverhampton and Leicester[78] rather above the
average for large towns; the intermediate position of Liverpool; and
the especially low figures recorded in London, Birmingham,
Sheffield and the Potteries.

TABLE ONE

19 towns ranked in order of the proportion of church attendances to popula-
tion in the religious census of 1851 and in censuses of 1881, 1886 or 1892.

	1851	1881		1851	1881
Bath	1	1	Hull	11	5
Ipswich	2	3	Liverpool	12	12
Northampton	3	7	Bradford	13	13
Leicester	4	8	The Potteries	14	18
Southampton	5	4	Coventry	15	6
Warrington	6	15	Bolton	16	11
Nottingham	7	14	London	17	17
Bristol	8	2	Birmingham	18	19
Wolverhampton	9	9	Sheffield	19	16
Portsmouth	10	10			

Three tendencies are again apparent in 1881: the concentration of
most of the towns of high churchgoing on the belt of high rural
attendance; the low figures recorded in most of the centres of
industry; and the placing of most large towns near to the bottom
of the scale. The significance of the second and third tendencies
can be seen from Table 2, and of the first from Map 1.

It will be noted that the percentage of attendances to population
appears to be related both to the size of town and to its social
composition as represented by population structure. But the relative
weight of these and of the regional factor can only be determined
by comparing towns that are similar in two dimensions but not in
the third. This is not easy to do, because the inadequate evidence
provided by nineteenth-century population censuses makes it hard
to know if like is really being compared with like; but it can be done
in a rough sort of way. *A priori*, it is the importance attached by
most students of this subject to the size of town that must provoke
most scepticism. But though the 'size' theory remains both unproven
and insufficiently explained, it does receive more support from

MAP ONE

Church Attendance in rural areas in 1851 compared with attendance in large towns in the 1880s

Rural areas and small towns: total attendances as % of county population (after excluding large towns)

83.3 + 104.6	
67.9−77.6	
56.0−65.7	
37.6−55.0	

Large towns: total attendances as % of population

BATH	46.3−60.9
HULL	36.9−42.4
Barrow	33.2−36.2
London	22.9−31.8

TABLE

Church attendances as a percentage of

	Population	Social Index
Bath	51,790	1
Scarborough	30,484	3
Peterborough	21,219	15
Bristol	206,503	8
Gloucester	36,310	10
Ipswich	50,762	4
Hastings	47,735	2
Southampton	60,235	5
Hull	154,240	14
Coventry	45,116	6
Northampton	57,553	18
Leicester	122,351	13
Darlington	35,102	23
Wolverhampton	75,738	17
Barnsley	29,789	22
Portsmouth & Gosport	149,583	7
Burnley	63,502	21
Bolton	108,963	19
Barrow	47,276	29
Rotherham	34,782	28
Liverpool	552,508	16
Stockton	41,040	26
Bradford	194,467	12
Nottingham	186,656	9
Warrington	40,960	27
Sheffield	284,410	24
London	4,058,735	11
The Potteries	118,579	25
Birmingham	579,709	20

the later censuses than from 1851: one large town (Nottingham) having fallen from a relatively high position, another (Birmingham) having fallen to the very bottom of the scale,[79] Northampton being placed some way below Kettering and Wellingborough, and Sheffield slightly below its more proletarian twin-town of Rotherham. Nonetheless, the very high figures in Bristol, the seventh city in England, as well as the relatively high figures in Hull, Leicester and Portsmouth, the only other towns of over 100,000 counted in 1881 and situated in counties where total rural attendances ex-

TWO

total population in 1881, 1886 or 1892

C of E	RC	Major NC	Other	Total
34·8	5·1	12·8	8·2	60·9
19·4	2·1	17·3	19·1	57·9
22·5	1·0	17·9	13·3	54·7
21·7	3·1	15·5	13·4	53·7
23·2	2·7	13·3	12·5	51·7
23·0	1·6	18·5	4·6	47·7
28·2	1·9	12·4	3·9	46·4
19·4	0·9	9·8	12·1	42·2
8·9	2·7	12·4	17·7	41·7
17·8	4·1	11·6	5·8	39·3
17·9	1·8	14·0	5·0	38·7
12·9	1·7	15·6	8·3	38·5
10·1	3·9	11·0	12·1	37·1
15·7	4·7	11·7	4·8	36·9
8·7	2·6	9·3	16·4	38·0
17·3	1·8	9·4	7·6	36·1
6·7	6·1	14·0	9·0	35·8
12·9	6·0	11·2	5·2	35·3
9·3	6·3	8·1	10·1	33·8
10·8	3·3	10·9	8·2	33·2
9·8	11·3	7·9	4·2	33·2
10·2	5·0	8·9	7·7	31·8
8·1	4·6	12·3	6·7	31·7
11·4	1·7	10·1	8·5	31·7
10·0	7·1	9·4	4·8	31·3
10·8	2·1	8·2	8·1	29·2
13·5	2·8	8·6	3·6	28·5
7·7	5·6	7·3	7·3	27·9
10·0	1·8	7·6	3·5	22·9

(Notes to Tables 2 and 3 will be found at the end of the chapter)

ceeded 60% in 1851,[80] indicate that if size was a factor it still operated within a distinctive regional context.

The significance of the second tendency is more obvious. The wide class differences in religion, as in all other areas of life, in nineteenth-century England are well known, and the fact that in every town far fewer of the working class than of other classes attended church has been established beyond any possibility of doubt.[81] It will be seen from Table 2 that nearly all towns with high percentages of churchgoers are towns of high social status, in so far as this is represented by the Social Index, and this is notably true of Hastings and Scarborough, both in regions of low churchgoing, but both towns favoured by the aged rich.[82] Yet, once again, a regional factor may be at work: for, as has already been noted, the major centres of nineteenth-century industry, and thus the major working-class concentrations, were nearly all in areas of low rural churchgoing. The only major exception to this rule was South Wales, and the two Welsh towns counted in 1881 returned very high figures.[83] Nonetheless, there is a minor industrial county with high rural attendance rates: Northamptonshire, a centre of small-scale production in the boot trade. Here were several towns with large working-class populations and high or very high attendance rates: Northampton, Kettering, Wellingborough and the railway and brick-making (as well as cathedral) city of Peterborough.[84] There are signs, therefore, that the connection between the industrial town and non-churchgoing was not invariable or inevitable, and that if class was the chief differentiating factor within each town, it was only one of several factors dividing one town from another.

V

The primary importance of class in forming the pattern of attendance *within* each town is clear enough when the larger cities are broken up into smaller and socially more homogeneous units. These figures could be used to illustrate either the continuing diversity of regional patterns, or else the centralizing trend. On the one hand, the figures from working-class areas of London, Birmingham, Sheffield and Protestant Liverpool are so similar that they could be taken for slightly different parts of a single system. On the other hand, those from working-class areas of Leicester and of Catholic Liverpool are significantly higher, and those from Bristol are on a level with middle-class areas of London or Birmingham (see Table 3).

Some of the figures for the wealthier districts will have been distorted by the chance matter of the placing of the most fashionable churches: for instance, the Leicester and Liverpool figures may have been exaggerated for this reason. But several points are evident: that churches of the Establishment and of the major Nonconformist denominations are invariably better attended in the wealthiest suburbs than in the poorest districts; whereas in the

TABLE THREE

Church attendances as a percentage of total population in the 1880s in districts of similar social type in various large towns

Areas of low status: Infant mortality, 160+

	Population	C of E	RC	Major NC	Others	Total
London: Shoreditch	46,476	5·7	4·1	4·8	2·1	16·7
London: St George's in the East	125,778	7·7	1·9	3·7	1·6	14·9
Birmingham: St Stephen, St Mary, St Bart	66,820	6·2	2·3	2·5	2·6	13·6
Birmingham: Duddeston, Nechells, Saltley	78,000	6·1	1·1	6·3	2·4	15·9
Liverpool: Exchange and Vauxhall	35,319	2·2	30·7	2·3	1·6	36·8
Liverpool: Scotland	70,606	4·0	22·8	1·7	1·1	29·6
Sheffield: North	38,982	5·3	4·7	3·8	0·7	14·5
Sheffield: Park	19,948	6·1	—	5·0	4·1	15·2
Sheffield: Attercliffe	26,965	6·9	1·6	8·2	9·0	25·7
Sheffield: Brightside	56,719	6·9	0·9	5·1	8·8	21·7
Bradford: South, North, Bradford Moor	38,120	5·9	0·8	8·3	2·4	17·4
Bradford: East Bowling and West Bowling	28,738	7·0	—	6·1	5·5	18·6
Nottingham: North-East	53,911	8·7	1·2	6·8	4·1	20·8
Leicester: North and Middle St Margaret's	47,208	8·3	1·8	6·9	11·0	28·0

Intermediate status; Infant mortality, 130–159·9

Mainly working class

	Population	C of E	RC	Major NC	Others	Total
London: Poplar	165,366	7·4	1·8	8·3	3·6	21·1
London: Battersea	132,695	10·3	1·3	5·9	3·8	21·3
Birmingham: Aston Manor	68,639	8·5	1·2	7·3	1·8	18·8
Birmingham: Bordesley and Balsall Heath	70,881	6·7	—	10·2	3·8	20·7
Liverpool: Kirkdale	58,145	6·4	4·2	10·6	1·4	22·6
Liverpool: West Derby	67,727	8·5	5·2	4·5	1·8	20·0
Bristol: Bedminster	37,741	14·5	—	7·3	16·0	37·8
Bristol: St Philip and St Jacob	50,108	12·5	1·7	10·2	16·8	41·2
Nottingham: Basford and Bulwell	26,712	9·6	—	13·5	10·8	33·9
Portsmouth: Kingston	39,127	10·6	—	6·3	6·3	23·2
The Potteries: Hanley	54,169	4·1	2·8	6·1	6·1	19·1
The Potteries: Longton	18,615	8·0	7·5	7·3	6·2	29·0

Intermediate status
Socially mixed

	Population	C of E	RC	Major NC	Others	Total
London: Hackney	185,211	14·6	1·9	13·5	3·4	33·4
London: Lambeth	264,451	14·8	1·3	9·4	2·9	28·4
Birmingham: Handsworth	32,756	16·5	—	13·2	3·9	33·6
Liverpool: Toxteth	106,660	10·6	7·6	10·2	2·9	31·3
Sheffield: Ecclesall	67,538	11·8	—	8·9	8·8	29·5
Sheffield: Nether Hallam	41,480	11·6	—	8·3	10·7	30·6
Bradford: Little Horton and Great Horton	28,617	8·7	6·2	13·9	5·1	33·9
Bradford: Manningham	20,340	18·9	—	13·8	4·8	37·5
Nottingham: North-West	39,574	14·9	0·8	12·3	12·9	40·9
Portsmouth: Gosport	21,571	20·8	2·2	11·4	3·1	37·5
The Potteries: Burslem	26,521	7·7	8·9	8·6	11·8	37·0
The Potteries: Stoke	19,274	18·0	7·3	9·0	5·4	39·7

High status: Infant mortality, under 130

	Population	C of E	RC	Major NC	Others	Total
London: Hampstead	53,856	26·3	2·0	11·3	1·3	40·9
London: Lewisham	78,365	28·5	0·5	12·7	3·8	45·5
Birmingham: Edgbaston and Harborne	26,135	20·3	10·2	6·5	1·5	38·5
Birmingham: Moseley and Kings Heath	11,339	27·1	—	13·3	0·2	40·6
Liverpool: Abercromby	41,997	22·9	6·2	16·7	11·2	57·0
Bristol: Clifton and Westbury	42,049	33·3	6·5	22·2	3·5	65·5
Portsmouth: Southsea	11,106	35·9	—	14·0	0·1	50·0
Leicester: East St Mary and East St Margaret	35,429	19·2	3·7	34·3	9·2	66·4

smaller denominations the reverse is more often true; that Roman
Catholic strength tends to be in the richest and poorest rather than
in artisan or lower middle-class districts; but that all the Protestant
churches, from the Anglicans to the Primitive Methodists, do better
in the newer than in the older working-class districts.

This break-down into socially more homogeneous units also
suggests that generalizations based on city totals may be misleading. Every city was composed of a lot of miniature cities, some set
on a hill and some on a marsh, often dramatically separated by
rivers or railway complexes. They have points in common: for
instance, both Clifton and Bedminster, however otherwise different, have higher church attendance rates than districts of similar
social type in most other towns, while Edgbaston and Saltley
share the reverse tendency. On the other hand, Edgbaston and
Clifton share with most other fashionable suburbs the fact that
Anglican worshippers were both numerous and, moreover, far
more numerous than any other kind of worshipper; while Saltley
and Bedminster are alike in that most worshippers were Nonconformists. In fact, any reference to a large town as 'Anglican' must
be qualified by the statement that the majority of worshippers in
working-class areas were very probably Nonconformist, and that
the Anglican majority was probably won in the wealthier suburbs,
with their very high attendance rates; similarly, even in such
proverbially Nonconformist towns as Bradford, Anglican worshippers were very numerous, and often the majority in the wealthiest
wards.

What was true of the Church of England was also true, though
in less extreme degree, of the Wesleyans and the other high-status
Nonconformist churches. For instance, Inglis uses the fact that
the total number of Wesleyan attendances in most of the northern
towns considerably exceeded those at chapels of any of the Methodist sects to justify his neglect of these bodies in his study of urban
working-class religion.[85] Yet, the Wesleyan preponderance was
often due to their ability to draw support from all parts of the
city, including those where churchgoing was highest, while the
other forms of Methodism had little support outside the working-
class districts. Bradford, where the Wesleyans were strong in all
parts of the town, would largely support Inglis' thesis. On the other
hand, in Leicester, where the Wesleyans were the largest of the
Methodist bodies, they were heavily outnumbered by the Primitives

TABLE FOUR

Distribution of Methodist attendances within various towns in the 1880s

	Social status	Wesleyan	WR	MNC	UMFC	PM	BC
London							
Shoreditch	Low	0·6	—	—	0·3	0·1	0·2
Poplar	Fairly Low	2·4	—	—	0·9	1·0	0·2
Battersea	Fairly Low	2·5	—	—	0·8	0·5	—
Hampstead	High	2·6	—	—	—	—	—
Birmingham							
St Mary, St Stephen, St Bart	Low	2·2	—	—	—	—	—
Bordesley & Balsall Heath	Fairly Low	3·9	—	0·3	0·5	1·6	—
Ladywood & All Saints	Fairly Low	0·3	—	0·9	—	0·5	—
Edgbaston & Harborne	High	1·5	—	—	—	—	—
Liverpool							
Kirkdale	Intermediate	4·6	—	—	—	0·7	—
Everton	Intermediate	2·0	—	0·4	0·3	1·1	—
Toxteth	Intermediate	4·5	—	0·2	0·4	0·4	—
Sheffield							
North	Low	1·9	0·5	1·7	1·8	0·6	—
Park	Low	3·6	—	0·9	3·6	3·6	—
Brightside	Fairly Low	3·2	0·3	1·1	0·8	2·0	—
Attercliffe	Fairly Low	2·9	1·9	0·9	1·3	1·6	—
Ecclesall	Fairly High	4·5	1·4	—	—	—	—
Nether Hallam	Fairly High	5·6	1·2	1·6	3·2	3·3	—

		Wesleyan	WR	MNC	UMFC	PM	BC
Bristol							
Bedminster	Fairly Low	2·7	—	—	4·9	2·1	3·0
St Philip & St Jacob	Fairly Low	4·1	—	—	2·9	1·9	0·9
Clifton & Westbury	High	7·9	—	—	1·1	—	—
Bradford							
W. & E. Bowling	Low	4·5	1·4	0·9	1·3	1·6	—
South, North & Bfd Moor	Low	5·0	—	—	0·8	1·5	—
Manningham	Fairly High	9·8	—	—	0·8	2·5	0·8
Nottingham							
North-East	Low	1·0	—	2·0	1·0	—	—
Basford & Bulwell	Fairly Low	4·6	—	2·3	2·2	1·8	—
North-West	Intermediate	2·6	—	1·0	3·4	1·5	—
Leicester							
North & Middle St Margt	Low	1·3	—	0·3	1·2	3·7	—
West St Mary & All Saints	Fairly Low	3·9	—	—	—	2·8	—
East St Mary & E. St Margt	High	3·5	—	0·9	—	0·1	—
The Potteries							
Hanley	Fairly Low	3·3	—	3·9	0·1	0·8	—
Longton	Fairly Low	3·4	—	3·9	0·6	1·1	—
Burslem	Intermediate	6·7	—	4·7	3·7	3·9	—
Stoke	Intermediate	5·8	—	2·3	—	2·5	—

WR   Wesleyan Reformers
MNC   Methodist New Connexion
UMFC   United Methodist Free Church
PM   Primitive Methodist
BC   Bible Christian

in three of the four working-class wards, and in Bristol, where the Wesleyans had a higher total in the city as a whole than all the Methodist sects combined, their majority was won in the city centre and in the wealthy and middle-class districts to the North and West, while the sects were far ahead in the working-class suburbs to the South and East. In the Potteries, the Wesleyans were the largest Nonconformist denomination, but in the most proletarian of the towns, Hanley and Longton, the New Connexion led. In Sheffield and Nottingham, where Wesleyans were the largest single Methodist body, but had fewer worshippers than the sects combined, a common pattern emerged: the Wesleyans had a few very well attended chapels in the city centre, and there they were comfortably in the majority; everywhere else, the majority of Methodist worshippers chose one of the low-status churches, but instead of being concentrated within two or three very big chapels, they were distributed among a number of small chapels, the best attended attracting no more than three hundred people to a service (as against six or seven hundred at the best supported Wesleyan services); at the same time, one of the Methodist sects might have several such small chapels in a single district. Wesleyans seem to have formed a majority of Methodist worshippers in working-class areas only in those towns such as London and Birmingham where working-class church attendance was rarest, or like Bradford where the Wesleyan denomination was especially strong[86] (see Table 4).

The volatility of a denomination's support seems to be related to its social constituency, and perhaps to the degree of scope for lay initiative. The Church of England, standing at the top end of the scale on the first count and the bottom end on the second had the least variable strength. The proportion of Anglican worshippers in the population appears to remain almost constant from one working-class ward or one middle-class suburb to another within each town;[87] and even between one town and another the difference between wards of a single social type is not very great. If Liverpool's central wards, with their predominantly Catholic population, are excepted, the working-class districts of London, Liverpool, Birmingham, Sheffield, Bradford and Leicester have Anglican percentages of 6%–8%—marginally less in some of the poorer districts and marginally more in some of the most 'respectable', and slightly higher generally in Leicester than in Bradford. In the two most Anglican of the major cities, this percentage rises to 11% in Portsmouth and to a maximum of 15% in Bristol. On the other hand (with Catholic areas of Liverpool again excluded) Nonconformist strength in the working-class wards varies from 5% in some parts of London, Birmingham and Sheffield to 27% in one area of Bristol, and the range even within single towns is much greater than in the case of the Church of England.

If the strength of the Wesleyans, Baptists and Congregationalists was more variable than that of the Church of England, that of the smaller Nonconformist churches was most variable of all. In Sheffield North they comprised 5% of all worshippers, and less than 1% of the population, and similar figures were recorded in some parts of London and Liverpool; in two districts of Bristol, on the other hand, they comprised 40% of worshippers and 16% of the population. And though Bristol is a freak among the great cities, the smaller Protestant churches, notably the Primitive Methodists and the Salvation Army, were also strong in working-class wards of Leicester (40% of worshippers and 11% of population) and in those Northern towns, such as Hull, Barnsley, Darlington and Scarborough, where church attendance was above the average.[88] It would seem that the percentage of the urban population who could be persuaded to attend an Anglican church was rather small, but that this section included many people with a strong sense of the obligation to attend church, whose habits were little affected by the distinctive quality of the local clergy or Anglican community. The larger Nonconformist churches, while being more dependent on conversions and on the personalities of their ministers, could also rely on the support of good many middle-class habitual churchgoers. Such bodies as the Primitive Methodists, the Salvation Army, and perhaps the other Methodist sects could rely on little support of this kind, and their following in many districts seems to have been minimal. On the other hand, their potential support seems to have been greater than that of Wesleyans, Congregationalists or Baptists. Like the Pleasant Sunday Afternoon movement, which also provided informal worship and a platform for those with little education or social status, they attracted people who would attend no other kind of church.[89] If large sections of the working class in late Victorian England were bored or antagonized by any form of religious service, there also seems to have been a considerable section which had no such fixed objection, but which was not attracted by the forms of organized religion it most com-

monly met – 'a floating population', as one of Charles Booth's inter-
viewers put it, 'both of men and women not habitual churchgoers
who can be brought to church if the services are made sufficiently
attractive and the sermon is of the kind they can understand and
appreciate'.[90]

If the class-based differences of denominational distribution
within each town were only to be expected, it is more surprising that
district by district breakdowns provide further evidence of the
regionalization of religious practice. The biggest and best of the
local church attendance counts, the *Daily News* census of Greater
London in 1902–3,[91] showed that church attendance rates were
closely linked to social status, upper- and upper-middle-class areas
having the highest and the poorest districts the lowest rates, but that
the pattern was upset in the Western and South-Western suburbs,
where attendances were low, and Nonconformity especially weak,
and in the North-East, where the situation was reversed. In twelve
North-Eastern districts, chapel attendances exceeded 10% of the
adult population in all but two, and in twelve South-Western
districts they fell below 10% in all but two.[92] The reason for this
probably lies in different patterns of immigration: each part of
London drew particularly heavily from the county adjacent –
Lewisham from Kent, Wandsworth from Surrey, and so on – and
whereas the counties immediately to the North of London formed
an area of high churchgoing with many centres of Nonconformity,
Middlesex and Surrey to the West and South were areas of low
churchgoing generally and had fewer Nonconformists than any
other part of the country.[93] So even the *most* heterogeneous and
and *least* localized of English cities was still some way from being
a single unit in its pattern of religious allegiance.

VI

Much of this will be familiar to 'religious sociologists' in the tradition of Gabriel Le Bras.[94] Boulard and Rémy, in their comprehensive analysis of contemporary French religious statistics lovingly
describe the regional peculiarities of urban Catholicism, and appear
to assume that these are a permanent feature of French society.
Yet they would scarcely find the English parallel encouraging. The
regional peculiarities that were so important in England of the
1880s had largely dissolved by the 1950s. If one aspect of this
change is the near-uniformity of class-based politics, another is

the breaking down of all distinctive religious traditions. By now, immigration from Ireland, Asia and the Caribbean has more bearing on the religious geography of urban England than the Anglican parish system or the diffusion of Dissent from the seventeenth to the nineteenth century.

NOTES

This is a revised version of a paper read to the University Association for the Sociology of Religion at LSE in April 1972, and I am grateful to those who attended this meeting for their comments. I am especially indebted for his advice to Dr David M. Thompson. He is not, of course, responsible for the use I have made of it.

1. F. Boulard and J. Rémy, *Pratique Religieuse Urbaine et Régions Culturelles*, Editions Ouvrières, Paris 1968, p.35. If very small units of population are excluded the range is from about 5% to 85%. The figures quoted in this book were mostly collected in the mid-1950s, since when there appears to have been a drop in Mass attendance in some parts of France (Ibid., pp.32–5), so that the upper extreme may now be lower.

2. C. Y. Glock and R. Stark, *Religion and Society in Tension*, Rand McNally, Chicago 1965, p.206, quoting a poll of 1956.

3. For instance, the contrast in Spain between the Catholic North and the anti-clerical South and East can be seen from the map in G. Brenan, *The Spanish Labyrinth*, paperback edition, CUP 1960, p.335, and from R. Duocastella, 'Géographie de la Pratique Religieuse en Espagne' in *Social Compass*, vol. XII, 1965; the chapter on Norway in E. Allardt and Y. Littunen, *Cleavages, Ideologies and Party Systems*, Helsinki 1964, discusses the distinctiveness of the South and West, marked by small farms, high church attendance, support for the temperance movement, and voting for the centre parties.

4. For contemporary churchgoing statistics, see David Martin, *A Sociology of English Religion*, SCM Press 1967, pp.43–5. Reliable information on this subject is scarce, but in all the towns that he quotes the proportion of weekly attendances to population falls between 7% and 20%. For links between religious affiliation and voting habits, see D. Butler and D. Stokes, *Political Change in Britain*, Penguin Books 1971, pp.158–71, which shows, among other things, that the link is much stronger with those brought up before 1918 than among younger voters. Glock and Stark (op. cit., chapters 10-11) use 1957 British Gallup Poll data to support their thesis of a worldwide link between religion and right-wing voting. These figures seem to me to beg more questions than Glock and Stark allow, but the relative weakness of the link in Britain can be seen when they are compared with similar figures from a country where religious affiliation definitely *is* politically significant: see E. Aver and others, 'Pratique Religieuse et Comportement Electoral', in *Archives de Sociologie des Religions*, no. 29, janvier–juin 1970.

5. According to Hippolyte Taine's description in *Notes on England*, English translation 1873, p.9.

6. Evidence of the Rev. J. Colbourne, Rector of Bethnal Green, to the Select Committee of the House of Lords appointed to inquire into the

Deficiency of Means of Spiritual Instruction and Places of Divine Worship, *Parliamentary Papers*, 1857–8, vol. ix, Q.524.

7. F. H. Critttall, *Fifty Years of Work and Play*, Constable 1934, pp. 40-55. Crittall became famous and rich by manufacturing the metal window frames that were a distinctive feature of houses built in the 1920s and '30s.

8. This omission is now being made good by interviews. R. Stark and C. Y. Glock, in *American Piety: The Nature of Religious Commitment*, University of California Press 1968, divide religion into five dimensions – belief, practice, knowledge, experience and consequences – in each of which the interviewee can be allotted a score.

9. The best known statement of the unorthodoxy, or at least the extreme diversity, of the theological ideas of churchgoers is Mass Observation, *Puzzled People*, Gollancz 1947. The same point was made some forty years earlier by C. F. G. Masterman, *The Condition of England*, Methuen 1909, pp.88–9, and by L. H. Courtney in his anonymous *The Diary of a Church-goer*, Macmillan 1904. Nineteenth-century 'agnosticism in the pew' is discussed in a short paper by P. G. Scott, 'A. H. Clough: A Case Study in Victorian Doubt', *Studies in Church History*, 9, ed. D Baker, CUP 1972.

10. In the upper class for most of the nineteenth century, the act of attending church services regularly was 'amongst the recognized proprieties of life' (Horace Mann's phrase in his report on the 1851 Religious Census, 'Religious Worship [England & Wales]', in *Parliamentary Papers*, 1852–3, vol. LXXXIX, clviii); in the working class, which recognized no such propriety, PSAs (Pleasant Sunday Afternoons) and church clubs, not to mention Sunday Schools, were more important links with organized religion than Sunday services.

11. The national pattern is that revealed by the census of attendance at churches and chapels on 30 March 1851, organized in association with the decennial population census in that year. The original schedules are in the Public Record Office (H.O.129), and the results are summarized in *Parliamentary Papers*, 1852–3, vol. LXXXIX The results of the census and their reliability have been discussed in a number of articles. National patterns have been studied by K. S. Inglis, 'Patterns of Religious Worship in 1851', *Journal of Ecclesiastical History*, vol. XI, no. 1, April 1960, and by W. S. F. Pickering, 'The 1851 Religious Census – A Useless Experiment?', *British Journal of Sociology* XVIII, no. 4, December 1967. Other studies have been primarily local: R. M. Goodridge, 'The Religious Condition of the West Country', *Social Compass*, vol. XIV, no. 4, 1967, and I. G. Jones, 'Denominationalism in Swansea and District', *Morgannwg*, vol. XII, 1968; while D. M. Thompson, 'The 1851 Religious Census, Problems and Possibilities', *Victorian Studies*, vol. XI, no. 1, September 1967, though focussed on the East Midlands, is mainly concerned with problems of methodology, and Thompson's unpublished Cambridge PhD thesis, *The Churches and Society in Leicestershire, 1851–1881* (1969), includes the most intensive study yet made of the returns. J. Gay, *The Geography of Religion in England*, Duckworth 1971, provides maps showing the distribution of the adherents of various denominations both nationally and within certain areas. Other studies in which aspects of the returns are analysed include H. Perkin, *The Origins of Modern English Society, 1780-1880*, Routledge 1969, A. Everitt, *The Pattern of Rural Dissent: The Nineteenth Century*, Leicester University Press 1972, R. Currie, 'A Micro-Theory of Methodist Growth', *Proceedings of the Wesley Historical Society*, vol. XXXVI, October 1967. As for the accuracy of the returns, three points should be made: that the term used on

the schedule was 'estimated attendances', and it is clear that most of the figures returned, especially in the larger churches, were no more than estimates; that the elaborate explanations provided by many clergymen and ministers for below average attendances suggest that the estimates they gave were provided in good faith (about one return in three gave average attendances higher than those on 30 March); and that local factors may reduce the comparative value of the totals – for instance, a high proportion of the returns from Birmingham and the Black Country blamed Mothering Sunday for low attendances, but none of those from London, Liverpool or Sheffield. However, as I shall argue, the regional distribution of attendances on census day is largely confirmed by other evidence.

12. Peel told a meeting of Conservative MPs in 1837: 'By Conservative principles we mean the maintenance of our settled institutions in Church and State', N. Gash, *Reaction and Reconstruction*, CUP 1965, p.132.

13. D. M. Thompson (*Churches and Society in Leicestershire*, p.57) found that in 1851 there was a clear progression from squire's villages in that county, where both Anglican and total attendances were at their highest, through those with absentee squires and 'divided' villages, to freehold villages, with the highest mean percentage both of Nonconformist attendances and of non-churchgoers. Church and chapel were not completely mutually exclusive alternatives. Some people attended either or both indifferently. (See, for instance, H. Pelling, *Popular Politics and Society in Late Victorian England*, Macmillan 1968, pp.23–5). But these sharp differences between the distribution of attendances in different types of rural community suggests that there were also a great many people who did not attend both. (This does not, of course affect the validity of Pelling's point, that most people regarded the *theological* distinctions between the main forms of Protestantism as immaterial.)

14. A good description of the 'Old Squire's' conception of religion is given in *Facing the Facts*, ed. W. K. Lowther-Clarke, Nisbet 1911, p.31: 'he does not ask whether he needs the comforts of religion, he is sure that society needs religion, and if society needs religion he, as one of the first in the social organization, must be there at his post ...'

15. In 1912 an evangelical vicar in South London looked back to the days when 'even in those cases where religious convictions were not very deep, they thought it their duty to attend church, if only to set an example to their children and servants': Rev. W. H. Langhorne, in the parish magazine of Holy Trinity, Sydenham, as quoted in *Lewisham Borough News*, 9 August 1912.

16. This was not the only or the chief reason for working-class non-churchgoing: there were not a great many working-class Nonconformists either, in spite of the radical associations of some chapels. But the fact that few working men identified themselves with the 'settled institutions' of the country, and many regarded them with bitter hostility, removed a motive for Anglican churchgoing that was powerful in other classes. To take examples from Robert Tressell, a militant Secularist, like Owen, was an oddity, but Linden, who was 'very patriotic' and whose wife was a keen Anglican, was also in a minority, and the general view was that 'this religious business' was 'the parson's trade, just the same as painting's ours, only there's no work attached to it and the pay's a bloody sight better than ours is': R. Tressell, *The Ragged Trousered Philanthropists*, Panther 1965, p.141.

17. The heavy concentration of Anglican attendances on South and

East, and of the highest total attendances on almost the same counties, can best be seen from Gay, op. cit., maps 3 and 8.

18. Sylvester, *The Rural Landscape of the Welsh Borderland*, Macmillan 1969, ch.8.

19. In 1962, Anglican Easter communicants were most numerous in relation to population in the dioceses of Hereford, Bath & Wells, Carlisle, Gloucester and Exeter, and were increasing significantly only in Truro and Sodor & Man: *Facts and Figures About the Church of England no. 3*, Church Information Office 1965, table 75.

20. R. Howie, *The Churches and the Churchless in Scotland*, Bryce 1893, p.91.

21. C. Tilly, *The Vendée*, Edward Arnold 1964, revolves round the contrast between Les Mauges, an area of small farms and isolated farmhouses, highly Catholic and a stronghold of counter-revolution, and the Valley of the Loire, with larger farms, more concentrated settlement, many small towns and more contact with the outside world, where few people went to Mass, and the Revolution made rapid progress. A similar contrast is drawn in G. Cholvy, *Géographie Religieuse de l'Hérault Contemporain*, Paris 1968.

22. E. Kadlecova, 'Religiosity in the North-Moravian District of Czechoslovakia', *Social Compass*, vol. XIII, no. 1, 1966, in which the author concludes (in spite of the dramatic fall in the number of 'believers' since 1946) that the 'social conditions for the doom of religion – as they were formulated in the classics of Marxism–Leninism – have not yet been attained in our society'; and for similar figures from Bulgaria, David Martin, *The Religious and the Secular*, Routledge 1969, pp.139-52. Both sets of figures refer to answers to such questions as 'Are you a believer?', and so are not strictly comparable to those from England, Scotland and France referring to church attendance.

23. J. Thirsk, *The Agrarian History of England and Wales*, vol. IV, CUP 1967, pp.409-12, 463. An analogous situation in a heathland area of Surrey, with no church before the late nineteenth century, was described in G. Bourne, *Change in the Village*, Duckworth 1912, p.295: Lower Bourne, the village described, was a community of heathland squatters 'free from interference by rich people or by resident employers. They had the valley to themselves; they had always lived as they liked, and been as rough as they liked'.

24. For accounts of areas where, in the nineteenth century, Methodism was strong and the church weak, see J. C. Atkinson, *Forty Years in a Moorland Parish*, Macmillan 1891, and C. J. Hunt, *The Lead Miners of the Northern Pennines*, Manchester University Press 1970; and for a community where the church dominated in the mid-twentieth century, but religious indifference seemed to have prevailed for several centuries, W. M. Williams, *The Sociology of an English Village: Gosforth*, Routledge, 1956.

25. Incumbents of rural parishes in the South often mentioned 'the poor' as non-churchgoers in Visitation Returns, e.g. Caversham, Berks. (Oxford Visitation, 1802, Bodleian), East Bedfont, Middlesex (London Visitation, 1883, Lambeth Palace). At Cuxton, Kent (Rochester Visitation, 1881, Greater London Record Office), 'labouring *men*' were identified as an absent group.

26. D. M. Thompson, 'The Churches and Society in Nineteenth-Century England: A Rural Perspective', *Studies in Church History*, 8, ed. G. J. Cuming and D. Baker, CUP 1972, p.270.

27. A term applied by seventeenth-century Puritans to the rural areas of the West, the North and Wales, where Protestantism was making little progress against the twin enemies of Popery and ignorance of all religion. See J. E. C. Hill, 'Puritanism and "The Dark Corners of the Land" ', *Transactions of the Royal Historical Society*, 5th series, vol. XIII, 1963. These areas (except for Wales) had few Baptists or Congregationalists in the nineteenth century.

28. Currie, op. cit., pp.67-8, showed that Old Dissent flourished in counties where the Church of England was strong, Methodism in counties where it was weak. Everitt, op. cit., pp.11, 42-6, 58-61, using the parish as his unit of study, has shown that in Kent and Leicestershire, Old Dissent established itself in precisely the type of parish where Methodism flourished in Cornwall or Yorkshire – those that were large with a scattered population, subsidiary settlements or industry; whereas Methodism, coming later, concentrated on the gentry-dominated areas previously untouched by Dissent or on the new railway- or canal-based communities.

29. In an article in the *Revue des Deux Mondes* of 1875, entitled 'Une Visite Aux Eglises Rationalistes de Londres', Comte Goblet d'Aviella discussed 'l'idée essentiellement anglaise qu'il n'est pas "respectable" de ne pas assister le dimanche ... L'opinion ne s'inquiète pas si cet office est anglican, catholique, dissident ou même rationaliste'. Quoted in S. Budd, *The British Humanist Movement*, Oxford D.Phil. thesis, 1969, p.324.

30. Oxford Visitation, 1802 (Bodleian). Reply of the Rector of Culham.

31. G. Gissing, *Born in Exile*, Gollancz 1970, pp.280-1 (first published 1892). Times were changing: there was some argument as to whether this were still true, though both speakers were agreed that it had been.

32. Booth Collection (British Library of Political and Economic Science), B265, 131-3. Interview dated 6 June 1899.

33. For an example of the distinction being made explicitly, see F. M. Leventhal, *Respectable Radical*, Routledge 1971, pp.17-18: the highly self-improving Somerset bricklayer, George Howell, arrived in London in 1855 with nothing but a letter of introduction to the Aldersgate YMCA; but when he got there, he was told that their members did not wear corduroy trousers and that they could get him a job as a clerk but not as a 'mechanic'. A classic statement of the unrespectability of working men in general is the evidence to the Royal Commission on the Housing of the Working Classes of the Manager of the Great Eastern Railway, in which he defended his company's discouragement of the working-class passenger: 'Of an afternoon when our City trains are going out between 5 and 6 o'clock, they run out of the suburban side of our station at the rate of 16 in the hour filled with well-to-do city men and their wives and daughters; and it is not an agreeable thing for them to hob-nob with these working men, excellent men, perhaps, in their walk of life, but the language that they naturally use is very offensive to most people. Again, they have a rough, boisterous way about them; it is difficult, perhaps, to say that it is wrong; it is natural to them. But it is very annoying indeed to a large section of our passengers': *Parliamentary Papers*, 1884–5, vol. XXX, Q.10207.

34. Differences in style of life between clerks and artisans with a similar income are mentioned by C. Booth, *Life and Labour of the People in London*, Macmillan 1902–3, 2nd series, III, pp.277-8, and repeatedly by D. Lockwood in *The Blackcoated Worker*, Allen & Unwin 1958.

35. Gissing (op. cit., p.119), in a scene set in the early '80s, refers to 'that growing body of people who, for whatever reason, tend to agnosticism, but

desire to be convinced that agnosticism is respectable; they are eager for anti-dogmatic books written by men of mark. They can't endure to be classed with Bradlaugh, but they rank themselves confidently with Darwin and Huxley'.

36. A striking example of this type of person is Robert Tressell, a severe critic both of Christianity and of 'respectability' in the sense of servility, whose attacks on the exploiting classes and their lackeys nonetheless make special play with their drunkenness, unintellectuality, sexual immorality and (most revealing of all) incorrect English. (The two socialists in *The Ragged Trousered Philanthropists* are the only characters who keep their h's and do not swear.)

37. Thus F. Houtart, who regards low Mass attendance rates in the city as a problem, concludes that either the church has failed to adapt to urban conditions, or else these conditions 'ne favorisent pas un comportement religieux normal', whereas Thomas Luckmann, who sees the *survival* of 'church-orientated religion' as the problem, finds his solution in the survival of social groupings 'peripheral to the structure of modern society'. F. Houtart, *L'Eglise et la Pastorale des Grandes Villes*, Etudes Religieuses, Bruxelles 1955, pp.13, 18, 22-4; *Sociology of Religion*, ed. R. Robertson, Penguin Books 1969, p.149.

38. The median may be more revealing than the more commonly quoted mean rural and urban attendance rates, since, if urban units are being studied, Colchester is as much a unit, and deserves as much weight, as London, and if regional differences are to be represented, thinly populated areas, such as Herefordshire and Westmorland, deserve as much weight as a densely populated county such as Essex.

39. Flora Thompson, in *Lark Rise to Candleford*, contrasts her own Oxfordshire hamlet-dwellers with those living in neighbouring estate villages in rent free cottages: 'A shilling, or even two shillings a week, they felt, was not too much to pay for the freedom to live and vote as they liked, and to go to church or chapel or neither as they preferred.'

40. Cuming and Baker, op. cit., p.276. Thompson also notes (ibid., p.270) that in the mid-nineteenth century, only 10% of Leicestershire villages had a resident squire, while 30% had a single absentee landlord. Everitt's analysis of parishes in four counties in 1860 shows that the proportion in 'one hand' or 'a few hands' was 52% in Leicestershire, 55% in Kent, 58% in Lindsey, and 67% in Northamptonshire. But the parishes where property was 'much sub-divided' tended to be both larger in area and more densely populated.

41. This is well illustrated by H. Miner, *St Denis: A French Canadian Parish*, University of Chicago Press 1939. St Denis was a community of small farmers, with little social differentiation, where nearly everyone was a practising Catholic, where tradition defined correct behaviour in wide areas both of work and leisure, and where there was very little crime. On the other hand, there was a small class of landless labourers, and they were 'more individualistic, less under paternal dominance, and tend to be less faithful Catholics' (Miner, p.88) as well as providing some of the farmers' sons with prostitutes (ibid., p.210). Cholvy (op. cit., pp.455-8), who calculated the differences between Mass attendance rates of adult male agricultural workers and industrial workers in the Hérault in 1962, showed that there was a difference, but that it was small – 6·4% for the former and 3·5% for the latter, as against 20·6% for farmers.

42. The response to some of the Roman Catholic evangelistic efforts in

Irish London in the '40s, '50s and '60s is described in S. W. Gilley, *Evangelical and Roman Catholic Missions to the Irish in London, 1830–70*, Cambridge PhD thesis 1971, pp.216-21, 233-7; the lack of response to the churches built free of pew-rents in the 1840s through the Bethnal Green Churches Fund, by B. I. Coleman, *Church Extension Movement in London, c. 1800–1860*, Cambridge PhD thesis 1968, pp.182-3. In 1846, Bishop Blomfield was already referring to Bethnal Green as 'the spot where it is said that we have sown our seed in vain'. (The 1851 census did, however, show that Anglican attendances were slightly higher in Bethnal Green than in any other East End district, except Whitechapel.)

43. Whereas the attendance rates in mainly agricultural counties vary surprisingly little from one Registration District to another, areas of industrial villages and small towns vary more widely. Thus in Staffordshire, where rates of 45–55% are typical, Dudley stands out, with a rate of 67%. In Lancashire, where rates of about 40% for industrial and 50% for agricultural districts are typical, in three districts to the North of the county – Haslingden, Clitheroe and Garstang – the rate rises above 70%.

44. Whereas London incumbents in their Visitation Returns quite often blamed the irreligion of their parishioners on infidel influences, those in the countryside (until the 1870s, when the agricultural unions tended to be seen as a disturbing influence) attributed it to 'carelessness', 'indifference' or 'drunkenness'; though at Bradwell on the Essex coast the incumbent complained of 'the circulation of irreligious tracts and journals chiefly brought in vessels from the metropolis'. London Visitation, 1842 (Lambeth Palace).

45. A Derbyshire girl who came to work in a shop in Bolton about 1890 attended every church and chapel in the town – 'a great experience' – before settling at a church with a 'refined and scholarly vicar'. See H. Mitchell, *The Hard Way Up*, Faber 1968, p.78.

46. E.g. by Perkin, op. cit., p.202.

47. A. Redford, *Labour Migration in England, 1800–50*, Manchester University Press 1926, pp.54-8, 159-60.

48. M. Anderson, *Family Structure in 19th Century Lancashire*, CUP 1971, p.37.

49. At Winson Green, an area of skilled metal workers, 22% of those heads of households born outside Birmingham were in 1861 natives of the Black Country, 30% came from the rest of Warwicks, Worcs and Staffs, and 13% from Salop, Hereford, Derbys or Leics, parts of which were within 30 miles of Birmingham. In Deritend, an area with many labourers, the figures were 22%, 37%, 12%. I owe these figures to Miss Mary Hutsby of Birmingham University.

50. G. Stedman Jones, *Outcast London*, OUP 1971, pp.147-8.

51. The tendency in 1851 for immigrants from particular villages to live in the same house or street and for households to include kinsmen from outside the nuclear family has been noted both in Preston and among the London Irish. Anderson, op. cit., pp.45, 101-2; Lynn Lees, 'Irish Slum Life in 19th Century London', in S. Thernstrom and R. Sennett, *Nineteenth Century Cities*, Yale University Press 1969, pp.374-83.

52. E.g. Victor Pritchett's father, after running away from his North Yorkshire home in the 1890s, went first to York, to stay with an uncle, and then to London, where he had a cousin in the rag trade; V. S. Pritchett, *A Cab at the Door*, Chatto & Windus 1968, p.23. Or, for an example of the family networks spread over several miles, see C. S. Davies, *North Country Bred*, Routledge 1963, p.25, in which her father, leaving school

in Rossendale at the age of twelve, walked ten miles to Bury to enlist as a drummer-boy, and on being rejected immediately walked another ten miles to Manchester, to find a job in a warehouse and to lodge with his uncle, with whom he remained for 6 years.

53. Leventhal, op. cit., pp.11-25.

54. Working men could not (with a few exceptions, such as the GER services from Liverpool Street to the Lea Valley suburbs), afford to travel by train, and only with the coming of electric trams could large numbers of them afford to live at some distance from their work. In 1890, only one wage-earner in four in the Southern suburbs of London used public transport to go to work. J. R. Kellett, *The Impact of Railways on Victorian Cities*, Routledge 1969, p.369.

55. For subjective expressions of this view of working-class great city life at the beginning of this century, see A. S. Jasper, *A Hoxton Childhood*, Barrie & Rockliff 1969, and R. Roberts, *The Classic Slum*, Manchester University Press 1970. Roberts speaks of the Salford where he grew up as a 'village' of 30 streets and alleys, 'perhaps as closed an urban society as any in Europe'.

56. The role of animals in the leisure of the urban working class was illustrated by a *Daily Telegraph* enquiry of 1905 into the British Sunday. Special articles on London reported rabbit coursing at Hounslow, whippet racing and bird-catching on Hackney Marshes, fishing in the Lea and, in Bermondsey, repairing rabbit hutches and chicken runs; *Daily Telegraph*, 6-13 October 1905.

57. E. P. Thompson, ' "Rough Music": Le Charivari Anglais', *Annales*, vol. xxvii, no. 2, mars-avril 1972, pp.306, 309, giving examples of rough musics in the second half of the nineteenth century in Woolwich, Gorton, and at Pudsey and Huddersfield, where this form of making deviants feel unwanted was said to be 'très repandu'.

58. London Visitation, 1858 (Lambeth Palace). Reply of Vicar of St Andrew, Bethnal Green.

59. Peterborough Visitation, 1881, as quoted by D. M. Thompson, *Churches and Society in Leicestershire*, p.344.

60. Oxford Visitation, 1854 (Bodleian). Reply of Vicar of Binsey.

61. Booth, op. cit., 3rd series, I, pp.174-5.

62. Flora Thompson, op. cit.

63. Atkinson, op. cit., pp.58, 63.

64. The importance attached to churching by working-class women in London is discussed by Booth, op. cit., Final Volume, 46, and by M. Young and P. Willmott, *Family and Kinship in East London*, Penguin Books, 2nd ed. 1962, pp.56-7, who found that 41 out of 45 mothers in Bethnal Green had been churched after the birth of their last child. The continuing insistence by working-class custom on this ceremony is particularly interesting, because many clergymen disliked or even disapproved of it. Keith Thomas, *Religion and the Decline of Magic*, Weidenfeld 1971, pp.38-9, discusses the seventeenth-century debates: it was regarded officially as an act of thanksgiving, but by the people as ritual purification, and by Puritans as a disgusting superstition. It was part of a long history of popular appropriation of the ceremonies of the church for purposes quite different from those originally intended. A more recent example is the taking of communion at the Front in the First World War by soldiers who never communicated anywhere else – apparently in the belief that for a certain period afterwards

they could not be hit. See D. S. Cairns, *The Army and Religion*, Macmillan 1919, pp.172-7.

65. Inglis, op. cit., pp.78-86; Pickering, op. cit., pp.402-3.

66. Everitt, op. cit., table III, shows that gentry-dominated parishes in Kent were more likely than those in Leicestershire, Lindsey or Northamptonshire to be without a chapel, and that freeholders' parishes in Kent were considerably less likely to have two or more chapels. Though the most favourable to Dissent of the four counties, because of the sub-division of property, Kent nonetheless had, in relation to population, the smallest number of Dissenters.

67. This is the difference between the rural (71·4%) and urban (49·7%) means for England and Wales. Other towns with rates more than 30% below the rural rates for the same county are: Manchester, Oldham, Preston and Portsmouth.

68. Cf. Liverpool 45·2% (rural Lancs 50·3%), Hull 49·6% (rural East Riding 64·6%), Southampton 61·1% (rural Hants 72·5%), Newcastle 40% (rural Northumberland, 41%).

69. Inglis, op. cit., p.82.

70. The ratio of attendances to population was 88·5% in Merthyr – far higher than in any English large town but Colchester. It will, of course, be argued that Welsh-speaking areas form a separate cultural unit. But this is to deny that size, working-classness and degree of industrialization are the sole differentiating factors between towns, and to beg the question of why all the English-speaking areas of England and Wales should, in 1851, be regarded as a single cultural unit.

71. Perkin, op. cit., p.200.

72. Rochdale 49·8%, Ashton 45·8%, Bury 44·1%, Bolton 36·8%, Manchester–Salford 35%, Oldham 31·7%, Preston 25·5%.

Huddersfield 59·6%, Leeds 47·4%, Bradford 42·7%, Halifax 41·4%, Sunderland 48·5%, South Shields 46·2%, Tynemouth 44·1%, Newcastle 40%, Gateshead 32·9%.

For Nottingham and Leicester, see D. M. Thompson, 'Problems and Possibilities', p.92.

73. Dudley 55·3%, Kidderminster 53·6%, Wolverhampton 53·1%, Walsall 43·4%, Birmingham 36·1%.

74. Whereas the 1851 census depended entirely on the estimates provided by officiating ministers, supplemented in a few cases by those made from local knowledge by the district registrar, the papers involved in the 1881 census often provided their own enumerators, and in other cases they generally invited the officiating minister to appoint someone to make a head by head count. The result is that while about half the returns made by individual churches in 1851 end with a 0, this is true of no more than one in five of those in most 1881 counts, and of one in ten in a few cases. All figures that I quote are those appearing in the paper holding the census, and not the summary published by the *Nonconformist* on 2 February 1882.

75. O. Chadwick, *The Victorian Church*, II, A. & C. Black 1970, p.228, refers to the counts made in 1881 as 'the nonconformist census'. This was true only in the sense that any count of church *attendance* exaggerated the relative strength of Nonconformity. Though the majority of the papers making these counts appear to have been Liberal, and some clearly had a sectarian intention, this was by no means generally true.

76. The Bath census was the only one in which Sunday Scholars, i.e. those taken as a group into the main service, were specifically included, and

to make the Bath figures comparable with those for other towns I have had to deduct an estimated proportion of Sunday Scholars.

77. For instance, the editor of the *Hastings and St Leonards Times*, whose paper conducted one of the more efficient censuses, asserted (26 November 1881): 'We stand in the presence, all over the country, of a serious declension of religious worship. How is it? Of the fact there is not the slightest doubt'. And the editor of the *Nonconformist* (2 February 1882) thought that church-going had become 'more than was formerly the case perfunctory' and 'less regarded as a religious duty' and that there was 'much religious feeling that is growing up outside the religious organizations, and that does not look for sustinance from the pulpit'. The *Daily Telegraph* (quoted by the *Nonconformist*, 23 February 1882) expressed similar opinions in more apocalyptic terms. Chadwick, op. cit., p.224, quotes Archbishop Benson and other contributors to the *Guardian* (the High Church periodical) to the effect that it was 'well known' that church attendance was increasing in the '80s and early '90s. It may be that both newspaper editors and contributors to the *Guardian* generalized on the basis of impressions received within their own rather different circles.

78. For Leicester I have used the total provided in the published summaries. However, D. M. Thompson, using the original schedules, ('Problems and Possibilities', p.92) has shown that these were added up wrongly and that Leicester should have been placed 7th rather than 4th.

79. Birmingham was counted six years after London and eleven years after everywhere else. During this time there may have been a drop in attendances, though in Liverpool, the only town to provide statistical, as well as literary, evidence, the decline seems to have begun in the '90s.

80. Except for Birmingham, which may, however, be regarded as a special case. The frontier between the East Midland belt of high attendance and the West Midland belt of low attendance ran through the middle of the county. Although the rural average for Warwickshire was 64·8%, this varied between 84·1% in Atherstone and 35·8% in Meriden. Birmingham stood to the West of this line, and, in any case, drew more of its population from the West than the East.

81. The one dissentient voice is B. S. Rowntree, who claimed, on the basis of rough estimates by the enumerators at his York censuses, that there was no difference between the classes in their proportion of churchgoers. *Poverty: A Study of Town Life*, Macmillan 1901, pp.347-8; *Poverty and Progress*, Longman 1941, p.423.

82. Though the strength of Primitive Methodism in Scarborough can be explained in local terms.

83. In Wrexham the percentage for the day was 66·9%; in Llannelly that for the evening only was 41·4%. It appears from Jones' figures (op. cit., p.93) that, in the Swansea area in 1851, Welsh-speaking agricultural areas had the highest figures; with Welsh-speaking industrial districts slightly lower; Swansea itself in an intermediate position; and English-speaking agricultural districts at the bottom; E. T. Davies, *Religion in the Industrial Revolution in South Wales*, University of Wales Press 1965, pp.34-6, emphasizes that the district of heavy churchgoing in Monmouth-shire was the industrial North – though this began to change from the 1870s onwards, with English immigration and social cleavage.

84. Kettering and Wellingborough have not been included in the tables because their population fell below 20,000. Their attendance rates were

47·9% and 49% respectively, with both Anglican and Old Dissenting services very well attended.

85. K. S. Inglis, *English Churches and the Working Classes, 1880–1900*, D.Phil. thesis, Oxford 1956, pp.45-6. See also 'Patterns of Religious Worship', p.86. Important as Inglis' work on the larger denominations is, this neglect does re-inforce a bias already present in his work towards the treatment of middle-class attempts at evangelization rather than the religious views of the working class itself. In view of his tendency to treat the Wesleyans as *the* church of industrial England, it is also worth noting that they were outnumbered not only by Methodist sectarians in many working-class areas of great cities, but by Baptists and Congregationalists in most industrial towns that fell outside the North and the West Midlands. The Baptists were the largest Nonconformist group in the 1880s in London, Nottingham, Leicester, Northampton, Ipswich; the Congregationalists in Bristol, Southampton, Coventry; the Wesleyans only in Portsmouth and Peterborough. The association between Wesleyans and industry, like the association between non-churchgoing and industry is, at least in part, a result of the fact that both developed in areas where both church and Old Dissent were already weak in the mid-eighteenth century.

86. Though even Birmingham provides some examples; in the city as a whole in 1892 the Wesleyans had three times as many attendances as all the Methodist sects combined. Yet in three working-class wards, Bordesley, Nechells and All Saints, the sects were in a majority.

87. At the end of the nineteenth century all large towns had a few Anglican incumbents – the majority of them being, probably, Anglo-Catholics – who made great efforts to evangelize the working class, and who had some success in doing so. See, e.g., E. R. Wickham, *Church and People in an Industrial City*, Lutterworth Press 1957, pp.145-7. But except on a very local scale, this success does not seem to have been reflected in significant differences between church attendance rates in one district and another. In Sheffield, for instance, in 1881, the figures were for the four entirely working-class sub-districts: North 5·3%, Park 6·1%, Attercliffe 6·9%, Brightside 6·9%; and for the two mixed districts: Ecclesall 11·8%, Nether Hallam 11·6% (two central districts with low populations had higher rates).

88. In Hull, the Salvation Army (attendance equalling 7·4% of total population) and the Primitive Methodists (6·2%) were respectively the third and fourth strongest denominations, and the low-status Nonconformist churches accounted for over 40% of all worshippers; in Barnsley they were the second and third strongest (6·8% and 4·5% respectively); in Scarborough they ranked second and fourth (11·1% and 5·8%); in Darlington, fifth and fourth (2·9% and 3·2%).

89. For one example of this function of the PSA, see Charles Booth's interview of 19 July 1899 (Booth Collection, B271, 79-99, British Library of Political and Economic Science) with an official of F. B. Meyer's Baptist church, which had one of the largest PSAs in London. Its members were said to be drawn from within a mile of the church and to be 'mostly of the roughest clas of working men', while the morning and evening congregations were two-thirds middle class and drawn from all over South London. Initially there had been much mutual suspicion which, the official thought, had now largely disappeared.

90. Booth Collection, A33, Report on District 10,5. A. L. Baxter's com-

ment on the success of J. E. Watts-Ditchfield, the Evangelical Vicar of St James the Less, Bethnal Green.

91. The results of which, together with comments by such authorities as Charles Masterman, were published in *The Religious Life of London*, ed. R. Mudie-Smith, Hodder & Stoughton 1904.

92. In South-West London adult chapel attendance exceeded 10% in Ealing (16·4%) and Wimbledon (13·8%) and fell below in Richmond, Wandsworth, Acton, Isleworth, Twickenham, Battersea, Chiswick, Hammersmith, Barnes and Fulham – socially almost a cross-section of London, with only the poorest districts missing. In North-East London, Tottenham (7·7%) and Edmonton (9·4%) fell below, with an equally wide range of districts above: Ilford, Hornsey, Wood Green, Stoke Newington, Walthamstow, Enfield, Hackney, East Ham, Leyton, West Ham. To compare total adult attendance rates in socially similar areas: it was 19·6% in West Ham, but 15·4% in Battersea; 18·6% in Edmonton, 12·9% in Fulham; 32·7% in Enfield, 20·2% in Acton; 40·6% in Hornsey, 32·8% in Wimbledon.

93. In 1851, the still largely rural areas of North-West Surrey and West Middlesex were marked by low church attendances, with very few Nonconformists – but so were most of North Middlesex and South-West Essex, which suburbanization turned into Nonconformist strongholds.

94. E.g. Boulard and Rémy, using Mass attendance statistics collected between 1954 and 1962, show that there is no correlation between Catholic practice in France and size of town, and only a weak correlation between the level of practice and the proportion of manual workers in the population. The only factor to which urban practice was clearly related was the level obtaining in the surrounding countryside. They also note local, as well as social differences in Catholic practice within towns such as Lyon and Angers, lying on the frontier between different 'régions culturelles'; Boulard and Rémy, op. cit., pp.43, 47, 60, 62.

95. The declining political importance of regional differences can be seen from a comparison between Butler and Stokes, op. cit., pp.171-82, and H. Pelling, *The Social Geography of British Elections, 1885–1910*, Macmillan 1967. Post Second World War studies of church attendance suggest a near uniform national weekly rate of 10–15%. We have 11% in High Wycombe, 15% in a Hertfordshire village, 16% in the whole of South Norfolk, all of which would have fallen within the belt of high attendance in the nineteenth century; 7% in Rawmarsh, 10% in Crewe, 15% in Billingham, which would have fallen outside this belt; David Martin, *A Sociology of English Religion*, pp.45-7; P. D. Varney, 'Religion in Rural Norfolk', *A Sociological Yearbook of Religion in Britain 3*, ed. D. Martin and M. Hill, SCM Press 1970, p.67.

NOTES TO TABLE TWO

1. The figures for Birmingham and London are those published by the *Birmingham News* on 1 December 1892 and succeeding days, and by the *British Weekly* on 5 November–17 December 1886 and 13–20 January 1888. Estimates have been made of the population of Birmingham in 1892 and of London in 1886.

2. In all other cases the population figures are taken from the 1881 census. The names and dates of the newspapers taking the censuses are given in the *Nonconformist*, 2 February 1882.

3. 'Major NC' comprises the four major Nonconformist denominations of relatively high status: Wesleyans, Baptists, Congregationalists, Presbyterians.

4. 'Others' includes all denominations not included under the other three headings, notably Primitive Methodists, Free Methodists, Brethren and Salvation Army.

5. The figure in the column headed 'Social Index' represents an attempt to grade the towns according to their social status. The index used is the ages of the population, as there is no other status indicator for which separate figures are available in the 1851 census for all the 29 towns. The method used is to deduct the percentage aged 60 and over from the percentage aged 9 and under, and then to rank the towns in the reverse of the order of their scores: thus Bath (6·50) is ranked no. 1 representing very high status, and Barrow, scoring 27·31, is ranked no. 29, representing the opposite extreme. If this may seem a rough method, there appears to be no generally applicable alternative. That the proportion of old people in towns, and more especially the proportion of children, was closely related to their social composition was shown by C. A. Moser and W. Scott, *British Towns: A Statistical Study of their Social and Economic Differences*, Oliver & Boyd 1961, Table 26. They used the 1951 census. It may be reasonably assumed that the relationship was even closer in 1881.

6. Only morning and evening services have been counted; attendances by Sunday Scholars and at prisons, workhouses and other institutions have been excluded. It has been necessary in many cases to estimate the number of Roman Catholics attending Masses other than that held at 11 a.m. The formula used in such cases has been to multiply the evening total by three to obtain the morning total. This approximates to the average ratio in those towns with complete Catholic figures, but it tends to be rather higher in major Catholic centres, and lower in towns with few Catholics. Examples of ratios of Mass attendances to attendances at evening service: Liverpool 5·9:1, Bradford 4:1, Warrington 3·1:1, Stockton 3:1, Wolverhampton 2·6:1, Hastings 1·5:1.

7. All towns of over 20,000 people counted in 1881 have been included, except for a few where the figures are incomplete, notably Newcastle, where only morning figures are available, and Derby, where several Anglican incumbents objected so much to the rabidly Liberal journal holding the census that they refused to co-operate.

8. London is taken as the area of the County of London formed in 1889, i.e. the old metropolitan area, without Penge and part of Kensal Green; Birmingham includes Aston Manor and Handsworth, but no other area outside the borough limits; The Potteries comprises Stoke, Hanley, Longton and Burslem; otherwise the boundaries are those determined by the newspaper holding the census – sometimes the municipality, sometimes the parliamentary borough.

NOTES TO TABLE THREE

1. The units taken are: wards for Birmingham, Liverpool, Leicester, Bradford; registration sub-districts for Sheffield, Bristol, Nottingham, Portsmouth; for The Potteries the component boroughs; for London the areas of the future boroughs, which came into existence in 1900 (except for St George's in the East, which is the registration district of that name). The

Birmingham districts include some from outside the borough, and the units are in these cases either boroughs or urban districts (Aston Manor & Handsworth) or parishes (Kings Heath & Moseley).

2. The populations for Birmingham are estimates made by the *Birmingham News*, the paper holding the census; those for London are estimates made for me by Mr Benedict Heal, on the basis of the census figures for these areas between 1801 and 1921; no separate figures for Southsea are available before 1889, and the population for 1881 has been estimated on the assumption that it bore the same relation to the population of Landport as it did in 1889 when it was detached from that district. All other population figures are taken from the 1881 census.

3. Infant mortality figures are taken from the reports of the Medical Officer of Health. I have taken the mean of the rates for 1880, 1881 and 1882 or for the three nearest subsequent years for which I have been able to obtain figures. For Leicester only the figures for the general death-rate are broken up by wards. For Birmingham and The Potteries no such figures are available, and the districts have been distributed either on the basis of their age structure (The Potteries) or of local observation (Birmingham). Because infant mortality is much higher in some towns than others, districts placed in the same category are not necessarily socially comparable, but this appears to be the only social status indicator for which figures are available on a ward by ward or district by district basis in the great majority of towns.

4. In most large towns about 20% of church attendances took place in the often depopulated central business district, where such institutions as the parish church, the Roman Catholic cathedral, the Old Meeting and other chapels of seventeenth-century origin, and the Wesleyan Central Hall, tended to be placed. The percentage of the population actually attending services within a residential ward was probably slightly higher, therefore, than the attendance rates calculated on the basis of attendances within the ward. This does not affect the value of comparisons between residential wards within the same town or in different towns

3 The Catholic Pentecostal Movement

John Moore

Because pentecostalism is essentially a spiritual experience founded in scripture rather than a doctrine, it can easily fit into the institutional structure of the historic churches, whether Roman Catholic, Lutheran or Presbyterian. Theoretically, at least, this is so. But in practice, pentecostalism, in its seventy-odd years of existence, almost invariably sounded the approach of schism and the establishment of sectarian groups, about which the sociological literature abounds. What Ronald Knox said of 'enthusiastic movements' is an admirable, if impressionistic, description of this church-sect progression:

> There is, I would say, a recurrent situation in the Church history – using the word 'church' in the widest sense – where an excess of charity threatens unity. You have a clique, an *élite*, of Christian men and (more importantly) women, who are trying to live a less worldly life than their neighbours; to be more attentive to the guidance (directly felt, they would tell you) of the Holy Spirit. More and more, by a kind of fatality, you see them draw apart from their co-religionists, a hive ready to swarm. There is provocation on both sides; on the one part, cheap jokes at the expense of over-godliness, acts of stupid repression by unsympathetic authorities; on the other contempt of the half-Christian, ominous references to old wine and new bottles, to the kernel and the husk. Then, while you hold your breath and turn your eyes in fear, the break comes; condemnation or secession, what difference does it make? A fresh name has been added to the list of Christianities.[1]

Knox, no doubt would revise that statement in the light of neo-pentecostalism, but one feels that his revision would not be all that considerable, since he sees enthusiasm as being inevitably institutionalized and the pattern of fission recurring 'as a fugal melody that runs through the centuries'.

Neo-pentecostalism began in the 1950s as an attempt to maintain membership in the historic churches with a pentecostalist expression in worship, and it is from this latter tradition that the Catholic Pentecostal Movement derives. This paper will attempt to analyse the origins, development and sociological character of this movement, which during its five years of existence, has been successfully transplanted from its American base to all five continents, with an as yet uncounted 'membership'. I have described it primarily as a 'cult movement', and certain of its unique features will be treated from a number of angles. Among these are the educational background of the participants, the fact that this neo-emotional movement has taken root in the highly formal and institutionalized structure of the Catholic Church, and the 'establishment' reaction which gave a relatively open approval and blessing to a phenomenon, which would have been anathema to it, even ten years ago.

As an introduction I shall first outline how the movement sees itself. This analysis is based on a study of its own literature, supplemented by unstructured interviews with London-based members, and participant-observation of a number of their London groups.

How the Movement Sees Itself

The Catholic Pentecostal Movement (CPM) – or as it would prefer to be called 'The Charismatic Renewal Movement' presumably because of the connotations of the word 'pentecostal' – sees itself as a leaven working for the renewal of the whole church called for by Vatican Two. Primarily a prayer movement, it seeks to re-create the atmosphere and worship-expression of primitive Christianity as described in the New Testament, by being 'open to the Spirit', which manifested itself in New Testament times by an 'outpouring of gifts' (charisms) such as faith-healing, prophecy, speaking in tongues, etc. This openness to the Spirit leads to 'peace' and 'joy' and a complete rejuvenation of the whole Christian life. That the Spirit *is* active still is proven by the countless testimonies of 'people from all walks of life' who publicly bear witness to the Spirit's presence in their life and work, and is further guaranteed by the same New Testament charisms again flowing freely in our time. This is a cause for joy and praise; and the movement feels that it has restored the element of praise to the orthodox catholic theology of prayer, the stress of which is on petition. Witness after witness recounts the conversion (*metanoia*) they have experienced under the influence of a CPM meeting and the commitment they now acknowledge to bring this message to more and more people, even if it means ridicule and suspicion: this in itself is a further proof of the Spirit's activity – a true follower of Christ must expect to be persecuted as Christ was. They are glad to be, in Pauline terms, 'fools for the sake of Christ'.

Persecution is, however, only a minor part of their joy, since their message is gaining rapid and widespread acceptance. The present, then, is a new era of the Spirit: the forgotten person of the Trinity is restored to prominence, and God is more authentically worshipped. Not that traditional liturgical practices are, or should be, ignored but their formal and unemotional character does not allow the total man, body and soul, to worship as befits his nature. The church is seen to have a hang-up about emotions. It is acceptable to jump and shout for joy at a football match, but if one attempts to do this in connection with religion one is regarded as a 'screwball'. This is especially true of men, where there is a 'John Wayne syndrome', outlawing any overt emotional expression.

The movement is acutely aware of the dangers inherent in emotionalism and is constantly urging groups to be on their guard against emotionally unstable members attaching themselves, thus giving the movement, as a whole, a bad name. It is difficult enough to overcome prejudice and secondhand knowledge of pentecostalism, without courting the danger of official church censure. And church reaction is very important to the movement: in many ways the primary witnesses are churchmen and the United States hierarchy's report is seen as giving tacit approval to their work. There can be no question of schism, which is the fatal trap of all charismatic movements. 'The history of the Church is filled with stories of spurious enthusiastic movements which began with power but which ultimately brought division, dissension and finally schism. On the other hand, we can look to examples such as the Franciscan renewal of the 13th Century to see the fruit for the whole church which faithfulness can bring' (*New Covenant*, January 1971).

Pentecostals and Neo-Pentecostals

As is obvious from the very title of the Catholic Pentecostal Movement, the pentecostal nature of it cannot be understood apart from the more general phenomenon of pentecostalism, which originated as a religious movement in the United States at the turn of the century and which was subsequently exported with remarkable success across the world. Indeed, even at this early stage, the origins, development and exportation of the catholic brand parallels the prototype in almost every respect, excluding, however, some very significant and characteristically catholic details, which will be discussed later. The first wave of revivals came out of that tradition within Christianity known as 'holiness religion' and resulted in the gradual formation of some twenty-five or thirty national or regional associations of which the Assembly of God is the largest. These are the pentecostal 'sects' described in sociological literature as appealing to the socially or economically deprived, to the socially disorganized and to the psychologically disadvantaged. It is also within these established pentecostal bodies that the simple sect-to-church development has been noticed.

Until about 1956 the movement was religiously and culturally confined, although not absolutely, to protestants of an evangelical or fundamentalist background. Since 1956 there has been a rapid growth of pentecostalism among the established denominations belonging to the World Council of Churches. Here there is a notable difference. Whereas those who accepted the 'pentecostal spirit' in the early years of the century were for the most part driven out of the established churches by ridicule, persecution, or excommunication, with the consequent establishment of new sects, the present wave of pentecostals, or 'spirit-filled' people refuse to withdraw and join a pentecostal denomination, but instead remain in the church to which they already belong. This new phase is commonly referred to as 'neo-pentecostalism'. This is attracting people from a much wider range of socio-economic and educational backgrounds, and its spread across class lines has resulted in the formation of as yet uncounted numbers of independent groups. Some of these have memberships of several hundreds and meet in converted theatres; some are larger independent churches, often designated as inter-denominational, and represent a socio-economic cross section, whereas the sub-groups and the independent groups are internally homogeneous as to socio-economic and educational backgrounds and may be found at all levels of the socio-economic scale. This is especially true of the catholic movement: it proudly claims that its members come from all types of background and races, but the individual group tends to be homogeneous, which in my limited personal experience is predominantly middle-class and educated. One prominent London member told me that it would be 'disastrous' if 'ordinary' catholics joined without adequate educational and theological preparation.

It is difficult to estimate the membership of these fissiparous and proliferating groups: none of them appear in the official statistics of Christendom's head-counters. A conservative estimate would be that there are possibly fifteen million on a world scale (*Time*, 28 July 1967) but there are no figures available that would indicate what proportion of these are in independent or indigenous churches rather than in the more highly organized pentecostal bodies with national organizations in the United States and international missionary programmes. Freeman found that the average size of a catholic group in the US was 59 but she calculates from a basis of 50 to a membership of over 10,000.[2] One year later, the organizers of their annual congress were preparing for 10,000 participants (including, admittedly some from overseas), thus indicating the rapid and phenomenal spread of the movement.

Having thus sketched the historical background of pentecostalism as a whole, it is important, I think, to note briefly the cultural and ecclesial milieu within which the catholic movement originated. The reasons for this will become apparent, I hope, in what follows.

Church and Culture in America

America, a fertile breeding ground of enthusiastic movements, is given to periodic religious revivals. The 1960s was no exception. Indeed, given its internal and external political conditions at the time, it would be surprising if there were none. However, the character of the revival was different from its predecessors. Unlike earlier revivals, which sought individual conversion by a return to fundamental biblical principles, within the accepted and essentially unquestioned dominant value-system of the American way of life, the current renewal (still out-going but receiving less media-exposure) is syncretic, drawing its inspiration from primitive Christianity, Johannine and Franciscan theology of love, a positive rather than a negative retreat from (or rejection of) city life, the drug culture, eastern mysticism – in short 'the counter-culture'. In so far as Christ figured in this counter-culture he was the 'meek and mild', anti-institutional, preacher of love. This 'Superstar' syndrome had its effect on the institutional Catholic Church of the States as well, a church already well-shaken by the Vatican Council.

The American church was a highly-efficient, highly authoritarian machine. It was a mixture of post-Tridentine garrison catholicism and American immigrant catholicism, leaving little doubt as to what was appropriate behaviour for either the priest or for the layman. The catholic sociologist Andrew Greeley, presenting a study of the priesthood to the US hierarchy, stated that the fundamental crisis facing them, in the wake of Vatican Two, was not structural, not sexual, not even in the primordial sense of the word religious, but rather 'theoretical'. 'Our theoretical structure not only collapsed suddenly, it also collapsed without the slightest warning.'[3] The old theory served well at a time when most catholics were uneducated immigrants, striving simultaneously to keep their faith and earn a place in American society. The grave weakness in such a rigid and inflexible theory was that if any piece of it fell into question, the whole structure would be open to doubt. Once one began to examine one assumption or one aspect of a model, then everything would be examined. The reforms of Vatican Two began such a chain reaction of examination. The people most intimately connected with the origins of the Catholic Pentecostal Movement (and who to a large extent control and administer what organization there is) are not garrison catholics of the old type: they are the new, post-conciliar catholics, educated, vocal and liberal.

It is essential, I think, to understand the impact the Vatican Council had on these young catholics in generating a climate in which a charismatic movement could take root, a movement which but a few years previously would have been complete anathema to them. The council's stress on the charismatic aspect of the church as complementary to the institutional side, the impetus it gave to historical and scriptural studies, its advocacy of ecumenism, its renewed liturgy, its declericalization of the church and its call for the layman to take an active role in church affairs, effected a profound psychological change on these catholics – nowhere more so than in the theological departments of the universities, the starting-point and power-house of the whole movement. (I shall return to this point in the next section when the movement itself will be studied.) Article after article in theological journals made the inevitable comparison between the institutionalized church and the primitive Christian community, with the inevitable question: how come that our church does not seem to be characterized by the presence and activity of the Spirit as the early community was?

Liturgical experimentation with small groups, completely Bible-oriented, and contact with neo-pentecostals, convinced them that the primitive spirit of spontaneous prayer, 'joy', 'peace' and 'fellowship' could be recreated given a 'willingness for, and openness to the spirit'. Universities in the Great Lakes area organized 'Antioch weekends', retreats to 'confront undergraduates with what it is to be a Christian'. In the enphoric post-conciliar years, Bible-vigils, retreats and do-it-yourself liturgies flourished, but by 1966-7 the momentum died down. However, what is important for our purposes is that a complex tangle of interlocking friendships had developed between people at Duquesne (Pittsburgh) and Notre Dame universities; a network of similarly attuned people, experienced in new prayer styles, was established. These were to be the conductors of the new movement: there was in Troeltsch's phrase, 'a parallelism of spontaneities'.

Early Days in Pittsburgh

Although 'charismatic prayer groups' started quite independently of Duquesne, and some prior to it, the movement generally was given birth in the one started by two lay members of Duquesne's theology faculty. They were 'actively engaged in various liturgical, spiritual and apostolic endeavours. They were disappointed, however, with the results of their efforts, and it struck them that they did not seem to have the ability to proclaim the gospel with power as the early Christians had done. They made a pact to pray for each other that they might be filled with the gifts of the Holy Spirit, and they agreed to recite daily the hymn from the Mass of Pentecost: Come, thou Holy Spirit, come!' The two men were faithful to this prayer for the rest of that year and students began to meet with them. O'Connor, himself an early participant, writes that this group 'experienced a profound religious transformation in their lives. Above all, they were brought into real, personal contact with the living Christ. This event was also marked by the appearance of charismatic activity like that known in the early church: many of them received the gift of tongues, several received other gifts also, such as prophecy, discernment of spirits, and the power of exorcism.'[4]

Within a month similar groups began at Notre Dame, spreading out to the universities of Michigan State, Iowa and Portland. These met with initial scepticism by fellow faculty members but this was overcome by 'the conviction, directness and deep faith' of the renewed believers. At this stage, it appears that it took a special grip on the graduate schools, and was seen by the Full Gospel Business Men's Fellowship, a key neo-pentecostal organization, as an intellectual fad, whose prayer-meetings were 'staid'. But it was Ray Bullard, the president of their South Bend chapter, who became the new movement's spiritual godfather. A meeting was arranged to discuss charisms. Bullard brought along some prominent pentecostal ministers to counter any objections from the 'intellectuals'. Then the pentecostals who were there gathered around the Notre Dame group, and began to pray for them. They prayed in tongues; and within a few moments one, then another, and finally seven or eight of the Notre Dame people were likewise praying in tongues. For twenty-five minutes they continued to pray with great joy. A retired missionary who was present asked the students, 'Now that you have received the Holy Spirit, when do you plan to leave the Catholic Church?'[5]

Thereafter, regular meetings took place and tentative contact was made with the local bishop. A weekend prayer-meeting at Michigan State University brought the movement to the notice of press and television. This pattern of events was soon duplicated across the United States.[6] Cases are also known of individual catholics who had received the 'baptism in the Spirit' and the gift of tongues many years before the beginning of any of the groups mentioned above. In most cases, this seems to have come about through the influence of some pentecostal neighbour, although it is risky to generalize about a phenomenon so diffuse and so private. There are also some cases in which this gift seems to have been received independently of contact with members of any denomination.

Sufficient has been said by now of the history of the antecedents and origins of the Catholic Pentecostal Movement to allow us to deal with it and its subsequent development in a sociological perspective. The following analysis will consider four main areas:

1. An attempt at explanation in terms of 'collective behaviour'.
2. A typology of the movement in terms of 'cult'.
3. Factors within the movement crucial to its diffusion.
4. Establishment reaction.

1. *Collective behaviour*

Reference has already been made to Troeltsch's 'parallelism of spontaneities' and this can be further elaborated by a theory of collective behaviour. This field concentrates on those occasions of human behaviour when the ordinary normative structures disappear, and co-ordinated behaviour arises and changes under the control of constantly emerging normative definitions.[7] Situations that are commonly treated in this area are crowd reactions, riots, crazes, fads, and mass social movements. The distinctive mark of all these phenomena is the suspension of the usual controls over impulses and feelings. The person in this situation frequently reports that he feels 'free for the first time in his life'. These episodes also tend to occur in setttings undergoing some dramatic change or restructuring. Given the picture of the American church painted above, there is no need to elaborate this point.

Smelser categorizes collective behaviour into five types: panics, crazes, hostile outbursts, norm-oriented movements, and value-oriented movements. Of these 'craze' is the most appropriate one for the Catholic Pentecostals since their primary interest is what we may term 'collective individualism': personal conversion within a group context, rather than in creating values. Terming this a 'craze' is not to regard it as a fad or as trivial. Rather, a craze is the mobilization of opinion towards the creation of a positive wish-fulfilment belief. This belief usually takes the form of guaranteeing a positive outcome in an uncertain situation by empowering some force (such as the Holy Spirit) with the ability to overcome the ambiguity and anxiety existing in the situation. In a sense, it is the expressed wish that some outside force intervene directly in human lives and produce a solution to some difficult problem. The founders of the movement, as already noted, were actively involved, personally and professionally, in religious struggles at a particularly ambivalent period in history. Through their network of friendship, this wish-fulfilment spread, needing only a bizarre demonstration of the authenticity of the direct intervention of the Spirit as the problem-solving force. This authentification came for the movement in the claimed charisms displayed by members: faith-healing, prophecy, and spectacularly in glossolalia – with a new addition: singing in tongues.

2. *A typology of cults*

The concept of cult has long been the Cinderella in the family of terms that constitute the typologies of religious organizations. 'Consistently overlooked in favour of her "big-sisters" – sect, church and denomination – she has been relegated to a minor place within the sociology of religion's "household" and entrusted with menial tasks.'[8] Recently, however, she has found a number of suitors, but it is not our purpose here to deal with the viscissitudes of the concept – a useful summary may be found in Hill[9] – but with the efforts of one particular Prince Charming, Geoffrey Nelson, at a redefinition of the concept. Nelson's resulting typology is suitable for an analysis of Catholic Pentecostals.[10]

Nelson postulates three major criteria by which cults can be distinguished from other types of religious groups:[11]

(a) Cults are groups based upon mystical, psychic or ecstatic experiences.

(b) They represent a fundamental break with the religious tradition of the society in which they arise.

(c) They are concerned mainly with the problems of individuals rather than with those of social groups.

There are two ways in which a cult may come into existence. In the first case a group may form around a charismatic personality, as when a group gathers round an individual endowed with mystical or psychic gifts. In such a case the disciples are attracted by the charisma of the leader and come either as pupils to learn from him the techniques of mediation, or they come simply to hear his 'words of wisdom' or to receive the message he transmits from the 'other world'. The groups that gather round such a personality may be referred to as *charismatic cults*. Frequently a group which starts as a group of disciples develops by attracting a wider range of followers. The disciples may themselves attract followers and may thus be more successful in spreading the cult than was the original founder. The second way in which cults may arise is from the already discussed 'parallelism of spontaneities', the informal gathering together of people having similar experiences, ideas and needs. These groups may be referred to as *spontaneous cults*.

The Catholic Pentecostal groups contain elements of both types of cult. Primarily, they would be of the second type (spontaneous), but analytically at least, at the very beginning they would be 'charismatic' in Nelson's usage, with the important qualification that the early participants by no means saw themselves as 'disciples' of the charismatic leader but rather he would be an 'emissary' and not an 'exemplary' figure. The 'emissary' or ethical figure is the agent of a personal God who makes ethical demands on men, whereas the 'exemplary' figure or prophet, on the other hand, is one who shows men how they may attain salvation by following a particular technique or living in accord with certain impersonal laws of nature. Strictly speaking, I think a case can be made for regarding the individual group of Catholic Pentecostals as a 'mystical group' and not a cultic one. But since I am here dealing with the movement as a whole, I propose to ignore this distinction.

All cults begin as *local cults,* small groups that meet informally, with little formal organization. If they fail to develop a formal structure they tend to disintegrate rapidly. Some local cults, however, are successful in developing even a rudimentary organization and this facilitates their survival and, in particular, it ensures that the functions of leadership are carried out. Such groups may be described as *permanent local cults.* Spontaneous cults of this type – and to a certain extent, charismatic ones as well – may develop by establishing relationships with other groups having similar beliefs and practices to their own. This may start as an informal relationship for the mutual benefit of the groups and develop a formal organization, usually in the form of a federation of groups. In certain circumstances this federation may grow into a centralized organization (a *centralized cult,* either *unitary* or *federal*). (See Fig. 1.)

FIGURE ONE

Cult—New Religion Continuum

Cult————*Permanent Cult*————*Centralized Cult*————*New Religion*

On the other hand, some cults may be described as *cult movements.* A movement is a diffused collectivity composed of isolated individuals and/or local groups united only in holding common basic beliefs. These may have no formal organization, but may contain within them highly organized groups.

Just as a sect *may* develop into a church or it may be arrested in its development and remain a sect, or develop only as far as becoming a denomination (Fig. 2), so too a cult may develop into a new religion (as have all the historical religions) or its development may be arrested at some intermediate stage. Catholic Pentecostalism is a 'cult movement' as here defined, but as can be seen from the briefest outline of its history it also fits into the cult-new religion continuum. Initially a 'local cult', it is adaptable enough to survive leadership changes and becomes a 'permanent cult', with regular meetings and an ad hoc structure. As its ideas and beliefs spread and it helps with the establishment of other groups a loose federation of groups is set up, with one of these (Ann Arbor, Michigan) becoming a sort of headquarters and missionary centre, and the locale of publishing activities. It would be unwise at this stage to push the movement further along the continuum to 'new religion' for reasons which we shall see presently.

FIGURE TWO

Sect————Established Sect————Denomination————Church

3. *Factors within the movement conducive to its spread*

The cultural and ecclesial *milieu* within which this movement arose has already been described. It is important, I think, to keep these factors in mind, particularly the ecclesial ones emerging in the aftermath of Vatican Two. They serve to explain the 'why?' and 'when?' questions of the genesis of the movement, but there are also factors 'within the movement' which are crucial to its growth and spread.

The anthropologists Gerlach and Hine, in a paper on the internal dynamics of a modern religious movement,[12] propose the following factors:

1. Reticulate, acephalous organizational structure;
2. Face-to-face recruitment along lines of pre-existing significant social relationships;
3. Change-oriented ideology;
4. Commitment generated through an act or experience.

Under the first two of these headings would come the organizational-structure and friendship-network already discussed. Although the

Ann Arbor group has become the movement's centre for information and publishing, it does not effect any direct control over other groups. Its personnel act as conference organizers, and it provides a rota of speakers and 'missionaries'. Through this activity, they have become the spokesmen for the movement as a whole, and in that sense constitute a leadership-structure. They act as watch-dogs of the movement, pointing out inherent dangers of schism and other forms of activity regarded as out of tune with 'authentic catholic pentecostalism'. Yet this framework of authenticity is extremely large, if not flexible. No two groups are identical, and local and cultural variations are allowed for. The 'leaders' are consciously aware of 'extinguishing the Spirit' by formalism and regulation.

This reticulate social structure facilitates the spread of the movement across class and cultural boundaries. Ideological interpretation, organizational polity, type of leadership, methods of recruitment, and even the manifestation of the charismatic gifts, vary widely among the different groups. This organizational smørgasbord makes it possible to meet a variety of psychological as well as sociological needs, and to adapt to a wide variety of situations and conditions. 'It must also be noted that this kind of acephalous, multipenetration network of reticulated, often inconspicuous and seemingly innocuous cells provides a flexibility and camouflage which makes recognition and suppression of a movement very difficult. This type of organization can make a movement appear to its opponents to be a hydra-headed monster, or conversely, to be a spontaneous combustion of the grass roots.'[13]

Ideology is possibly the key to the infrastructure of the movement; whatever differences may exist among groups, their core belief in the non-human leader and his conceptual authority serves to unite them at the very deepest level. The effectiveness of a doctrine does not come from its meaning but from its certitude. The members are convinced of the Spirit's activity in their lives and if people regard them as mad they are content to be 'fools for the sake of Christ'. This activity of the Spirit is their recreation, their renewal, their rebaptism and it demands a total dedication and commitment to a new way of life, which consequently means that they must reject any ideal-real gap. A philosophical acceptance of the ideal-real gap is typical in social institutions designed to accommodate themselves to the world, as Troeltsch noted, and

Christianity's ethic, 'Be perfect as your Father in heaven is perfect', is of little concern to the churchgoer because of its seeming impossibility. But to the pentecostalists it is of importance, because the movement's ideology enables the believer to make the perfection ethic possible. Hence the seriousness with which they approach the basic scriptural texts, hammering out in discussion the application of ideological principles to specific situations. This intense focus on ideology functions as a mechanism for renewal of commitment and for increased involvement in the social structure of the movement.

Ideology also motivates action. But it engenders a positive fatalism. As Festinger[14] has pointed out, belief systems are real and work for their adherents. Pentecostalists believe that the Spirit is directing, guiding and empowering their members, so failure is explained as a consequence of the failure of the potential recipient to give thanks to God for answering his need. Like all belief systems worth being termed such, Catholic Pentecostal beliefs cover most, if not all, eventualities. What objectively *is* failure is reinterpreted as redirection by the Spirit or as a temporary testing of devotion and courage. In this, of course, it resembles the orthodox theology of prayer!

4. *Commitment*

Charisma, which in its strict analytical sense is assigned by sociologists and anthropologists only to inspired leaders of emergent movements, flows freely through the ranks of the Catholic Pentecostals. The fact that less extraordinary individuals can be led through a social process into an experience of commitment, with all its personal and social ramifications, and can influence others in turn, is significant to the study of the movement. The capacity to influence others and to arrive at sophisticated techniques of persuasion is observably traceable to the commitment experience. Pentecostals themselves verbalize one of the rewards of the baptism in the Spirit experience as the power to witness effectively.

In the catholic branch, as in pentecostalism in general, glossolalia is a phenomenon that performs such a function for many participants. The unique side of the catholic movement is the high educational background of the glossolaliacs, who should be seen against the background of a society where the phenomenon is regarded as very definitely beyond the pale and where the predominant form of religious expression is characterized by an almost extreme passivity and cool rationality (excepting, perhaps, the miraculous elements associated with apparitions of the Virgin). However, as Virginia Hine has stated, theories which explain glossolalia as indicative of psychological pathology, suggestibility, or hypnosis, or as a result of social disorganization and deprivation, are inadequate to explain recent data on the pentecostal movement.[15] She finds that concepts of glossolalia as learned behaviour and as part of a process of personality reorganization are more useful: it is one component in the process of commitment to the movement. Since glossolalia is characteristic of all pentecostal movements and is a recurrent theme in anthropological studies, we need only very briefly discuss it here.

For some participants, the experience of speaking in tongues occurs only once and is considered a sign of 'Baptism in the Holy Spirit'. For most it is a recurrent experience felt to be a more direct communication with God and usually accompanied by a sense of joy, release and power. Though the original Pentecost evoked a speaking of tongues that were readily understood by all who heard the apostles, the phenomenon as it emerged in this century, par excellence in pentecostalism, is quite the reverse: it now involves utterances of varying length, producing a range of sounds from animal-like grunts and 'gibberish' to well-patterned articulate ones.

Cross-cultural studies of religious behaviour support the assumption accepted by most anthropologists that the capacity for ecstatic experience and trance, or other associated behaviours, is universal. Only the interpretation of it, the techniques designed to facilitate or inhibit it, and the form it takes, differ cross-culturally. When such states and behaviours are valued in a society (as they are in many non-western societies), this capacity can be systematically encouraged in some or all of its members. When they are devalued, they can appear as deviant behaviour, setting the practitioners apart and making what Aberle called 'religious virtuosi of the ordinary worshippers'.[16]

The Church Reacts

The foregoing analysis of the movement would not be complete without mentioning the reaction of the official church. Initially it was more one of surprise and hesitation than of alarm. This contrasts sharply with the reports of both the Episcopalian (1958) and

Lutheran (1962) churches on neo-pentecostalism among their own ranks. Speaking in tongues was their main source of disquiet and they manifested a basic unhappiness with the appearance of the phenomenon. Unlike the later examinations by the Presbyterians and Catholics, both these reports seem to identify pentecostalism with tongues. The Presbyterians in 1970 adopted 'a position of "openness" regarding the neo-pentecostal movement within our denomination. The advent of it into our denomination may be one aspect of reformation and renewal.'[17]

The reaction of the mainline churches is not surprising. Given all the obstacles to an objective evaluation, particularly the strong tendency of the early neo-pentecostals to take over the cultural baggage, exegesis, and doctrine from classical pentecostalism instead of integrating the experience into their own theological traditions, it is hardly to be wondered that the historic churches took a basically negative stance. The report of the committee on Doctrine of the National Conference of (US) Catholic Bishops (1969) concludes that even though judgment of the movement is hampered by emotionalism and 'somewhat socially unacceptable norms of religious behaviour' it should not be inhibited but allowed to develop, and given certain safeguards, such as episcopal supervision, to avoid the mistakes of classical pentecostalism. This report has been used by the movement as one of their most potent testimonies, and seems to have calmed the fears of many catholic would-be members. Individual bishops have also expressed interest in, and encouragement of the movement. The September 1971 issue of their monthly magazine *New Covenant* (originally a mimeographed newsletter but by now a more professionally produced magazine, containing individual and group 'testimonies', news of new groups, articles about the theology of charisma – some very sophisticated and scholarly) asked a number of bishops for 'opinions' about the movement: what the editors got, to their delight, were 'testimonies'.

I think the reason for this open attitude on the part of the official church can be found in the fact that the movement is self-consciously aware of being 'catholic'; aware of the strangeness of their worship; aware of the danger of substituting religious experience for religious doctrine – a common American phenomenon. The 'leaders' and originators are not naive advocates of a new religion, but theologically-aware, committed Catholics, who found that their needs were not being satisfied by existing liturgical and ecclesial structures.

Tremendous efforts are made in their various publications to prove that their theology is fully in line with traditional teaching (albeit, that of the patristic period), and that this new experience does not mean a betrayal of traditional worship. On the contrary, they highlight that this charismatic experience has enlivened the faith of many nominal Catholics, increasing their appreciation of the Mass, and various Marian devotions, and has been the rescuer from 'morbid introspection' of numerous priests, hung-up on identity crises. For them, schism is unthinkable-but-possible. What they needed was not a new religion, but a renewed one, a charismatic one.

On the one hand, therefore, we have these protestations of loyalty to the institutional church, and on the other, theological and most certainly sociological possibilities of schism. Thus, the ambivalence of the bishops' report, which comes out clearly in this extract:

> *It must be admitted* that theologically the movement has legitimate reasons for existence. It has a strong biblical basis. *It would be difficult to inhibit the working of the Spirit...* Certainly, the recent Vatican Council *presumes* that the Spirit is active continuously in the Church (my italics).

Outside the 'plausibility-structure' of the group,[18] life is not easy for the individual Catholic Pentecostals. Their experiences and behaviour are ridiculed by fellow Christians and suspected by official churchmen. Deviants from accepted norms, they are ever in danger of being victims of a self-fulfilling prophecy, pushing them nearer and nearer to schism, but the movement as a whole is anxiously aware that it is on a very slippery continuum. The frequent defamation and even persecution of new organizations and religious orders within the church has often resulted in this being purified before they have come to be fully accepted as positively valuable.

Cults are tolerated only when the beliefs in the traditional religious system have broken down to a point where the functionaries of that system can no longer dominate the socia-cultural context. In consequence, since they can no longer enforce their belief system on to individual members of society, they are forced to tolerate the existence of relatively independent groups in their midst and frequently make a virtue of necessity. But then, perhaps, the Catholic Pentecostals are saints of a new kind and the church, as in the past, does not know how to deal with them.

NOTES

1. R. A. Knox, *Enthusiasm*, Clarendon Press 1950, p.1.
2. E. Freeman, 'Directory of Catholic Prayer Groups', The Communications Centre, Notre Dame 1970.
3. A. Greeley, 'Blunt Speaking', *The Tablet*, 26 February 1972, pp.184-5.
4. E. O'Connor, *The Pentecostal Movement in the Catholic Church*, Ave Maria Press, Notre Dame 1971, pp.13-15.
5. Ibid., p.48.
6. K. and D. Ranagham, *Catholic Pentecostals*, Paulist Press, NY 1969.
7. N. Smelser, *Theory of Collective Behaviour*, Free Press, NY 1963; W. McCready, 'The Pentecostals', *Concilium*, vol. 2, no. 8, pp.112-16.
8. C. Campbell, 'The Cult, the Cultic Milieu and Secularization' in *A Sociological Yearbook of Religion in Britain 5*, ed. M. Hill, SCM Press 1972.
9. M. Hill, *A Sociology of Religion*, Heinemann 1973, ch. 4.
10. G. K. Nelson, 'The Concept of Cult', *Sociological Review*, vol. 16, no. 3, pp.351-362; 'The Analysis of a Cult', *Social Compass*, vol. xv, no. 6, pp.649-81; 'The Spiritualist Movement and the Need for a Redefinition of Cult', *Journal for the Scientific Study of Religion*, vol. vii, no. 1, pp.152-60.
11. Nelson, art. cit. (in *Sociological Review*).
12. L. Gerlach and V. Hine, 'Five Factors Crucial to the Growth and Spread of a Religious Movement', *Journal for the Scientific Study of Religion*, vol. vii, no. 1, pp.23-40.
13. Ibid., p.30.
14. L. Festinger, *When Prophecy Fails*, Harper & Row, NY 1956.
15. V. Hine, 'Pentecostal Glossolalia', *Journal for the Scientific Study of Religion*, vol. viii, no. 2, pp.211-26.
16. Quoted in ibid., p.225.
17. O'Connor. op. cit., p.26.
18. P. Berger, *A Rumour of Angels*, Allen Lane The Penguin Press 1970.

4 Methodism as a Religious Order: A Question of Categories

Michael Hill

The familiarity of most sociologists with the typology of organizations which has been developed in the sociology of religion has in recent years bred a fair degree of contempt. As a result of this its original basis and the context in which it was first applied have been overlaid by a series of secondary versions, summaries, parodies and the inevitable statements that the categories included in the typology have no heuristic value in empirical research. While I would not wish to dispute that some applications of this typology have had confusing and occasionally bizarre consequences, especially when these abstract types have been mistaken for weapons with which to threaten religious opponents, I think that it deserves a better fate than the one it is currently facing. If nothing else, the typology of religious organizations epitomizes the historical development of sociology. In most fields of sociology it is possible to trace the initial development of large, often dichotomous type concepts – such as mechanical and organic solidarity, sacred and secular, Gemeinschaft-Gesellschaft, status-contract – and their gradual specification in the form of sub-types with a more contextual frame of reference.

The church-sect typology fits perfectly into this pattern. The terms 'church' and 'sect' originally derived from theological controversy and were used to distinguish established religious institutions from schismatic offshoots. 'Church' carried the connotation of *real* Christianity while 'sect' implied a group of religious elitists who had somehow 'rocked the boat'. An excellent example of a more recent polemical interpretation of Christian history in these terms is Ronald Knox's book *Enthusiasm*.[1] Initially Weber, in a comparative context, and subsequently Troeltsch, in the context of Christianity, attempted to reformulate this value-ridden but potentially useful distinction in the shape of polar ideal types which could then be used in empirical research.[2] In exactly the same way Weber adopted the term 'charisma' – 'the gift of grace' – from the vocabulary of early Christianity, and especially from the use which had been made of it by Rudolph Sohm in his *Kirchenrecht* (1892) and recast it as a sociological category.

Two observations can be made about the origins of the church-sect dichotomy. Firstly, since the terms 'church' and 'sect' were previously evaluative labels, it might be expected that the problem of value would intrude on their sociological usage. This seems to have been the case when sectarian religion has been viewed as authentic Christianity and the church as 'compromised'; or, by contrast, when the universal church has been seen as transcending its social environment while sectarian religion represents a 'philosophy of sour grapes'.[3] Secondly, the origin of the church-sect typology demonstrates how an aspect of the 'meaningful reality' of participants in a religious institution may be incorporated in a sociological construct. A phenomenological component seems to have been built into the categories of church and sect by basing them on such religious 'in'-thinking.

In this short paper I wish to apply exactly the same approach to some aspects of Wesleyan Methodism in the eighteenth century. There has been some disagreement about precisely where Methodism can be located in a typology of religious organizations; not surprisingly, since Methodism is a complex movement incorporating a number of distinct religious elements as it developed from its virtuoso Anglican base.[4] On the one hand, Methodism has been seen in its origin as a sect and in its development as moving towards a church type of organization.[5] On the other hand, there is a firm statement of Martin that: 'The history of Methodism together with that of the Congregationalists and to some extent the Baptists begins in a "Spiritual Brotherhood", or "Holy Club" which in turn becomes *Ecclesiola in Ecclesia*, and finally a denomination, but at no point approximates to a sect.'[6] The category of *ecclesiola in ecclesia* links the sect with the denomination, and also with the church, since it occupies an intermediate position. Wach introduces the concept in terms of the relative autonomy which protest groups within an institutional church may achieve without sectarian schism. Significantly, *two* of the three forms taken by the *ecclesiola* are seen by Wach to apply to Methodism.

The least autonomous form is the *collegium pietatis*, which typically practises an intensified devotion rather than seeing itself as an ideal community, and its characteristic observance is the 'meeting'. Both Methodism *and* Tractarianism are included as examples. A more autonomous level of protest is the *fraternitas*, with its important notion of egalitarian fellowship: again, the Methodist groups are given as examples, and Wach points out that these eventually formed an organization outside the parent church. Finally, the *order* represents a highly crystallized and autonomous 'protest within'. Wach does not see Methodism as having reached this degree of formal autonomy within an institutional framework. And yet part of the disagreement over categories might be accounted for in these terms since, as I have argued elsewhere, the order is a quasi-sectarian organization within a church.[7] Is there any sense in which Methodism can be seen as a religious order? And was the parallel seen by Wesley's contemporaries and by others in the English church of the eighteenth and nineteenth centuries? There is evidence that it was, especially by the High Church Anglicans.

There are a number of indications that eighteenth- and nineteenth-century observers noted a resemblance between Methodism and a religious order. For instance, when he made his plea for Protestant sisterhoods in 1829, Southey took as his audience the Quakers and the Methodists rather than looking for a response to the Church of England.[8] Pusey certainly thought that Wesley had come near to founding a religious order, to the extent of using the parallel of the Methodist separation of the eighteenth century to give a warning to the church of the nineteenth: 'The Church of England should be large enough to contain every soul who would, with devoted heart, labour for her. We mourn now that Wesley was not led to form an order within the Church, rather than rend those thousands upon thousands from her. We mourn here the loss of deep devoted fealty, of strong intellectual energy, of clear-sighted faith, of ardent piety, lost to us... Let us take heed how it is repeated.'[9]

The question whether Wesley might have formed a religious order is, of course, a matter of conjecture. What is very interesting is the fact that it continually reappears in the literature, from the eighteenth century until the present. Anson, for example, finds the analogy significant enough to include in his account of the 'call of the cloister' in England in the seventeenth and eighteenth centuries.[10] He argues – very hypothetically, it should be added –

that if Wesley had not broken away from Count Zinzendorf (about 1745) he might have founded quasi-communities on the lines of the Moravians in England. The 'Holy Club' was in Weberian terms a virtuoso community, and Wesley was apparently impressed with the Moravian settlement at Herrnhut. Another point of convergence is that Wesley spoke in his later life of the attraction which Nicholas Ferrar's quasi-religious community at Little Gidding had had for him, though he rather characteristically transposed the analogy: 'When I was young, I was exceedingly affected with a relation in Mr *Herbert's* Life; an account of Mr *Farrar's* family at *Little Giddings*, in *Huntingdonshire*: a very particular description of which is given in the Arminian Magazine. I longed to see such another family, in any part of the three kingdoms. At length I had my desire: I did see exactly such another family: I saw a family full as much devoted to God; full as regular in all their exercises of devotion, and at least as exemplary in every branch of Christian holiness.'[11]

Bishop Lavington is noted for his condemnation of Methodist other-worldliness as 'Popery'[12] and, like the earlier Quakers, the Methodists were sometimes labelled as Jesuits. Although contemporary pamphleteering is far from being a reliable source of useful analytical comparisons, it cannot be entirely dismissed – after all, both Quakers and Methodists took their names from popular taunts – and the comparison of Wesley with Ignatius Loyola[13] is at least supported by Wesley's qualified admiration for the saint: 'Surely one of the greatest men that ever was engaged in the support of so bad a cause.'[14] Much more frequent, however, has been the comparison of Wesley with St Francis. One of Hogarth's caricatures of a Methodist preacher portrays him with his wig falling off to reveal a friar's tonsure underneath. Though Wesley referred to Francis as 'a well-meaning man, though manifestly weak in his intellect',[15] the authors of the *New History of Methodism* find sufficient parallels to conclude that 'John Wesley was, in fact the St Francis of the eighteenth century.'[16] The points of comparison which can be cited are: (1) both the Franciscan and Methodist movements were fundamentally movements of the laity (though a more recent writer has accurately pointed out that this is the 'Francis of Sabatier rather than of Thomas of Celano'[17]); (2) both were democratic movements which sprang from the lower classes; (3) Francis Wesley used similar methods in so far as they concentrated their mission on those who needed it most – in both cases the urban poor; (4) both equated perfection and joy, and spread this belief among their followers. Apparently the parallels have been frequently noted, because comparisons between Wesley and Francis often appear.[18]

Parallels between Methodism and monasticism have also been drawn by several historians – who are sometimes apt to confuse monks and friars – and this is particularly true of the 'Holy Club'.[19] Once again, it is Workman who presents the most clear outlines, and we can summarize them as follows:[20] (1) in both, and especially in the early stages of Methodism, there was a common emphasis on the renunciation of self as a condition for the effective work of God; (2) as worked out by Benedict, monasticism was essentially social, and this was true also of Methodism.[21] (3) monasticism, especially in its origins, was the witness to a sacerdotal age that holiness is a fact of character rather than an imputed act, and this was very characteristic of Methodism; (4) both were predominantly lay movements; (5) both were movements which emphasized personal prayer and worship rather than the simple observance of externals; (6) there was also the organizational parallel, in that the annual Conference of the Wesleyans came to play a very similar function to the General Chapters of religious orders. One might add to this list the observation that Wesleyanism began as a virtuoso movement *within* the wider institutional framework of the Church of England – a feature on which great emphasis was placed in the elaboration of the ideal type of the religious order. Another similarity can be seen in the form of group confession which Wesley instituted in his classes and which was not unlike the 'Chapter of Faults' of a religious order.[22]

There are indeed ideological and organizational parallels between Methodism and the Catholic religious orders, but it is important to qualify these by saying that they are not the result of any conscious intention on the part of Wesley to imitate the latter. On the other hand, he was very much impressed by the tradition which he saw among both the High Church Anglicans and the Moravians of Religious Societies. From his Oxford days onwards, Wesley was convinced of the need for such societies of pious Christians to restore a decaying Christianity, and he explicitly stated that this was the origin not only of the Oxford 'Holy Club' but also of the Methodist Societies in general.[23] In fact, these Religious Societies, which grew up under the influence of an Anglican, Anthony Horneck, were *ecclesiclae in ecclesiae* of church members with a high degree of commitment and zeal, and are in this respect similar in some ways to religious orders,[24] though they lacked a common organization and a systematic definition of discipline and obedience. But they did attempt to perform in many respects the same function within the Church of England as religious orders performed within the Roman Catholic Church. As Methodism grew in size there was a shift in interest away from the original private meetings to the public service on Sunday, and Lawson sees this process as the development of a denominational form of organization: 'The private Religious Society of disciplined zealots.. [turned] into a looser denominational congregation, yet a congregation which [possessed] the closely-knit group of "Members of Society" as an inner directing "cell". Here may be seen gradually developing in the latter decades of Wesley's life the polity which became typical of nineteenth-century Methodism.'[25]

This discussion confirms that Troeltsch made a significant contribution to an analysis of the Methodist revival. He saw it as 'an attempt to leaven the life of the National Church with the influence of smaller groups or genuine and vital Christians'.[26] He argued that Methodism belonged essentially to the sect-type and not to the church-type, despite its strong desire to remain within the Church of England.

If, as has been argued, religious orders share several important features with sects, then early Methodism – which in certain general features approximates to a religious order within the Church of England – did indirectly approximate to a sect, though it later developed into a denomination. And this is Troeltsch's solution, for he sees Methodism as being something between a religious order, 'established upon a foundation of unconditional obedience and minute mutual control', and a society of earnest Christians with an experiential faith and 'founded upon entirely voluntary membership in which the members have a permanent share'.[27] He continues: 'The two sociological forms of the sect-type, the Religious Order and the voluntary association, are here combined; at the same time they are made elastic for the reception of increasing numbers, without, however, allowing the opposition to the popular piety of the church-type to disappear.'[28]

Methodism was indisputably a complex movement which combined elements of various traditions to produce a highly original amalgam: above all, Methodism was dynamic. Nevertheless, in Wesley's organization of Methodism from the beginning was an explicit concern to revive the religion of the established church through the activity of small, face-to-face groups of virtuosi *within* that church. This, it has been argued, gives early Methodism a status close to that of a religious order in the Church of England.

NOTES

1. R. A. Knox, *Enthusiasm*, Clarendon Press 1950.
2. There appears to be a certain amount of confusion about the precise origin of the church-sect typology, largely due to the proliferations of versions, translations and acknowledgments in footnotes, but it did in fact originate *in sociology* with Weber. It first appeared in *The Protestant Ethic and the Spirit of Capitalism* (originally published in 1904–5), where Weber noted that the distinction had simultaneously and independently been used by Kattenbusch in the *Realenzykopädie für protestantische Theologie und Kirche*. Weber subsequently used it in an article of 1906 in the *Frankfurter Zeitung*. Troeltsch acknowledges in *The Social Teaching of the Christian Churches* (first German edition, 1911–12) that the dichotomy had been first developed by Weber (p.433); and in a 1920 rewriting of his 1906 article Weber noted: 'The present rewriting is motivated by the fact that the concept of sect as worked out by myself (as a contrasting conception to "church") has, in the meanwhile and to my joy, been taken over and treated thoroughly by Troeltsch ...' (H. Gerth and C. Wright Mills, *From Max Weber: Essays in Sociology*, Routledge & Kegan Paul 1948, p.450).
3. W. Stark, *The Sociology of Religion. A Study of Christendom*, vol. 2, 'Sectarian Religion', Routledge & Kegan Paul 1967, p.130.
4. M. Hill and B. S. Turner, 'John Wesley and the Origin and Decline of Ascetic Devotion', in *A Sociological Yearbook of Religion in Britain 4*, ed. M. Hill, SCM Press 1971.
5. E. D. C. Brewer, 'Sect and church in Methodism', *Social Forces*, vol. 30, no. 4, May 1952, pp.400-8; J. C. Chamberlayne, 'From *sect* to *church* in British Methodism', *British Journal of Sociology*, vol. xv, no. 2, June 1964, pp.139-49. *Jм Тигк̣л · Ком Jос̌ик̠ Клл Ld/нлСл̃л 1563*
6. D. A. Martin, *Pacifism*, Routledge & Kegan Paul 1965, p.211. The concept of *ecclesiola in ecclesia* is taken from J. Wach, *Sociology of Religion*, University of Chicago Press 1944, ch. 5, section ii.
7. M. Hill, 'Typologie sociologique de l'ordre religieux', *Social Compass*, vol. xviii/i, 1971, pp.45-64.
8. See A. M. Allchin, *The Silent Rebellion*, SCM Press 1958, pp.33-4.
9. *Report of the Proceedings of the Church Congress of 1862 Held in the Sheldonian Theatre and Town-Hall, Oxford*, J. H. & J. Parker 1862, p.143.
10. P. F. Anson and A. W. Campbell, *The Call of the Cloister*, SPCK 1964, pp.22-3.
11. Allchin, op. cit., p.33.

12. George Lavington, *The Popery of Methodism: Or, The Enthusiasm of Papists and Wesleyans Compared*, Leeds 1839.

13. For sources, see W. J. Townsend, H. B. Workman and George Eayrs, *A New History of Methodism*, 2 vols., Hodder & Stoughton 1909, vol. 1, p.163 (footnote).

14. Knox, op. cit., p.427, quoting from Wesley's Journal for 16.8.1742.

15. Quoted in Townsend et al., op. cit., p.44.

16. Ibid., p.44. See also the sections in H. B. Workman, *The Place of Methodism in the Catholic Church*, London 1921.

17. Rupp in R. E. Davies and G. Rupp, *A History of the Methodist Church in Great Britain*, vol. 1, Epworth Press 1965, p.xv.

18. For example, Frank Baker quoted in T. Dearing, *Wesleyan and Tractarian Worship*, Epworth Press/SPCK 1966, p.59: 'With its devotional timetable and its work of charity, the Holy Club seemed to be a kind of University monastery of the Franciscan Order with John Wesley the acknowledged Superior'; S. C. Carpenter, *Church and People, 1789–1889*, SPCK 1933, p.205: 'It was, of course, a tragedy that, whereas a mediaeval Pope had approved of the Mendicant Orders, the English Bishops could not entertain Methodism. Yet it was practically impossible for prelates of that period to comprehend what Wesley was about, or, in so far as they comprehended it, to view it with favour'; Rupert E. Davies, *Methodism*, Penguin Books 1963, p.18: 'Francis did for his age what John Wesley did for his, and the resemblance between the work of the two men is all the more striking when the considerable difference between their personal characters and abilities is remembered.'

19. For example, Martin Schmidt says of the early Wesley: 'It is evident that he is held by the ideal of monasticism. It is not freedom but restraint which he values; not spontaneity, but discipline; so much so that he can disdainfully and expressly reject a life without rules as a type of Christian freedom which is too high for him. What is being described in every one of his sentences is none other than the monastic state with its advantages and its weaknesses. Its aim has rarely been so sympathetically appraised from outside Roman and Byzantine Christianity.' (*John Wesley. A Theological Biography*, Epworth Press 1962, vol. 1, p.121.)

20. Both in Townsend et. al., op. cit., pp.41-3, and in Workman, op. cit., 1921.

21. E. P. Thompson thinks that the strong communitarian basis of Methodism was one of the reasons for its popularity in the period of rapid industrialization and urbanization. (*The Making of the English Working Class*, Penguin Books 1968.)

22. G. R. Cragg, *The Church and the Age of Reason*, Hodder & Stoughton 1962, p.147, notes: 'The conscience of the individual was reinforced by the concern of the class meeting. Each member was expected to report his victories or defeats, and his way of life was subjected to searching scrutiny. As he advanced in responsibility he was expected to submit to an increasingly stringent discipline. The penalty for failure was expulsion and this was no empty threat.'

23. Davies and Rupp, op. cit., p.215ff., deals with this aspect of Wesley's organization.

24. A. C. Outler, *John Wesley*, OUP, NY 1964, brings out the similarity in the case of Methodism very strongly indeed: 'Wesley's idea of Methodist societies serving the Established Church even against the good will of her leaders was a distinctive adaptation of the pietistic patterns of the "religious

societies" (*ecclesiolae in ecclesiam*) which Anthony Horneck had brought from Germany to England in 1661 and which had served as a refuge for "serious Christians", discontent with apathetic and nominal Christianity. The Methodist notions of corporate Christian discipline were derived, at least in part, from Wesley's interest in the Roman Catholic religious orders – the Society of Jesus in particular' (p.307).

25. Davies and Rupp, op. cit., p.205.
26. E. Troeltsch, *The Social Teaching of the Christian Churches*, 2 vols., Allen & Unwin 1931, vol. 2, p.721.
27. Ibid., p.723.
28. Ibid., p.723.

5 A Millenarian Movement in Korea and Great Britain

Mark Cozin

Traditional Korean Religion

Before Christian missionaries went to Korea in the late nineteenth century there existed no dominant religion, but rather a system of belief consisting of elements of Shamanism, Confucianism, and Buddhism, a checkered ethos which reflected the political and military struggles which beleaguered this peninsula nation. Shamanism, the term applied to indigenous Korean religion before the arrival of Confucianism and Buddhism, has in the writings of Korean ethnographers been used as an inclusive label to describe a great variety of ritual activity, the core of which is the animistic 'belief in the presence of spiritual beings'.[1] These spirits comprised a vast number of gods, demons, and demigods who controlled the powers of good and evil and demanded worship. The importance of this belief in the spiritual cosmos should not be underestimated. Everyday occurrences and the problems of life were determined by having a proper relationship with these spiritual entities. Commenting on the omnipotence of this highly elaborated cosmology of spirit beings one author states: 'Shamanism is the primitive ethos of the Korean people. It is the basic instinct of the masses, especially in the countryside. All Korean religious ideas and ceremonies are influenced by it and at some point coalesce with it. All successful religious movements in Korean history, including the "New Religions" have drawn upon strong Shamanistic underpinnings.'[2]

Confucianism was introduced to Korea when the Chinese of the Han Dynasty established the Four Chinese Colonies in 180 BC. Four hundred years later Buddhism was introduced, also by way of China, and continued to gain in importance until the Koryo Dynasty (920–1250) when Buddhism and Confucianism struggled for dominance, Buddhists generally holding the upper hand of the royal court until the fall of the dynasty in 1392. Then, at the start of the fifteenth century, under the Yi Dynasty, Buddhism met with increasing hostility. Buddhas and temples were destroyed and monks were stripped of status. In 1420 a ban was imposed on the building of monasteries and an edict passed forbidding monks to attend or pray at funerals, and Confucianism once again became the state religion.[3]

In general, Confucianism can be said to have had a more enduring influence on Korea than Buddhism.[4] More important, however, than the pre-eminence of one religious belief system over another was the fused character with which these religions permeated Korean beliefs and ritual. Shamanism, with its conviction of the presence of spirit beings, Confucianism, with its reverence for established authority based on the five relationships of king–subject, parent–child, husband–wife, elder–younger brother and friend–friend, and Buddhism, with its ideal of relieving the world of evil by eliminating desire, were often mixed in the minds and practice of the Korean people. It was not uncommon for a Korean at times 'to take part in the ceremonies of ancestor worship, at times to offer Buddhist prayers, and at times to call on a magician for help in placating the spirits that were supposed to be threatening his safety and happiness'.[5] This heterogeneous religious soil, coupled with a series of historical events, and the prevailing social structure in Korea before 1882 accounts for the rapid gains which Christianity made in converting Koreans between 1882 and 1910.

Japan, Korea's near island neighbour, had traditionally with China vied for political and military control of Korea. In 1876, shortly after Japan had herself opened her ports to Western ways, and adopted an expansionist stance, she forced a treaty on Korea.[6] To offset this Japanese move, the Chinese Viceroy advised Korea in 1879 to open its ports to the Western nations, which she did in 1882, signing a treaty of amity and commerce with the United States. For some time before this pact an internal political schism had been developing within Korea. Aware of the growing influence of Japan and the United States outside 'the Hermit Empire', a progressive faction had become impatient with the Confucian principled government machinery which had developed during the Yi Dynasty.

At the apex of the government was the king, his authority based on the ethical norm of Confucian filial piety. Below him was a social structure consisting of four rigid classes; the royalty and nobility (Yangban), a small middle class (the Chungin), the commoners (Sangmin) composed of farmers, merchants, artisans, and constituting the majority of the population, and the 'lowborn' class (Ch'omnim).[7] For some time this social structure had been exceedingly rigid. This was caused by an examination system which had originally been intended to serve as a vehicle for choosing the class of government officials. By the beginning of the reign of King Myong in the mid-sixteenth century, however, 'passing the exams became more dependent on the socio-politico background of the aspirant than on his intellect',[8] and by the end of the nineteenth century, the rigidity of the class structure had strengthened even further, so that the most highly skilled class of all, the middle class of doctors, accountants, lawyers, interpreters and astrologers, were not even able to take the exams which might have gained them a high political appointment.

This group, which was both politically ambitious and deprived – and among which were included the illegitimate sons of concubines of the nobility, who suffered humiliation and ineligibility because of the pollution they suggested in a society based on purity – along with Korean women, 'were particularly amenable to new ideas, even alien religious ideas, which could improve their social and psychological situation'.[9]

On 4 December 1884 at a dinner party celebrating the opening of a new post office, the progressives attempted a coup, managed to lure the prince outside the reception hall and nearly stabbed him to death. Horace Allen, a missionary who was also a physician, was summoned, withstood thirteen Korean doctors 'who wanted to pour black wax into his gaping wounds', sewed the prince up, and he slowly recovered.[10] Subsequently, Allen became extremely popular with the Korean court, as did other Christian missionaries, and just at the turn of the century, the emperor and the court were baptized.

Other factors beside those of royal sanction and the appeal ideologically that the Christian message of equality before God regardless of social station had for some segments of Korean society helped to generate a high rate of conversion. John Ross, of the United Presbyterian Church of Scotland, had translated in 1883 the New Testament into han'gul, or the Korean language which had been devised in 1450. This was a unique advantage, as it was the language of the common people, as opposed to that of the nobility who preferred the use of Chinese. Christianity had the benefit as well, because of the politically neutral policy of the United States, of being proliferated without the taint of colonialism.

In part, the widespread acceptance of Christianity must also be attributed to the early missionaries' ability to graft certain Christian concepts on to the traditional bias.[11] The laws of evil and benign causality between human and spiritual personalities contributed a basis upon which the concepts of sin and punishment in the Christian doctrine could stand. The mirror image of God in the Christian religion was provided by Hananim, the supreme spirit in the spirit pantheon and heavenly king of Confucianism. He was aided by the merciful supermen which appear in the legends of old Korean history and thus was easily transferable to the Christian concepts of God and the messiah. The concept of a future existence in Buddhism made it easy for the Korean Christians to spread their belief in eternal life.[12]

By 1910 (the time of the Japanese annexation) there were an estimated two hundred thousand Christian converts,[13] a figure which rose to some seven hundred thousand (somewhat more than half Protestant) by 1944, despite a climate of regimentation and suppression which limited Christian missionary activities during the Japanese protectorate. With the liberation of the country at the end of World War II, freedom of religion was officially guaranteed and at the termination of the Korean conflict a renewal of missionary effort occurred. From 1953–1962 the evangelizing efforts of the Christian churches was evidenced by a doubling of the Korean Christian population to over one and a half million.[14] By 1966, (when the total population was 29,193,000) the official figures were given as follows: Roman Catholics 628,546; Protestants 900,000 (500,000 Presbyterians, 150,000 Methodists); and a total of 40 denominations.[15] In 1971 these figures had increased to 779,000 Roman Catholics, 3,192,621 Protestants (1,415,436 Presbyterians, 300,107 Methodists) and 79 Denominations.[16] Official figures given for the same year included 4,943,059 Buddhists and 4,423,100 Confucists.[17]

The 'New Religions'

In the aftermath of the Second World War and the Korean War there emerged in addition to the growing adherents of the already existing Christian denominations a number of religious groups which have since been labelled the 'New Religions'. In itself, this is not an unusual occurrence. There exist numerous and universal accounts of religious and social revitalization movements occurring subsequent to the confusion wrought by a vastly altered social structure struggling in the wake of war or rapid social change.[18] At the conclusion of the Korean War, there were five million refugees and half the visible assets of the Korean peninsula had been destroyed. By 1966, there existed some 'several hundred miscellaneous cults',[19] and in this respect the Korean situation parallels the emergence of new religions since 1945 in neighbouring Japan.[20] The Korean case is far less documented and in this respect it reflects its position in Asia as 'the stepchild of ethnologists'.[21]

Numerous causal explanations for millenarian movements – which a high percentage of the new Korean religions are – have been offered ever since Mooney's early anthropological accounts of the Ghost Dance and that of Williams on the Vailala Madness.[22] The ethnological and theoretical material concerning these movements has now reached voluminous proportions. Little consensus exists, however, among scholars as to the causes and functions of the movements. Inevitably, recent works have tended to refute particularistic theories and have sought refinements in the form of taxonomies and classifications, detailing the descriptive and structural qualities of these social-religious phenomena.[23]

At the core of most of the causal debates remains the concept of relative deprivation. The foremost recent refinement of this concept is that of Charles Glock.[24] In particular it is the resolutions sought for psychic deprivation (one of five types of deprivation), a consequence of severe and unresolved social deprivation, 'the social propensity to value some attributes of individuals and groups more highly than others and to distribute societal rewards such as prestige, status, and the opportunity for social participation', which are most likely to lead to a religious response. However, the problems with deprivation theory are manifold, and it has received harsh yet justified criticism.[25] Relative deprivation does not account for alternative ways of responding to psychic stress, such as anomie, psychosis, or apathy, and it relies too heavily on the ethnographer's interpretation of what constitutes 'a felt disadvantage'.

However, even with the disabilities revealed by its critics (its psychological ally 'cognitive dissonance' suffers from much the same criticism) it remains historically validated that a corporate religious response, its function either manifest or latent, often appears subsequent to the dislocation of a culture's social and valuative structure. It is not surprising, therefore, that in interpreting the 'New Religions' of Korea commentators use deprivation theory as an explanation of the attraction which these religions hold for the citizens of a country which had experienced incalculable damage by any standards twenty years ago.

The almost half-century of occupation and war which Korea experienced was followed, as in the rest of Western Asia, by rapid industrialism and urbanization, largely influenced by the more industrially advanced West. Commenting on these turbulent years, Moos, a leading Western scholar on the 'New Religions' of Korea says:

> At such times of intense stress, i.e. war, foreign occupation, conditions become fertile for the emergence of new expressions of religion, economic, and political feeling and aspiration. Under such conditions of stress, for many, the formal established traditional religions fail to provide answers to the problems of a modified more 'modern existence'. New aspirations had to be satisfied, new answers were sought. In addition, in the case of Korea, religious freedom was granted to the Koreans, really for the first time at the close of W.W.II. Until 1945, religious activities, other than those serving the interests of the Japanese during her thirty-six year occupation were discouraged to say the least ... so that these new religious cults in Korea not only helped to fill the psychological vacuum resulting from the end of the Japanese occupation and the subsequent liberation of Korea in 1945, but also have succeeded in providing a seemingly hopeful and more psycho-economic future to many hitherto economically depressed and hopeless individuals.[26]

The Tong-Il Movement, which will be described shortly, though distinctive, shares many similarities with other new religious groups in whose congregations are an estimated 10% of the entire population. However, it is neither the fastest growing nor the most publicized: these honours belong to Park Chang No Kyo or, as it is more commonly known, the Olive Tree Movement.[27] This religious movement was begun in 1955 by Park Te Sun who claimed to have received a vision from heaven that he was 'the one from the East'. Almost immediately he began to attract a large following, due in the main to his reputation for healing by a method known as 'the touch of peace' whereby a vigorous massage by Park transmitted his divine power to the afflicted individual. Although he spent a year in gaol for charges of fraud and injuring sick followers, his following grew and by 1964 the movement had some two million members and 303 congregations.

The movement possesses an extraordinarily articulate organizational system. This was begun when a 'boomtown', Christian Town I, was built for more than 20,000 of Park's followers. By 1962, this town also enclosed fifty large factories, six apartment house complexes, and schools from kindergarten to high school. It has its own post office, a police station, a motor pool and a fire department, all manned by government personnel who are at the same time members of the Olive Tree Movement. On July 1962, a second Christian Town was begun on a 900 acre piece of property adjacent to the first development (ten miles from Seoul). The town is completely autonomous and is headed by the Zion Federation, a name which the movement adopted for 'external relations'. All the goods manufactured in the factories are given the Zion label. Among the items produced by Olive Tree labourers are fluorescent lamps, artificial flowers, cosmetics, pianos, engines, and all the underwear and soya sauce for the Korean army. Ideologically the movement professes a superdenominational Christianity and believes that the last day of the world will come within Park's lifetime. Tobacco and alcohol are proscribed, as they are in the Tong-Il movement, as well as the eating of pork and peaches: the latter was banned because it was the fruit which caused Adam's Fall in the Garden of Eden (the apple is a cash crop of the movement).

The Tong-Il Movement

The Tong-Il Movement is an international millenarian movement which was founded by Moon Sun-myung, a Korean who is now fifty-two years old. On Easter morning in 1936, Jesus Christ appeared to him and told him that he was destined to remake the world.[28] During the next few years he received revelations from God about the world, its future, and the role that he was to play in this drama. These revelations were subsequently transcribed and are contained in a volume known as *The Divine Principles*.[29] In 1945, after the liberation from Japan, Moon established an independent church in P'yongyang. Three years later, he was accused by ministers of the existing Christian churches of disturbing the social order and was placed in Hungnam prison, being released in 1950, when the United Nations' forces captured Hungnam. Moon then proceeded to Pusan with two of his followers and began to spread his teaching. In 1954 a church, under the name of the Holy Spirit Association for the Unification of World Christianity, was established. The following year Moon and several other members of the church were charged and gaoled for 'injuring public morals'.[30] Three months later they were released, having been found innocent of the charges, and in May 1955 received a registered certification as a legal social organization.

In January 1964, the movement claimed some 32,491 members most, with the exception of a few hundred, living in Korea and Japan.[31] The movement was brought to the United States in 1959, and after a few difficult years now seems to have gained a membership numbering several hundred.[32] In the mid-1960s 'missionaries' for the movement began to proselytize in Europe, and by the summer of 1972 Moon had approximately three hundred followers in Europe (including Britain), the largest groups being those of Germany, France, Holland, Italy, and Great Britain. The last-mentioned country, where I was engaged in research as a participant observer, had fifty-five members in May 1972, four years after it gained its initial convert. The movement is often known by its short title, the Unified Family.

The beliefs of the movement are succinctly contained in its sacred text, *The Divine Principles*, the revelation of the movement's leader, Sun Myung Moon (the surname is reversed in English). This text, containing twelve chapters, serves as a sacred manuscript, and as an ideological corpus with the potency to regulate, interpret, and create a world view.[33] It also functions as a proselytizing instrument, taught chapter by chapter to people who demonstrate, after initial probing questions by movement members, an interest in the 'message'. The core of *The Divine Principles* is a historical account borrowing predominantly from the Old and New Testaments (*The Divine Principles* are referred to as 'the Completed Testament') narrating the behaviour of biblical figures from the time of Adam up until the present. This narration is preceded by an introductory chapter which superimposes certain axiomatic procedures which have regulated this biblical history, and a preface by Young Oon Kim, who brought the 'teaching' to the United

States in 1959, and translated the *Principles* from Korean to English. She sets the tone of the volume by proclaiming that 'Revelation, the last volume of the New Testament, is being fulfilled, a new heaven and a new earth is being established, and complete revelation has now been given to mankind, the ultimate solution to the questions of life and the universe has been revealed.'[34]

The Unified Family[35] interprets the events of the Bible as having taken place within three stages of existence, the formation stage, the growth stage, and the perfection stage. Originally it was God's intention to create man and have him progress to the perfection stage where God's dominion is manifest. As he approached the perfection stage Adam had sexual intercourse with Eve.[36] Mankind, his descendants, because of Adam's indiscrete act, fell 'physically' from the top of the growth stage to below the formation stage, or the 'non-principled realm'. Also at this early time another significant event transpired. Lucifer, the archangel, attracted by the beauty of Eve, 'ventured to join together with Eve', stood against God, was cast down and became Satan. By this act he alienated Adam and Eve 'spiritually' from God.

The fact that man fell both 'physically and spiritually' because of the actions of Adam, Eve and Lucifer is of utmost importance, for it contains the fundamental Unified Family axiom, namely, that there are two worlds, the spirit world, and the physical world, the latter often referred to as the 'earth plane'. This is explicitly stated in *The Divine Principles*: 'God created the visible physical world as an object corresponding to the invisible, spirit world. The latter is the world of cause and purpose, the former that of effect ... whatever happens in the physical world has its cause in the invisible world.'[37] Armed with this principle, Unified Family members are able to interpret much of their daily experiences, as well as newsworthy world events, in terms of having been controlled by Satan or his allies, evil spirits, 'who are either fallen angels or evil people on the spirit side of life'.[38]

History, since the time of the Fall, is a record of man's struggle to achieve the perfection stage, loose himself from the control of Satan and re-establish God's original intent of a kingdom of heaven on earth. In order to understand this ascent back to the perfection stage, a climb to which over one-third of *The Divine Principles* is devoted, another axiom, that of 'restitution', must be understood. Because Satan claimed man as his own, physically and spiritually it was (and is) necessary for man to reject Satan's unrelenting attacks and return to God by acts of restitution, or as they are usually termed by 'indemnity' or 'setting condition'. In terms of biblical figures, these acts of restitution usually took the form of sacrifices or acts of suffering. However, all of these holy agents followed a similar pattern by erring in some fashion so that those who followed them had to seek restitution by further indemnifying behaviour. This pattern was begun by Cain, who was capable of making restitution for the Fall by subjugating himself to Abel. However, because of his jealousy and the later killing of his brother, a 'foundation of faith' could not be laid in Adam's family. In a similar manner, neither was Noah, Abraham, Jacob or Solomon (all of whom transgressed to a degree) able to construct this foundation of faith. By the time of Jesus and the events of the New Testament, mankind's progress had reached only the upper portion of the formation stage. Jesus, too, largely because of the transgressions of John the Baptist and because of his own failure to take a wife, was only able to grant man spiritual salvation. It was not until some two thousand years after the death of Christ (the precise date is 1960) that man was able to reach the perfection stage and enter into a proper relationship with God. *The Divine Principles*, therefore, are able to parallel the two-thousand-year-period from Jacob to Jesus, a period marked by the confines of the formation stage, or the Old Testament Age, with the two thousand years since his crucifixion, a period terminated by the First World War and labelled the growth stage, or New Testament Age.

The final chapter of *The Divine Principles* is the climax to this historical analysis since Original Sin. It is a description of the forty years before 1960 which were a 'historical encapsulation of the 400 years since the Protestant Reformation and serves as restitution to God for the entire 6,000 year history of man's satanic behaviour on earth'. In three global encounters Satan was defeated. First, Satan's allies during World War I, the Germans, were beaten to make restitution against Satan for Adam's failure. In World War II, Hitler was defeated in retaliation against Satan for the only partially completed mission of Jesus. Lastly, communism, Satan's attempt to thwart the fulfilment of God's providence, must and will be reversed. These three periods of Satanic activity are paralleled with three significant events of Moon's life:

In a Satanic world, that which is false always appears first and imitates the truth, thus confusing people. God's final dispensation, that of the Second Advent of the Lord, has developed in three stages. The first stage was the arrival of the Lord of the New Age to the world. This was preceded by the counteracting force of William II who caused World War I. The second stage was the start of his ministry, which was preceded by the counteracting force of Hitler who caused World War II. The third stage is the initial fulfilment of his mission, the role of Jacob in the realm of Cosmic Restoration, which was marked by an event in 1960. This was preceded by the counteracting force of the Communist regime of the Soviet Union. The Lord of the Second Advent will conquer the Satanic world and unify it by Divine love and power, thus completely fulfilling the providence of God.[39]

Indemnifying acts, however, are not limited to the stage of biblical actors, chronologically arranged below Moon. Although Satan is being defeated, he is still active and is making, in these final days, a 'last stand'. He forces people to be late, causes doubts and depressions, prevents people from hearing *The Divine Principles*, and generally acts in ways which prevent the Unified Family from gaining a large following. In order to rebuff Satan completely, all Unified Family members 'set condition'. The most common of these are praying for a particular length of time each day, periodical fasting, taking cold baths, and 'witnessing' to a stipulated number of people each day. The importance for each individual in the movement to 'set condition' is perhaps best summarized by one member writing in their monthly pamphlet. 'You can not enter the Kingdom of Heaven until every ounce of evil has been torn from your heart and mind, until the rottenness within you has been dragged into daylight and cut out with the fiery sword.'[40]

The concluding pages of *The Divine Principles* are concerned with who the Lord of the Second Advent is, and where he will come from. The first condition is that he will come from the 'East', for Revelation 7.2–4 implies this (biblical excerpts are given throughout *The Divine Principles* to support their assertions). As well, 'this nation must have been tried for a long period in its history through suffering and persecution', and 'in the last days, the suffering of this nation will become more intense and much of their blood will be shed'. Finally, in order to be a symbolic representation of the whole world, which is now divided between Cain and Abel (the good and Satanic forces), so too must the chosen nation be divided into two sections. 'The establishment of the Kingdom of Heaven and the destruction of Satanic rule will be effected in this country first and from there it will spread universally.'[41]

Clearly, the Tong-Il Movement, though smaller both in number and enterprising expanse clearly possesses many affinities with the Olive Tree Movement. Both appeal to a strong ethnocentric nationalism. Korea is the most lauded nation in the world because it is the homeland of the Lord of the Second Advent (a title both Park and Moon claim). It is the promised land, as Israel once was, for as Christ sacrificed for that nation, so do Park and Moon sacrifice for Korea. The building of paradise on earth will begin in Korea and, as it spreads, that nation will be recognized as the fatherland of mankind. Another similarity is the heavy emphasis given to Christian doctrine, and especially to the book of Revelation, typical of almost all millenarian movements.[42] That Christian dogma should lend itself so easily to millennial interpretation is a reminder that Christianity itself once flourished in the millennial spirit. However, it is not, as many have assumed, the ideological groundwork for all millenarian movements.[43] What does render it extremely malleable in a prophet's hands is the remarkable innovation which Eliade has noted, namely that unlike the cyclic eschatological regenerations which other religions posit, the Judeo-Christian apocalypse will occur only once. 'There is a Judgment, a selection, only the chosen will live in eternal bliss. The chosen, the good, will be saved by their loyalty to a Sacred History; faced by the powers and the temptations of this world, they remained true to the Kingdom of Heaven.'[44]

Unlike the Olive Tree Movement and most of the new religions of Japan, the Tong-Il Movement does not emphasize healing.[45] People have been healed, but this has happened spontaneously, and only to those who understand and fully accept *The Divine Principles*. In Britain, no mention was ever made of healing. Perhaps the most distinctive quality of the Tong-Il Movement is the sacrosanct emphasis it places on the family unit. Its importance is expressed in axiomatic form. 'Originally Adam and Eve and their children, with God, would have made up the basic family unit of the Kingdom of Heaven representing the four heavenly directions: east, west, south and north.'[46] It was not until Moon married in 1960 (he had been married once previously) that mankind was restored physically and spiritually. The year 1960 therefore has a special significance, for it represents the crossing function between good and evil. 'Evil, which had formerly taken an aggressive stand is now in a defensive position, and good, which had been on the defensive, is now taking the aggressive position.'[47] This wedding, now known as Parents' Day (one of four holidays), has been succeeded by other joint wedding ceremonies among his followers, which by the increasing number of couples has signified the growth of restoration. A joint wedding of three couples followed Moon's wedding ceremony, which was followed by a second ceremony for 36 couples in 1961, of 72 couples in 1962, 430 couples in 1967 and 777 couples in 1970,[48] all of which have symbolic significance (e.g. 430 represents the 430 years Israel spent in the desert). Those blessed in divine marriage 'can automatically go to the Kingdom of Heaven'.[49] All marriages which have not been blessed by Moon are considered as Satanic, and previously married members of the Unified Family live as unmarried individuals in the Unified Family centres where a distinct division of labour exists and sexual activities are taboo.[50]

From East to West

The popularity of a doctrine which emphasizes the sacramental quality of marriage and family life may have particular appeal in Korea, where the structure of the traditional nuclear and extended family was seriously disrupted by the Korean War. Traditionally marriages were arranged completely by the parents, to whose home the sons, and particularly first sons, returned with their brides. In the past twenty years this model has undergone significant modification. Marriage is no longer left to the match-making of parents, there is a growing tendency, especially among urban couples, to live apart from their parents, and there is a notable trend in the increase of divorce.[51] The British Unified Family, while less likely to appeal directly to a populace which feels unease at changing kinship patterns, nevertheless interprets the increase in disrespect for parental authority, increasing divorce rates, and sexual liberalism tolerated by the press and visual media, as evidence of the evil influences which percolate in our 'permissive society', proof that we are approaching the last days.

The Unified Family also finds it necessary to readjust and legitimize the claimed spiritual ascendency of Moon. In Korea, where Shamans are still prominent, the Tong-Il Movement, which recognizes the causal potency of the spirit world, emphasizes evidence which they have given to Moon. Choi Syn-duk states: 'They [the Tong-Il Movement] also take witches and fortune-tellers seriously. These witches and fortune-tellers, even though they bear wicked spirits, may perceive Moon more correctly than people in other established churches. Just as men who were possessed by devils in Jesus' time shouted "You, Son of God", when they saw Jesus, so today, witches and fortune-tellers testify concerning Moon and who he really is.'[52] For the Unified Family, the concept of a spirit world, in a milieu where – in contrast to Korea – not many people believe in the active engagement of spirits on empirical events, this principle is one which is both central to its ideology and one of the hardest concepts for them to popularize.

It is not surprising, therefore, that many of those who are initially attracted to the Unified Family are those who have knowledge of, or have belonged to, spiritualist circles. For their benefit, an often-quoted and printed bit of evidence is provided by the famous 'sensitive' Arthur Ford and his 'spirit guide' Fletcher, who attest to Moon's spiritual powers. An excerpt quoted from an 18 March 1965 spiritual session in which Moon was present along with Ford and Fletcher quotes Ford as commenting on Moon to the others present: 'In another setting I would insist that my instrument and the rest of you should take off your shoes. But spiritually you can create the humility that will enable you to know that you are in the presence of truth incarnate.' In another session dated 13 May 1964, in which 'representatives of the US and Korean Divine Principle Movement were present', Ford says of Moon: 'This person is going to have a great influence not only on your life but on the lives of a great many people ... he has tremendous spiritual power and also psychic power ... he is a prophet who will bridge the gap between the east and west and the past and future.' Speaking of Korea, Ford says: 'Out of your country will come a great spiritual urge. It will be a blending of the ancient with a new revelation and it is not far off – it is near.'

This legitimizing information, however, does not negate the fact that there exist fundamental ideological differences between the democratically organized spiritualist societies and the hierarchically organized Unified Family, which appear to be unbridgeable impediments that deter many spiritualists from becoming Unified Family members.[53] By a process of dislocating and grafting certain

principles of the Tong-Il Movement from its Korean context to that
of Western society, and in this case Great Britain, the Unified
Family have made the revelations of Moon an exportable com-
modity. While it is not possible fully to examine the success of the
Unified Family, whose transfer of the Satanic force of communism
from the guise of the Chinese (in Korea) to that of the Soviet Union
(in Great Britain) is an extraordinarily interesting process, in its
ability to transmit a millennial message and become a thriving
religious movement,[54] I do wish to examine one fascinating aspect
of transmission, that of Sun Myung Moon's charisma.

One of the most significant aspects of charismatic authority, 'a
rule over men, whether predominantly external or predominantly
internal, to which the governed submit because of their belief in the
extraordinary quality of the specific person'[55] as opposed to traditional authority, which depends upon customarily recognized status,
and bureaucratic authority, which depends upon impersonal and
specified rules and procedures, is its 'irrationality', its foreignness
to rules, whereby authority is legitimated solely on the recognition
of the leader's extraordinary quality by a following. Because the
emergence of a charismatic leader and his ability to generate a
sympathetic response is a historical process, the relationship between a man like Moon, who as a messiah (a term he uses in
reference to himself) and prophet, which for Weber represented the
archetype of charismatic leader,[56] should be open to scrutiny.

It is difficult to assess with certainty how Moon has acquired and
sustained a charismatic following in Korea, especially without an
awareness of his persuasive or speaking ability in Korean. One
possible suggestion is Tucker's concept of 'situational charisma'
(exemplified by Churchill in the Second World War and Roosevelt
in 1933) when 'a leader's personality of nonmessianic tending evokes
a charismatic response simply because he offers in a time of acute
distress leadership that is perceived as a source and means of
salvation from distress'.[57] One may choose to question Tucker's use
of 'nonmessianic' in a particularly narrow and ecclesiastic sense.
It is highly debatable whether in fact all charisma is not situational,
especially in the light of Tucker's own statement (first employed by
Erik Erikson) that 'there are certain historical periods when people
are charisma hungry: (*a*) during times of fear, (*b*) during times of
anxiety, (*c*) during times of existential dread, i.e. distress experienced by people in which rituals of their existence have broken

down' (all three periods relating in some measure to the Korean situation in the mid and late '50s). There is little evidence here of any advance beyond Weber's statement relating necessary if not sufficient historical periods of distress with the concomitant rise of a charismatic leader likely to embody and express relief from such distress.[58]

The manner in which a charismatic relationship between Moon and Unified Family members is established is a discernible process. Significantly, special care is taken in neglecting to mention the name of Sun Myung Moon and in the removal of all symbolic and ritualistic paraphernalia (such as photographs of Moon) from prospective Unified Family members until they have heard the complete text of *The Divine Principles*. Moon's name does not appear anywhere within the *Principles*, except in the preface, which is not part of the initial 'teaching', where he is mentioned as a 'dedicated religious leader and philosopher in Korea'. Only at the conclusion of the climactic section of the *Principles*, entitled 'The Qualifications of the New Messiah', is the listener told that the messiah is Sun Myung Moon.[59] A process then begins which can accurately be termed a 'charismatic education'.

The key to understanding the dynamics of this charismatic validating procedure is the creation and repetition of a series of myths concerning Moon, and the implicit and explicit associative content these myths have with revered historical and biblical figures endemic to British culture.[60]

In understanding myth in this instance as a dramatic diachronic narrative, I will be emphasizing the power of myth to serve as history, and in the Unified Family case, a history justified by the power of a retooled, near literal, interpretation of the Bible.[61] I will leave for the present the analysis of these myths by the structuralist formula of binary contradiction, mediation, and resolution.[62] Such a lengthy undertaking would defuse the kerygmatic function these myths serve in the Unified Family situation, a situation which because of its biblically literal idiom is not demythologized, and seeks, with the prime exception of Moon's mission, no resolutions.

This legitimation of Moon's charisma by myth is not begun immediately but is preceded by the viewing of photographs of Moon, dressed in both traditional Korean and Western clothes. Little, if any, response is evoked by the first sight of these photographs. A typical response was, 'he looks quite ordinary'. After these photographs have been viewed, a short biographical sketch is read aloud, which I will quote in part, which initiates the process of charisma building. It is prefaced by a statement claiming that 'this has been compiled from the testimony of Sun Myung Moon's earliest followers and other witnesses. Very little of it is taken from his own words. He himself has never fully revealed his life to his disciples. Most of his story is still shrouded in mystery, much of it will remain so for eternity.'

Only a few months after the liberation of Korea from Japan, God directed Sun Myung Moon to begin preaching his new revelation in Pyung-yang, the capital of Red-held North Korea. In the same manner that Abraham had been called to leave his native land of Ur and journey to Haran, in the same way that Jacob had to flee to Canaan to suffer in Haran for twenty-one years, in the same manner that the Israelites began their journey from the Satanic land of Egypt, and in the same manner that Christianity began under the persecution of the Roman Empire, Sun Myung Moon began his mission of bringing the world back to God in the capital of an atheistic land. He was called upon to establish the foundation for the Kingdom of Heaven under the most adverse conditions ... As he continued to preach the Divine Principle in the capital of North Korea, he converted a number of communists. When this came to the attention of the communist authorities, they were very disturbed that a God-accepting ideology was being spread so successfully in the capital of a Communist-held territory.

As a result, one day without warning he was taken to the Dae Dong Communist Police Department where he was brutally tortured. He was given what is known as a water treatment, where water is continually poured into the nose; he was made to stand on his feet day and night without allowance for sleep, and finally, he was cruelly beaten with clubs. He was so brutally beaten that he was injured internally and began to throw up quart after quart of blood. He was thought to be dead and the bloody mass of his body was tossed out into the cold winter night. His sorrowing disciples found his body and began funeral preparations, but within three days he mysteriously revived, and although the blood had nearly drained from his body after his beating and he was badly bruised and aching, he immediately arose and began to preach out his powerful message, the Divine Principle. When his recovery became known to the Communist authorities, he was re-arrested and this time sent to a Communist fertilizer factory at Hung-nam, an east coastal town in North Korea ... Sun Myung Moon had been sent to a living hell. The moment he entered the prison camp, he knew that the communists had sent him there to die, and that under ordinary circumstances no man could endure such existence for any length of time. He determined to subsist in spite of all these obstructions, however, but his method of survival was entirely different from what one would imagine. From the very first day he entered Hung-nam, he set aside one half of each meal and divided it among his fellow prisoners. The total portions alone were not adequate to feed even a small child, yet for three months Sun Myung Moon lived on half of the meal that he was served.

Though many of his devout followers walked more than a hundred miles to the prison to bring him food and clothes, he never kept any of their gifts for himself but always distributed them among his fellow prisoners. So concerned was he for the suffering of his companions that he forgot his own suffering and hunger. Instead he wore the clothing whose tatters hung from his body dripping with sweat. On his back, the number 596 was clearly seen. This number was not a coincidence. In Korean it is translated, 'Oh goo ryuk' which means 'innocent'. He was indeed innocent, a man 'smitten and afflicted' for the transgressions of all humanity ... At the most, a prisoner at Hung-nam lived for six months but Sun Myung Moon endured nearly three years of unbearable physical hardship and in the process even gained a small amount of weight ... On June 25 of 1950, the Korean War broke out and UN Forces began to march into North Korea in their drive toward the Yalu River. US B-59 strategic bombers proceeded to bomb all the industrial areas of North Korea of which Hung-nam was one of the prime targets. As the air raid signals began to sound, a strange incident occurred. Wherever Sun Myung Moon took shelter, the shelling would miraculously miss him. When the prisoners in his compartment noted this, they began to gather around him as chickens gather around a mother hen. Wherever he moved, they followed after him like a flock of sheep ... it was not in the plan of God for him to die. Though historians may attribute the Korean conflict to a variety of causes the real cause was to free that one man of God so that he could continue with his divine mission of establishing the Kingdom of Heaven on earth. His time was now full and on the fourteenth of October 1950, he was liberated from Hung-nam prison by the UN forces ...

The strikingly similar parallels between the accounts of Moon's life and of biblical figures is readily apparent, and in the first paragraph explicitly stated. His call from God, his sufferings, his doubts, his Christ-like rise from death, his sense of mission, his unselfish concern for others characterizes and personifies qualities of the most sacred biblical cast, and especially Christ. These traits aid in amplifying what is explicitly stated in *The Divine Principles*, that Moon's omnipotence stems from his prophetic lineage of Abraham, Jacob, Moses, and Jesus and because of his superiority, is even in excess of theirs. These characteristic hues of sacrifice, perseverance and courage against overwhelming odds are not limited to linking Moon with biblical characters, but also with historical ones. During many of the fervent and ecstatic prayers reference is constantly made to men such as William Tyndale, George Fox, John Knox and John Wesley. Articles appear from time to time in the *Unified Family Monthly* sketching the lives of British heroic figures, their qualities of martyrdom and heroism constantly alluded to.[63] In one instance, quoted in a Unified Family missionary pamphlet, George Fox himself appeared in a vision to a member of the audience listening to one of Moon's lectures. 'She saw George Fox and other Quaker elders kneeling with their faces to the ground. On being asked, "Why don't you look at Mr Moon?", George Fox replied "I was so sinful in my life that I can not look directly at him so bright is his light. I envy you and all the others who can." '

References to 'proofs' of Moon's extraordinary qualities are not merely limited to written testimonies, for there also exists an oral mythology. An original member of the American Unified Family who brought the movement to Great Britain and who with her husband leads the movement here, was fond of retelling how when Moon first came to the United States in 1965, he travelled to forty-eight states in forty days, his spiritual energy sustaining him throughout the journey with the minimal food or rest. It was often said that he only slept an hour or two every night, and although he visited and stayed with the Unified Family for a week in March 1972, this fact could hardly be verified, the only contact he had with rank and file members being typically distant, except during periods when he spoke directly to the Family as a group.

Lastly, by constantly referring to heroic figures who have suffered because of uncompromised faith, Unified Family members have constant reminders that even though they, who lead fairly spartan lives, and receive ridicule (as one would suspect, they are well insulated within the primary reference group, but open to derision when promulgating their beliefs publicly), these trials are meek by comparison with those of Moon, Fox, Tyndale, and Wesley. By allying Moon with the sacred figures and values of Britain, the Unified Family is able not only to create a charismatic aura about Moon but also generate a model to emulate and with which to compare their sufferings.

NOTES

1. Yun Kuk Kim, 'The Korean Church', *Korean Affairs*, February–March 1962, Seoul, Korea, pp.81-105.
2. Spencer Palmer, *Transactions of the Korean Branch, Royal Asiatic Society*, vol. XLIII, Seoul 1967, p.5.
3. Cornelius Osgood, *The Koreans and Their Culture*, Ronald Press, NY 1951, p.247.
4. Ibid., p.246.
5. Kim, op. cit. p.94.

6. Spencer Palmer, *Korea and Christianity*, Hollym Corporation, Seoul 1967, p.54.

7. Gregory Henderson, *Korea, The Politics of the Vortex*, Harvard University Press 1968, pp.36-59.

8. Palmer, op. cit., p.41. See also William E. Griffis, *Corea, The Hermit Nation*, Scribners, NY 1889, pp.228-41.

9. Palmer, op. cit., p.46.

10. Palmer, op. cit., p.51.

11. Hwang Song-mo, 'Protestantism and Korea', *Korea Journal*, 1967.

12. Chung, 'Christianity in Modern Korea', *Korean Quarterly*, vol. 5, no. 2, 1963, pp.136-7.

13. Osgood, op. cit., p.250.

14. Kim, op. cit., p.59.

15. Korea Annual 1966, Seoul, Korea.

16. Korea Annual 1971, Seoul, Korea.

17. Ibid.

18. A bibliography of millenarian movements, revitalization movements, and 'crisis cults' is provided by Weston La Barre, *Current Anthropology*, February 1971, pp.3-45.

19. Korea Annual 1966, Seoul, Korea.

20. For example, see H. Neil McFarland, *The Rush Hour of the Gods*, Macmillan 1967; Harry Thomsen, *The New Religions of Japan*, Tuttle 1963; Clark Offner and Henry Van Straelen, *Modern Japanese Religions*, Leiden 1963; L. Carlyle May, 'The Dancing Religion: A Japanese Messianic Sect', *The Southwestern Journal of Anthropology*, vol. 10, 1964; 'Heaven Beyond A Golf Course', *Daily Telegraph Colour Magazine*, 17 March 1972.

21. Felix Moos, *Transactions of the Korean Branch, Royal Asiatic Society*, vol. XLIII, Seoul 1967.

22. La Barre, op. cit.

23. For example, see M. W. Smith, 'Toward a Classification of Cult Movements', *Man*, vol. 59, 1959, pp.8-12; F. W. Voget, 'The American Indian transition: Reformulation and accommodation', *American Anthropologist*, no. 58, 1956, pp.249-63; Yonina Talmon, 'Pursuit of the Millennium: The relation between religious and social change', *European Journal of Sociology*, vol. 3, 1962, pp.125-48; A. J. F. Kobben, 'Prophetic movements as an expression of social protest', *International Archives of Ethnography*, vol. 44, 1960, pp.117-64; Igor Kopytoff, 'Classification of religious movements: Analytical and synthetic', *Proceedings of the American Ethnological Society*, 1964, pp.77-90; *Millenial Dreams in Action*, ed. Sylvia Thrupp, Shocken 1970.

24. Charles Glock, 'The Role of Deprivation in the Origin and Evolution of Religious Groups', *Religion and Social Conflict*, ed. M. E. Marty, OUP 1964. See also David Aberle, 'A Note on Relative Deprivation Theory as applied to Millenarian or other Cult Movements', S. Thrupp, op. cit., pp.209-15.

25. See Weston La Barre, *The Ghost Dance*, Allen & Unwin 1972; Bryan Wilson, 'Millenialism in Comparative Perspective', *Comparative Studies in Society and History*, vol. VI, 1963-4, pp.93-114; Bryan Wilson, review of Stark and Glock's *Religion and Society in Tension* in *Journal for the Scientific Study of Religion*, vol. 5, no. 3, pp.461-3.

26. Moos, op. cit., p.116.

27. Felix Moos, 'Some Aspects of Park Chang No Kyo – A Korean Re-

vitalization Movement', *Anthropological Quarterly*, July 1964, vol. 37, no. 3, pp.110-20.

28. *Sun Myung Moon, A bibilographic sketch* (no author), The Holy Spirit Association for the Unification of World Christianity, Seoul, Korea.

29. *The Divine Principles*, translated by Yong Oon Kim, The Holy Spirit Association for the Unification of World Christianity, San Francisco 1963.

30. Choi Syn-duk, 'Korea's Tong-Il Movement', *Transactions of the Korea Branch, Royal Asiatic Society*, vol. XLIII, Seoul 1967, p.169.

31. Ibid., p.169.

32. An account of the movement's early activities in America is given in John Lofland's *The Doomsday Cult*, Prentice Hall 1966.

33. See Gary Schwartz, *Sect Ideologies and Social Status*, University of Chicago Press 1970.

34. *The Divine Principles*, p.iv.

35. The most commonly used title for the British Chapter is the Unified Family, and I will refer to it as that from now on.

36. *The Divine Principles*, p.27.

37. Ibid., p.17.

38. Ibid., p.37.

39. Ibid., p.207; for a full descriptive account of the power which the notion of Satanic forces has see Lofland, op cit., pp.193-203.

40. *The Unified Family Monthly*, February 1972.

41. *The Divine Principles*, p.213.

42. See P. G. Rodgers, *The Fifth Monarchy Men*, OUP 1966, esp. pp.4-13.

43. See V. Lanternari, 'Messianism, Its Historical Origin and Morphology', *History of Religions*, vol. 2, pp.52-72 and Shirley J. Case, *The Millenial Hope*, Chicago University Press 1918.

44. Mircea Eliade, *Myth and Reality*, Allen & Unwin 1963.

45. Offner and Van Straelen, op. cit., p.28.

46. *The Divine Principles*, p.22.

47. Ibid., p.39.

48. See *Time Magazine*, November 1970, p.33 (mistakenly gives the figure as 791 couples).

49. Lecture by Sun Myung Moon to the Unified Family, 16 March 1972.

50. For example, the females do all the cooking and light housework, the males the harder tasks. There is a general tone of subordination directed to the females, as they play an inferior role to men in the restoration process. In America, Lofland has written to me that this has met with opposition from some, due perhaps to the recent women's liberation movement.

51. See Lee Hyo Chai, 'The Changing Family in Korea', *Bulletin of the Korean Research Center*, no. 29, December 1968, pp.86-99, Seoul; Gordon W. Hewes and Chin Hong Kim, 'Korean Kinship Behavior and Structure', *Research Monographs on Korea*, series F, no. 2, February 1952, Pyong yang, Korea; Lee Hyo Chai, 'Patterns of Change observed in the Korean Marriage Institution', *Bulletin of the Korean Research Center*, no. 26, pp. 34-56, 1967.

52. Choi 'Syn-duk, op. cit., p.179.

53. Geoffrey K. Nelson, *Spiritualism and Society*, Routledge & Kegan Paul 1969, esp. p.123; 'Spiritualists have consistently advocated that criminals should be reformed rather than punished'. This is in sharp contrast to the Unified Family, who favour the return of capital punishment, a cause for which they have produced a pamphlet, 'The Unarmed Friendly Bobby

or Gun Law?' Family members differ also in that they reject contact with any spirit other than Jesus and God (*The Divine Principles*, p.xii).

54. Two models for such an analysis are provided by Luther Gerlach and Virginia Hine, 'Five Factors Crucial to the Growth and Spread of a Religious Movement', *Journal for the Scientific Study of Religion*, vol. 7, pp.23-40, and E. R. Babbie, 'The Third Civilization – An Examination of Sokagakkai', *The Review of Religious Research*, vol. 7, pp.101-21.

55. Max Weber, *Essays in Sociology*, ed. H. H. Gerth and C. Wright Mills, Kegan Paul, Trench, Trubner & Co. 1947, p.295.

56. Dorothy Emmet, 'Prophets and Their Societies', *Journal of the Royal Anthropological Institute*, vol. 86, p.14.

57. Robert Tucker, 'The Theory of Charismatic Leadership', *Deaedalus*, vol. 97 (1965), p.744.

58. Weber, op. cit., p.245.

59. By accentuating the product rather than the person, the Unified Family tactics approach Waddell's 'rational originality'; see R. G. Waddell, 'Charisma and Reason, Paradoxes and Tactics of Originality', *A Sociological Yearbook of Religion in Britain* 5, ed. M. Hill, SCM Press 1972.

60. This associative methodology of charismatic validation was suggested to me by Ann and Dorothy Willner, 'The Rise and Role of Charismatic Leaders', *The Annals of the American Academy of Political and Social Sciences*, March 1964, no. 358, pp.77-88.

61. See Percy Cohen, 'Theories of Myth', *Man*, new series, no. 4, 1969, pp.333-53; K. O. L. Burridge, 'Levi Strauss and Myth', *The Structural Study of Myth and Totemism*, ed. Edmund Leach, Tavistock Publications 1967.

62. See Edmund Leach, *Genesis as Myth and Other Essays*, Jonathan Cape 1969; Claude Levi-Strauss, *Structural Anthropology*, Anchor Books, NY 1967, esp. pp.202-29.

63. *The Unified Family Monthly* of October 1971 has an article on John Knox; that of January 1972 an article on Nelson.

6 Aspects of Latter Day Saint Eschatology

Douglas J. Davies

The importance of religious influences in the formation of individual and group world-views was of fundamental significance in Max Weber's work on the protestant ethic and on the major world religions. More recently the concept of the orientation of religious groups to the world has been usefully employed in discussing the development of religious institutions, and especially of sectarian forms of religion.[1] While the initial response to the world of those persons involved in establishing a religious movement will be an important influence on the inner social structure of the sect, it is also likely to form the basis of a pattern of theology which serves to restrict the range of subsequent thought and speculation. In most cases of the inauguration of new religious movements the initial dissatisfaction felt with the prevailing socio-religious realities will be expressed by means of current religious terminology. It is characteristic of emergent religious groups that the leaders articulate their solution to the unformulated confusion of their followers by rearranging and re-emphasizing beliefs and practices already familiar to the potential disciples.

In this paper the change in orientation of the Mormon church to the world is outlined with specific reference to its eschatological doctrines on the premise that sectarian eschatology is perhaps the clearest and most unambiguous expression of their basic orientation. The initial reaction of the prophet Joseph Smith to his environment of religious confusion resulted in the Book of Mormon and certain other texts which have tended to provide a normative meaning for eschatological problems which the church has only slowly been able to reinterpret by means of numerous qualifications centring on the initial intention of the prophet. It is through a study of the development of the church and of its changing pattern of interaction with an ever changing 'Gentile' world that differently emphasized views of eschatology become clear. It is here argued that any change of emphasis in eschatological doctrines will be related to changes in the orientation of the church to the world resulting from changing patterns of the social organization of the church both internally and *vis à vis* the world.

The whole one hundred and forty year history of the church may conveniently be divided into three major phases with respect to eschatological doctrines. The period of initial orientation to the world, 1830-1900, was one in which the Second Coming of Jesus Christ was eagerly expected; the construction of a holy society, a chosen people in an American Zion, was seen as a necessary preparation for this imminent Advent.

In the second period, that of transition of orientation during the years 1900-50, a change in emphasis occurred both as a result of the fact that no Advent occurred and in order to make sense of the Mormon groups which still remained in Europe and had not been assimilated into the central Utah community by emigration.

The third period in the post-1950s saw a complete reinterpretation of Mormon eschatological doctrines as well as a new mobilization of the church's personnel for action in a newly perceived world situation. It was a reinterpretation of eschatology which validated the proselytizing activity of the missionary programme in the second half of the twentieth century and which justified the establishing of a world-wide Mormon community. Some of the occasional conservative nineteenth-century interpretations of eschatology still occur in the missionary periphery of the church, for although in Utah Mormonism is cultural orthoxody, in Europe it is a form of sectarianism. This peripheral conservatism which extends to a host of doctrines may be regarded, in part, as a form of compensation for geographical isolation from Utah and the centre of Mormon life. It is noteworthy that this conservatism has not been emphasized as much in the case of the Second Coming as in other doctrines. This is understandable as the logical conclusion of such belief is emigration to the American Zion in expectation of the Advent. Such a move is not so well received by affluent twentieth-century Europeans: for their forebears who lived in European poverty, however, the call to economic and spiritual salvation in America held a peculiar fascination.

Initial Orientation

From the very beginning of Joseph Smith's preaching he was success-ful in winning followers as well as opponents. Converts were organ-ized into a core group which served as a point of attraction for all those who were to hear the prophet's message of the forthcoming millennial advent and reign of Christ. Smith's purported revelations are here regarded as originating in the intellectual ferment of the Frontier situation and, as synthesized by Smith,[2] they attest to the fact that Smith – in common with many people in up-state New York – considered the millennial advent to be imminent. The task for which he believed himself peculiarly chosen and anointed was that of preaching this message so that men would believe it and join themselves to the group which Smith was organizing in pre-paration for the Lord's coming. The Lord was to come to America to establish his Zion, but before this the Latter Day Saints were to make some prior arrangements. Smith therefore exhorted his hearers to prepare themselves for the advent; his message was urgent and found a ready response in many areas. 'Prepare ye, prepare ye, for that which is to come, for the Lord is nigh ... Let them, therefore, who are among the Gentiles flee unto Zion ... Go ye out from among the Nations, even from Babylon from the midst of wickedness which is spiritual Babylon' (DC 133 : 12 and 14).[3]

Smith's idea of the world was that it was impure and evil and therefore those who would be awaiting the Lord should actually leave its corrupting influence by coming together in a holy congre-gation. 'And blessed are they who shall seek to bring forth my Zion at that day!' (I. Nephi 13.37). Those who joined the prophet began their great work by going out to continue the preaching of this message. The thousands of converts who were made were organized into Zion, a moving group of dedicated persons who were seeking a geographical location where their Zion could be completely estab-lished. The persecution and opposition which befell them made this task difficult and it was not until after the prophet's death that this dream was ever realized in any lasting way. This realization occurred in the colonization of the Great Salt Lake Valley in Utah during the decade of 1850.

The first missionaries to England in 1840 found a ready response to their message. Wales, however, did not embrace millennial hopes until the arrival of Captain Dan Jones in December 1844. The proselytizing activity of this fluent, Welsh orator was very success-ful. In 1849 he led a group of 249 converts to America and by 1852 he had returned to Wales and, in four years, converted 2,000 people of whom 703 left for America with him in 1856. This was his last visit to Wales and he died in 1861 the father of six children and husband of three wives. Jones' preaching gained considerable impact by virtue of the prevailing social conditions of the Welsh industrial towns, and most of all by the ever-present threat of death from cholera. This disease had killed 1,400 persons in Merthyr during the one year of 1849 when the population of the town was 25,000. The message of millennial hope and present economic advantage in an earthly Zion found a responsive audience in South Wales. Accordingly the emigration of converts continued until the end of the nineteenth century, depleting the number of Saints re-maining in Wales but strengthening the church in Utah. Even though this loss was occurring in Wales and even though the Mormon leader at Swansea could write in 1870 'the emigration of so large a number last season from this conference rendered my duties for the past year more like those of a teacher ... it is difficult to get up a congregation of more than ten or twelve' (MS 1870: Sep),[4] nonetheless the major theme and belief of the Welsh Saints, and of the church at large, was of moving to Zion.

This desire is well expressed in a hymn of Mary Ann Davies, who was a convert at Tredegar and wrote these words in 1882. The hymn was published in the *Millennial Star* for December 1883.

> Let Zion from the dust arise,
> And in her brightest beauty shine.
> Jesus descending from the skies,
> Shall fill her heart with joy divine.
>
> In gloomy darkness long she lay,
> Depressed with care and grief unknown.
> But now behold a glorious day
> Of Gospel light begins to dawn.
>
> Put off ye Saints your mourning dress
> And hail the long expected morn.
> Let robes of joy and righteousness
> The happy church of Christ adorn.
>
> Darkness involves the nations round,
> Gross darkness veils the peoples' eyes.
> But they who dwell in Zion's land
> Shall see the sacred light arise.

On her his glory shall be seen,
Her love, her zeal, her pious care
Shall witness to the sons of men
That God with all His grace is there.

Sinners shall flock to Zion's gate
And know the Gospel's joyful sound.
Peace shall confirm her happy state
And fruits of holiness abound.

Another writer produced the following as a New Year hymn for 1850:

Ye Latter Day Saints to Zion flee away,
For there shall be safety for all who will pray,
For this is God's promise through Joseph the Seer,
Flee then, ye righteous, in the present New Year.

A further specimen of a Welsh Saint's response to the church and his view of both it and the world with which he was familiar is given in this linguistically mixed hymn.

Hiraeth y Sant Tylawd	*The Longing of the Poor Saint*
Hiraethu wyf yn Mhabilon Am fyn'd i Seion wiw, Yn disgwyl am y newydd llon Yn amser da fy Nhuw.	In Babylon I pine and grieve For Zion far away, But I shall go I do believe, In God's appointed day.
Dywedair prophwyd Brigham Young In English tongue so grand, A welcome you shall have among The Saints in Zion's Land.	Then says prophet Brigham Young (etc.)

If these verses may be regarded as an example of the way in which Welsh converts regarded the church and the world then they demonstrate how the old Welsh culture and society were described as being part of evil Babylon. The use of the Welsh verb meaning 'to pine, grieve' in the first line of the last poem is indicative of this change of attitude because it is a verb which the Welsh consider to be untranslatable and which refers to a Welshman's feeling of patriotic homesickness. The transfer of this idea to Zion in Utah is indicative of the extent to which the preaching of millennial hopes had been received by some of the Welsh converts.

The influence which the emphasis of the doctrine of the Last Things was having in Wales is clear in that in causing many to emigrate it greatly weakened the Welsh branches of the church.

This trend began to diminish with the last two decades of the last century as the church in Utah began to encounter the opposition of the American government concerning polygamy. While the missionaries continued to preach the necessity of 'gathering to Zion', the people were responding less. In 1886 the missionaries were warned not to be discouraged by the lack of converts: 'A great harvest has been gathered from Wales and the elders who come here now really found this to be a time of gleaning and warning but with limited results for their labours' (MS 1886: Jan). Thus, while the emphasis of the doctrine remained strong, response to it slackened. This change was partly due to the changed conditions of the Utah church and the resurgence of Welsh Nonconformity. The revival activities of 1904, about which British Mormon leaders had much to say, provided a sense of immediate salvation and an accompanying change in the moral and social life of many communities in Wales. Leisure time activities became chapel centred and were supervised by the religious organizations. No evidence seems to exist to show whether many nominal Mormons went over to the chapels or not. However, for those who felt a need for it, a religious focus for life was provided which integrated many persons into the community and supplied an immediate answer to the problem of salvation which did not involve moving to a new country.

A few Saints remained faithful to Mormonism in Wales over this period and in Merthyr Tydfil, which had been a major centre of activity, the Saints came almost entirely from two families. In England rather more were still meeting together. The state of the church was, therefore, a delicate one. It had a centralized core membership in Utah, a dispersed membership in Britain and Scandinavia and it seemed that the dispersed group was not going to move to Utah. The advent expected by Mormons had not occurred. The church responded to this situation not by making any direct references to the coming of Christ, but rather to the nature of Zion. Zion had been, from the early days of Smith's preaching, the place where Christ was to be received and from whence he was to reign. Although the precise site of Zion was the cause for some speculation it was nonetheless always regarded as being in America. The response of the church leaders was to adopt a somewhat different perspective concerning the geographical location and social composition of Zion.

Transition in Orientation

What was the purpose of the church? Its initial purpose as understood by Joseph Smith had been accomplished. Converts had
gathered from America and Europe and had been preparing
Temples in preparation for the Lord's return. Now that it seemed
unlikely that the Lord was at the door of the Temple, what was to
be done? Some of the more conservative Mormons knew the
answer and it was the same one that Smith himself had used, the
call to be prepared. Thus George Q. Cannon preached to the Saints
at Salt Lake City in 1901 and explained how he viewed the situation: 'I have felt impressed of late to talk to our people in relation
to preparing ourselves more than we have done for the coming
of the Lord' (MS 1902: Jan). One month after this address he
again spoke his mind even more clearly when in October he assured
the Tabernacle congregation that 'Many are now within the sound
of my voice have been promised that they shall live, if they have
faith, to behold the Second Coming of the Lord'.[5] This view could
not have been totally accepted by the leadership of the church, for
in 1903 the Saints in Britain were told that they 'should be in no
hurry to emigrate. We desire that strong branches be built up and
that the local priesthood should help the leaders from Zion' (MS
1903: Jan).

As the emphasis on emigration declined, so the leaders began
to direct their attention to the process of strengthening the church
structure which had developed in Britain. The goals of the church,
which had been to strengthen the Utah church, were still present
in the British church but now the mode of strengthening that
church changed as the policy became one of drawing together the
Saints *in situ*. Had the church still considered the advent to be
imminent their exhortation would have been to come to America
with haste. The position was made more clear in the 1904 *Star* in
which the editor told the elders, who in the 1903 editorial had been
referred to as coming 'from Zion', not to preach the necessity of
emigration. The authorities were becoming aware, if they had not
been aware for quite some time, that Zion, that bastion of purity
awaiting final redemption, was itself polluted. 'Although the emigration is not preached by the elders and in some cases those who
desire (to emigrate) are positively counselled not to, nevertheless
many imagine that they are possessed of the true spirit of gather-

ing ... they refuse to believe that the emissaries of evil, that vice and crisis, sabbath breaking and a host of other sins are to be found in Salt Lake City as much as anywhere else on the face of the earth. In fact the temptations of satan ... reach their climax almost under the shadow of the Temple.' This admission that evil abounded in the geographical Zion was the first step in the process of 'spiritualizing' the concept of Zion.

The next phase in this process came with the direct interpretation of Zion as consisting of the 'pure in heart', not only in the United States but also in Britain and throughout the world. Scriptural warrant for this interpretation was found in DC 97:21 which says. 'Therefore, verily, thus saith the Lord, let Zion rejoice for this is Zion THE PURE IN HEART' (capitals original). When Smith had written this verse his own understanding of Zion was of a place rather than an inward state of the spiritual lives of Saints. This is clear if this verse is placed in its context where Smith refers more specifically to Zion in rather pragmatic terms. 'Behold I say unto you, concerning the school in Zion, I, the Lord am well pleased that there should be a school in Zion'; 'Verily I say unto you that it is my will that a house should be built unto me in the land of Zion like unto the pattern that I have given you' (verses 9-10).

By 1915 this new view of Zion was better established. It was the universal Mormon church which was the pure in heart. 'Do not delay. Come out from Babylon. Seek safety in the acceptance of the Gospel. Join the church of Jesus Christ' (MS 1915:153). This change of attitude thus brought those dispersed groups of Mormons into the same category as those who had emigrated to Utah. Thus the new myth of a spiritual Zion overcame and resolved the paradox of a divided 'geographical' Zion.

Certain leading Saints have commented on the gradual change in the understanding of the nature of the church which Mormons had to face. Dr John Widstoe wrote; 'At first the people of the Lord had to be brought together to give them strength. The prophecies of old have been fulfilled. We have become well known and strong. Now our duty is to spread over the earth. We still have the right, if we desire, to go to America. There is no force in the church of Jesus Christ; but many of you have your mission here' (MS 1932: 631). It is surprising that such an authority could regard the initial gathering as only intended to give the people strength. Such an interpretation after the event is obviously necessary unless the writer explicitly comments on the fact that the expected millennium did not come into being. In defence, Mormons could argue that Smith never set an actual date for the Second Coming and that if any other Saint made explicit statements such as that of George Q. Cannon then they would be speaking beyond their authority. Even though such statements are made it is an inescapable fact that the whole ethos of the early church was one of expectancy of the advent and subsequent millennium.

This view which is prevalent in current Mormon circles was made explicit as long ago as 1937 by John McNight when he wrote that 'The Millennium is perhaps our conception of the perfect social order ... it will not descend from heaven upon the earth and destroy this World but rather will grow into it ... through our enlightenment we still achieve the goal that we as individuals and as members of our social order set for ourselves' (MS 1937: 190). Thus the church sees its present mission as one of converting the world and thereby changing the whole ethos of human life.

With apologies to Professor C. H. Dodd it would be tempting to give the term 'realized eschatology'[6] to the changed view of Zion and the millennium but this must be resisted because the Mormon church is still committed to a belief in the literal second coming of Christ and would not subscribe to the idea that it has already come in a different form. That this belief is rather attenuated in the church life is shown by Robert Rapoport's comment that 'the Mormon lack of apocalyptic compulsion and urgency is a further contributing factor to the short term failure of the Mormon mission (among the Navaho Indians)'.[7] In the first four decades of the life of the church there would have been no lack of urgency and apocalyptic.

Welsh religious life was not without influence in assisting the Mormon leaders to make direct statements concerning the millennium, for with the development of the 1904 revivals in Wales the church leaders in Britain were more or less compelled to comment on the manifest workings of some sort of power and influence in Wales. Such comment was necessary because many thousands of persons were now joining religious bodies only a short time after the Mormon authorities had closed the Welsh Mission because of the ineffectiveness of its missionaries. Once again the editorial of the *Star* made everything clear: 'It has been told us by our prophets that when the millennium begins it should begin with the people of God. Moreover it should come to pass naturally and simply and without any particular heralding ... only those who take part in that Spirit and power would know of its existence, others about them should be ignorant of this power' (MS 1906: 193). Fifty years before this there was scarcely a month passed without some Saint or other being convinced that the 'signs of the times' were right for the heralding of the millennium. However, the authorities had to ensure the remaining Saints in Britain that God was not starting some special work without reference to them. Accordingly the Welsh revivals were regarded as the result of evil influences which were at work among the Welsh as a result of their former disobedience and hard heartedness towards the Mormon gospel.

Of course, to say that the emphasis given to the doctrine of the Last Things and to the idea of Zion has been altered in its content is not to say that nothing remains of the idea of a literal millennial advent of Christ. Such a view would be alien to the thousands of theologically conservative Mormons who believe the tenth Article of Faith which says that 'Zion will be built upon this (the American) continent; that Christ will reign personally upon the earth; and that the earth will be renewed and receive its paradisiacal glory'. There still appear, on occasion, the more conservative types of statement as in the *Star* of July 1970, in which a twenty-two-year-old British Saint states his belief that 'the Second Coming of Christ is upon our very doorstep, for I am a great believer in the signs of the times'.

While all these changes in emphasis concerning the millennium and the doctrine of Zion had been proceeding the official teaching of the first presidency remained the same. Thus it is not the statement of faith or official doctrine which has been changing but rather the more individual interpretation of these authoritative texts. The factors stimulating new interpretations arose from the changing circumstances in which different parts of the church found themselves. Over this period of change the structure of the church has altered very little. Those offices and organizations which were operative when the church entered the Salt Lake Valley are still present today. Of course, some changes in the institutions of the church did occur after the 1850s, as the development of the Mutual Improvement Associations for the young men and women of the church demonstrates. One of the greatest changes which occurred and which was to deeply influence the type of message preached by the missionaries, was the change in the type of missionary sent out. In the years following the First World War and even more so the Second War the missionaries were young men. In the early days of the church the missionaries were persons who had been personally, affectively, converted to the church but this later generation had to a large extent been born into church families. Their commitment was not dependent upon a millennial aspiration of salvation as had formerly been the case for early converts. Accordingly their preaching was far more persuasive when their topics concerned the nature of the church as the only true one. The change in emphasis on the millennial doctrines was thus suited not only to the needs of post-war Britain and successful Utah but also to these younger missionaries.[8]

The nature of the church in the last century and in the present may usefully be compared by giving two accounts of the activities of the church in these two periods in the form of ideal types. For ease of comparison the first type refers to that period between the founding of the church in 1830 and the close of the century. The second is taken as beginning about 1930 and continues to the present. These dates are arbitrary in that a variation of ten years from each date might make little difference to the picture. The important factor to be considered is that there appears to be a period of transition between two general sets of orientations of the church to the world, and generally speaking, that this period lay between 1890-1940.

Initially, the orientation was one of a revolutionary religious enthusiasm. The present world order was wrong and evil, not because men were themselves basically evil, but because truth and the priesthoods had been absent from the earth for such a time. It was necessary to change this state of affairs because Christ was soon to return to the earth to begin a reign of righteousness. All men should repent and unite in preparing a society fit for the reception of the Saviour. Such converts should separate themselves from all who did not repent. They should unite under the leadership of the prophet and build Temples in which to prepare themselves in a ritual way for the millennium. In order to achieve these ends revivalist preaching was used in reaching a mass public and door-to-door visiting was also practised. Religious services and meetings were of an emotional type, this reaching a climax at the dedication of the Kirtland Temple when glossolalia was experienced by some Saints, including Brigham Young. Bible teaching and preaching from the other standard works was of a fundamentalist and literalist nature. Education was something to be utilized at every opportunity, and not to be despised if it was liberally associated with Mormon theology. This orientation involved a negative attitude towards the world in that the societies of the world were corrupt and to be kept apart from the Mormon community. The use of education, politics and technological skills were not discouraged but advocated if they furthered the cause of Mormonism.

The second major phase of development was one in which the former revolutionary zeal had lost its eschatological emphasis and in its place there had appeared a proselytizing zeal, the aim of which was to win converts to the only true church. The major form of proselytizing had become that of door-to-door canvassing with occasional open-air preaching. Later sophistication in contacting likely converts through current members made the missionary system more effective and 'business-like' and much less random. While there still remained as the dominant attitude a fundamentalist-literalist approach to the Bible and standard works, there developed a small number of more liberal Mormons, mostly among the academics. Commitment to the church involved a more emotional tie for the individual, not necessarily taking the form of a conversion experience but usually demonstrated while 'giving one's testimony' at a special meeting. The members are not expected to shatter their ties with their locality and old way of life in order to separate themselves from unbelievers by emigrating to a place apart. They are, however, expected to be different from the Gentiles among whom they live, this difference being expressed by the dietary proscriptions of avoiding tea, coffee, alcohol and tobacco. Similarly the leisure activity of the Saints is expected to revolve around the church, to which total commitment is expressed through the paying of the tithe. The aim of the church is to extend its organization and the 'leavening' power of its priesthood throughout the world so that the latter may become an improved place for the life of mankind. In that the church is no longer envisaging and encouraging a separatism and Mormon communitarianism which had formerly been epitomized in the capitalistic-communitarianism of the United Order, its orientation to the world may be seen as becoming less negative. As part of its influence on the world, church members sometimes involve themselves in serving the Gentiles if only through the production of concerts, plays and pantomimes as in parts of Britain. The leaders of the church in America are also prepared to associate themselves with national politicians in the cause of opposing communism which they see as an enemy of freedom and religion.

It was proposed at the beginning of this paper that the eschatological beliefs of a religious group could be used to indicate the ideological orientation of that group to its wider social environment. The changes that have taken place in the interpretation of eschatological doctrines by Mormons may be understood in terms of the changing orientation of Mormons to their social environment. During this period of change there has been practically no change in the official doctrines of the church. The major change has been in interpretation of doctrines and scriptures and this change has occurred as the Saints have had to rationalize the position of what had been an actively millennial church in a situation in which that particular millennial perspective was no longer relevant. Thus as far as the Mormon church is concerned the proposition that 'the eschatology of sects is (perhaps) the most emphatic expression of their basic orientation'[9] would seem to be entirely validated.

NOTES

For his patient supervision and many vital insights during my research on the Mormons I express my sincere thanks to Dr Bryan R. Wilson of All Souls College, Oxford.

1. The central importance of a sect's 'attitude to the world' has been employed by B. R. Wilson as a basis for the classification of such religious groups. See *Sects and Society*, Heinemann 1961.

2. The influence of Sidney Rigdon on Smith is stressed by George B. Arbough, *Revelation in Mormonism*, University of Chicago Press 1932, and that of Smith's psychology and social environment by W. F. Prince in 'Psychological Tests for the Authorship of the Book of Mormon', *American Journal of Psychology*, vol. XXVIII, July 1917, and by I. W. Riley in *The Founder of Mormonism*, Heinemann 1903.

3. The abbreviation DC is used for the *Doctrine and Covenants*, one of the standard works of the church.

4. MS is an abbreviation for *Millennial Star*, a Mormon magazine which was published in Britain between 1841 and 1971, and is an invaluable source of data.

5. No actual date was ever given by Mormons for the Second Coming. Joseph Smith had one revelation concerning it but its nature was vague. 'I

was once praying very earnestly to know the time of the coming of the Son of Man, when I heard a voice repeat the following. Joseph, my son, if thou livest until thou art eighty-five years old thou shalt see the face of the Son of Man.... I was thus left unable to decide whether this coming referred to the beginning of the millennium, to some previous appearing or whether I should die' (DC 130: 14ff).

6. C. H. Dodd, *The Apostolic Preaching and its Developments*, Hodder & Stoughton 1937, p.198.

7. Robert N. Rapoport, 'Changing Navaho Religious Values: A Study of Christian Missions to the Rimrock Navahos', Harvard PhD. thesis 1954, p.51.

8. Douglas J. Davies, 'The Mormons at Merthyr-Tydfil', Oxford B.Litt. Thesis 1972, ch. 7.

9. Bryan R. Wilson, 'Social Aspects of Religious Sects', London PhD. Thesis 1955, p.1198.

7   The Sectarianism of Scientology

Roy Wallis

The concept of the sect is one of the most frequently deployed and ardently debated concepts in the sociology of religion. There is little definitional agreement amongst those employing the term, although a certain minimal working consensus over a number of component features appears to exist.[1] Amongst these are that the sect is (1) a voluntary association in which membership is achieved rather than ascribed; (2) that it is exclusive in that membership is by proof of merit and may be withdrawn for infraction of group norms; (3) that its members regard themselves as an 'elect' or elite, with unique access to the truth or salvation; and (4) that they are hostile to or reject their social environment, and often also the state. Further features sometimes specified are: (5) that the sect is egalitarian, operating as a 'priesthood of all believers'; (6) that the sect's message is ethical and ascetic in character; and finally (7) that the sect is totalitarian, attempting to embrace every aspect of the lives of its believers, and demanding a high level of commitment. These characteristics are the most frequently mentioned amongst those writers such as Troeltsch, Becker, Johnson, Yinger and Wilson,[2] who have contributed most directly to this issue.

These writers have all largely been concerned with religious groups standing in some relatively easily identifiable relation to the tradition of Christian belief. There have been attempts, of course, to apply the concept in a variety of other religious traditions, with a greater or lesser degree of success. More recently, however, there have been those such as Susan Budd, Robert K. Jones and Roger O'Toole,[3] who have employed the concept in the analysis of a variety of groups and movements lying at the margins, or altogether outside the traditionally religious sphere – respectively to the Humanist Movement, Alcoholics Anonymous, and 'political sects'. These analyses have clearly suggested that 'sect' is not an exclusively religious concept, and pointed to close affinities between a variety of religious and non-religious organizations.

An interesting case in this respect is a currently controversial and flourishing religio-therapeutic system – Scientology.[4] Founded in 1950 by L. Ron Hubbard, a former American science-fiction writer, Scientology began life as a psycho-therapeutic system, Dianetics. After early attempts to secure recognition for Dianetic techniques from the medical and psychiatric profession, which met with sharp rebuff and a certain amount of hostility and attack from the profession and the state, Dianetics progressively developed a supporting religious philosophy based on notions of an immortal Thetan and transmigration, and the formal, corporate structure of a church – The Church of Scientology.[5]

Scientology manifests a variety of dissimilarities from traditional forms of sectarianism. It is almost entirely instrumental in orientation, offering a theory to explain failure in this world, poor interpersonal relations, mental and physical ill-health, etc., in terms of engrams, that is, the physiologically or neurologically recorded experience of trauma in early life, the womb, or a past life, now unconscious, which may be 'restimulated' by a crude association of ideas in a current situation. The reactivation of such an engram will result in the appearance of the appropriate physical, mental, or social symptoms. For example:

> Here's how an engram can be established: Mary, age 2, knocked out by a dog, dog bites. Content of engram: anaten;[6] age 2 (physical structure); smell of environment and dog; sight of dog jaws gaping and white teeth; organic sensation of pain in back of head (hit pavement); pain in posterior; dog bite in cheek; tactile of dog fur, concrete (elbows on pavement), hot dog breath; emotion; physical pain plus endocrine response; audio of dog growl and passing car.
> What Mary does with the engram: she does not 'remember' the incident but sometimes plays she is a dog jumping on people and biting them. Otherwise no reaction. Then at age 10 similar circumstances, no great anaten, the engram is restimulated. After this she has headaches when dogs bark or when cars pass that sound like *that* car, but only responds to the engram when she is tired or harassed otherwise. The engram was first dormant – data waiting just in case. Next it was keyed-in[7] – stuff we have to watch out for. Then it was thereafter restimulated whenever any combination of its perceptics appeared while Mary was in slight anaten (weary). When forty years of age she responded in exactly the same way, and still has not the slightest conscious understanding of the real reason.[8]

Whilst the notion of the Thetan plays a quite important part in the explanation and therapy employed by Scientology and the entities themselves are held to be supernatural in attributes, they are not the occasion of worship. The Thetan is the essential and persistent element through the variety of bodies it inhabits. The ultimate aim of Scientology technique is to erase fully the effects of the engrams built up over thousands of past lives in a variety of traumatic situations, leaving the individual 'clear', and free to act unimpeded as an 'Operating Thetan', able to dissociate itself at will from the body which it temporarily inhabits unrestricted by mundane considerations of time, space, mass and energy, and capable of fully employing its superhuman powers. Reaching this sublime state,[9] however, requires extensive sessions of auditing (the name for the technique of therapy) and the completion of numerous courses, at a cost of something between £1,500 and £3,000.[10]

We now turn to consider Scientology in the light of the characteristics of the sect outlined above.

1. *Voluntary and achieved nature of membership*

Although the Church of Scientology has begun the practice of baptizing children into the church, this ritual appears to be of very little moment, and the number of baptisms, as of marriages, performed by the church is relatively small. Membership in the church is voluntary and necessarily achieved, since the major prerequisite for affiliation is the ability to pay for auditing and courses (or by gaining employment with the organization). Scientology is quite clearly geared to making a very substantial profit." L. Ron Hubbard is of the opinion that knowledge of scientology is one of the most valuable assets on the planet, and consequently well worth whatever the market will bear. Standard prices are established for each facility offered by the church, and membership is open to all who can afford it. Currently the physically ill are required to undergo treatment prior to admission, the psychotic are not allowed to affiliate, nor those detailed below in the next section. Some return on the investment in therapy and training is available for those who choose to practise as, and take the appropriate course to become, professionally practising auditors. Membership is also, of course, achieved in the sense that it involves the acquisition of the considerable body of doctrine and practice taught in its courses. These are structured in a hierarchical manner and often examined, success in the examination being a prerequisite for entry to more advanced courses.

2. *Exclusiveness*

The universalistic nature of its membership criterion mitigates the degree to which Scientology is able to be exclusive on entry. It aims to convert the world, and thus is eager to accept almost anyone presenting himself for membership. Hard-sell advertising techniques are an established feature of its practice. Personal salesmanship, public display advertising and extensive use of mail advertising are principal sources of recruitment – as well as through the sale of Ron Hubbard's numerous books, each of which contains the addresses of local Scientology organizations. Only those conclusively rejected as enemies by Scientology will not be permitted to affiliate. The final page of *Dianetics: Evolution of a Science* states: 'Membership in the Hubbard Association of Scientologists International is open to anyone who is not antipathetic to Scientology.'

While no stringent criteria for membership are established initially, Scientology operates a quite rigorous practice of expulsion of its deviant, uncommitted, unproductive or fractious members. Final exclusion is the last of a series of sanctions employed in the exercise of social control. Inadequate work performance (if one is employed in one of the Scientology organizations), questioning Hubbard's findings or theories, publicly derogating Scientology, Hubbard, or his wife, and a host of other 'crimes' are grounds for action by the Ethics Officers of the church whose job it is to uncover and extirpate sources of inefficiency or subversion within the organization. Individuals who consistently or seriously infringe the norms are declared 'suppressive persons' and not only are they ejected from Scientology, but Scientologists of their acquaintance are required to 'disconnect' from the guilty party, to have no further contact with him, and publicly declare to him by letter their intentions.

There are, of course, degrees of affiliation, and while little extensive commitment is expected of those simply undergoing auditing and the early courses, those who take the advanced courses – usually held only at regional or national headquarters of the organization, or who take the courses for professional auditors, are expected to commit not only substantial amounts of money but also of time. These courses often require full-time involvement for several weeks or even months, thus obliging such students to give up normal jobs, home, friends, and family, through disconnection (avowedly no longer practised due to the bad publicity to which it gave rise in the press) or as a result of the need to move closer to the Advanced Organization for training. Applicants for more advanced courses are vetted before acceptance to prevent infiltration by the potentially hostile.

3. *Self-conception as elect*

Scientologists claim to have 'the only route to Total Freedom', to be engaged in the most important mission in the world today, and to be producing the most able beings on the planet. Such claims are strongly indicative of a self-conception as an elect or elite, and that the Scientologists regard themselves as having unique and highly privileged access to the Truth. The following claims have appeared in promotional literature:

> Scientology is the study of knowledge in its fullest sense.
> Scientology brings you truth.
> Scientology brings you Total Freedom.[12]
>
> Scientology is ... the Greatest Movement in History.
>
> No man in history has ever been able to do for others what a Class VI (Auditor) can.
>
> Scientology brings ability, spiritual freedom and immortality.
>
> This is the first and *the* successful workable system of philosophy. Man has not had before even a single step of this route.
>
> Scientology: the bridge from chaos to total freedom.[13]

Or to quote an apostate from Scientology whom I interviewed:

> The frightening thing about Scientology is that it builds up your ego to such a fantastic extent that you begin to feel you're a supergod... I got to feeling that everyone else was a lesser mortal and that it didn't matter what one did to them ... because you are one of the chosen Few almost ...[14]

4. *Hostility towards social environment and the state*

Scientology manifests a certain ambiguity on this criterion which might be more fruitfully examined by considering each component in turn. Hostility in Scientology is largely reserved for competitors or potential dangers to itself. Whilst Hubbard is virulently anti-communist he is almost as virulently anti-fascist (actually conflating the two into a world conspiracy opposed to the liberalizing effects of Scientology), and Scientology is largely non-political except as a pressure group in its own interest.[15] It also manifests little hostility towards other churches, often inviting ministers to take its courses[16] The established denominations are seen as no real threat, although interview data suggest that active membership in alternative ideological collectivities is denigrated, and adherents while 'on course' or receiving auditing are required to follow a set of regulations including:

> Do not receive any 'treatment', 'guidance', or 'help' from anyone in the 'healing arts', i.e. Physician, Dentist, etc., without obtaining the consent of the Director of Training.

> Do not engage in any rite, ceremony, practice, meditation. diet, food therapy, or any similar occult, religious, naturopathic, homeopathic or chiropractic treatment or any other healing or mental therapy while on Course without the express permission of the Director of Training.[17]

Similarly, while on course, drinking alcohol and engaging in sexual relations with a student or staff member other than one's wife are prohibited.

Scientology does not directly oppose the values and social behaviour of the wider society, except in so far as the only important thing worth doing is Scientology and everything else – family, career, holidays, hobbies, etc. – is expected to take a very secondary place. Scientology is not, as we shall see below, an ascetic movement. Salvation is to be gained through application of Scientology technique and not through frugality or working hard in a calling. Few social habits or cultural values are proscribed by Scientology except in so far as they conflict with its own aims, and although valued cultural goals and social standards of success are relegated to a position of considerably less importance than involvement in Scientology itself, it is at the same time believed that Scientology will enable those who apply its techniques the more easily to acquire these cultural goals, and social success.

A rather similar attitude has been taken to the state. Only in so far as it attempts to circumscribe or investigate the activities of Scientology is it seen as an object of hostility. There is no aversion to the state *per se*. Scientologists are not opposed to inoculation, blood transfusion, public education of their children, nor are they opposed to war. Conflict with the state has been occasioned by threatened or implemented investigation of its activities – Scientologists taking the view that all form of mental healing, including institutional psychiatry, should be investigated at the same time, and arguing for example in America that as a religion such investigation is a violation of its constitutional rights. Its claim to therapeutic efficacy in cases of both physical and mental illness (now obscured beneath a patina of religious rationalization), have resulted in a variety of conflicts with the state. Scientology claims to be able to cure 70% of all man's illnesses on the basis of its theory that most illnesses are psychosomatic, i.e. engrammic in character.

The movement has been subject to periodic harassment by state and medical agencies. Proceedings were instigated by the New Jersey Board of Medical Examiners as early as January 1951 'for conducting a school, which, it was charged, was teaching medicine, surgery, and a method of treatment, without a licence.'[18]

In 1958 the American Food and Drug Administration became involved with the Church of Scientology in Washington where it was selling a vitamin mixture called 'Dianozene' as a preventative and treatment for radiation sickness. 'In a seizure action, FDA charged that the medicine was falsely labelled, and some 21,000 tablets were destroyed by court order.'[19]

In January 1963 the FDA instigated further action in connection with the E-meter,[20] charging that 'these devices were misbranded by false and misleading claims to treat effectively 70% of all physical and mental illness, and that the labelling did not bear adequate directions for such uses, as required by the Federal Food, Drug and Cosmetic Act'.[21] After a US District Court initially found in favour of the FDA in April 1967, the verdict was reversed by the Court of Appeals in February 1969 on the grounds that the FDA had not refuted the Scientology claim to be a religious organization.

Its therapeutic claims provide one of the major grounds for investigation by the governments of the State of Victoria in Australia, Canada, South Africa and the United Kingdom. Learning from experience gained in the courts, it now publicly describes its healing activities as devotional and the E-meter, the principal diagnostic tool, as a 'confessional instrument'. The incorporation of Scientology as a church, and ordination of ministers, was in considerable measure occasioned by conflicts over this issue since proscription of healing activities by unlicensed practitioners does not generally extend in the United States to ordained clergy.

Another major source of conflict with the state has been concerned with its activities in relation to minors. The introduction of elements of its technique into the curriculum of a private school led to investigation by Education Authorities in the United Kingdom,[22] and a major source of contention, particularly in Australia and New Zealand, has been over the claimed 'alienation of affection' that preceded the disconnection of teenage adherents from their parents (as well as wives from their husbands). Scientology gave way readily on this issue, claiming to have abandoned the policy of disconnection.

It was apparently the therapeutic claims of Scientology and practice of disconnection highlighted by the Report of the Victoria Board of Inquiry and subsequent banning of Scientology in Victoria, amongst other things, that led to the action by the British Government in the summer of 1968 of banning aliens – including Hubbard himself – from coming into England to pursue Scientology training.[23]

These sources of conflict have not been uncharacteristic of other sects – Christian Science,[24] Jehovah's Witnesses and the Exclusive Brethren being further examples.

A less contentious issue has been the unwillingness of the state in some countries to recognize Scientology as a religious body with the right to tax and rate exemptions – this seems to be the current position in the United Kingdom. However, politicians and civil servants are largely regarded by Scientology as foolish rather than evil. The state, whilst possibly mobilized by evil men, has simply been too stupid to recognize the benefits Scientology has to offer. Hubbard has been only too willing to suggest improvements, ranging from the offer of processing (i.e. auditing) to its leaders, to tax schemes involving a standard rate of income tax at 5% and the abolition of indirect and corporate taxation.

Evil lies less in the state or the social environment than in the medical profession, and particularly psychiatry. No dramatization of the Anti-Christ has displayed more horror and virulence than Scientology's portrayal of the psychiatrist. Indeed, so important and pernicious a threat is psychiatry, that a news-sheet, generally distributed free, has been founded specifically as a vehicle for the exposure and elimination of this evil – *Freedom*. Here psychiatry and psychiatrists, and supporters of mental health movements are described in scathing, if not paranoid terms:

> Institutional psychiatry ruthlessly promotes its own power and prestige. When psychiatry lies it is called mental health information.[25]

> It is now firmly established and generally known that the greatest menace to world peace, to the general well-being of all people, to the education of our children, to the sanctity of our Churches, and to the administration of justice in our courts, is the headshrinking cult of psychiatry.[26]

> It is no coincidence that psychiatric front groups teach that men are only animals to be herded and used at whim.[27]

> With a goal of control, by the reduction to zombie level of those in their clutches, with their sonorous predilections to stop religious belief, with their 'blood sports' raging fast and furious, and with their thoughts resembling the thoughts of Chairman Mao, it cannot be long before they all go the way of Hitler and Goebbels.[28]

> ... psychiatrists ... are false experts in a field which butchers, kills, rapes and practises all manner of licence contrary to the Nuremberg Code.[29]

One plausible conclusion would seem to be that this vitriolic attack mounted against psychiatry is motivated by the fact that psychiatry is a major competitor for many of its clients, and that it has radically rejected Scientology as a specious (and potentially dangerous) form of therapy. Perhaps more important, however, psychiatry also appears to act as a 'contrast-conception'[30] for Scientology. Sectarian groups, to maintain their own boundaries intact, need to distinguish themselves clearly from those ideological communities to which they might otherwise be assimilated. The greater the ideological proximity, particularly when both groups appeal to the same constituency, the greater the likelihood of animosity.

Since Scientology is right, psychiatry is not only different, but evil. Psychiatry aims to cure the psychotic, Scientology to make the able more able. Psychiatry is concerned with psychological healing, Scientology with spiritual healing, its techniques directed to the 'thetan' rather than the 'psyche'. Psychiatry employs constraint, pharmaco-therapy, electro-convulsive therapy and psycho-surgery, all characterized by Scientology as invariably therapeutically ineffective, evil, and motivated by malice. Evidence of malpractice, therapeutic failure and administrative error in psychiatry is eagerly sought by Scientology for publication in *Freedom*, which seeks to mobilize opposition to institutional psychiatry, presenting it in the blackest possible light.

However, this is not to say that Scientology's polemic is not motivated by a genuine revulsion against institutional psychiatry, its often crudely empirical forms of treatment and constraint on individual liberty, and a fear of state psychiatry as a monopoly, which is shared by many of the more marginal 'humanistic' psychologists – encounter group therapy, Jungian analysis, Reichian therapy, and the like, and by figures of such prominence as Ronald Laing and David Cooper in Britain, and Thomas Szasz[31] in the United States. (Thomas Szasz is currently the only psychiatrist whose books are promoted by the movement.)

Regarding the additional features of the sect:

5. The 'priesthood of all believers'

A 'priesthood of all believers' suggests that access to salvation is not mediated by a distinct professional hierarchy. In some sects such as the early Quakers, this implied a theoretical egalitarianism: indeed, Weber argued that 'pure sects also insist upon "direct democratic administration" by the congregation and upon treating clerical officials as servants of the congregation'.[32] Scientology is not altogether egalitarian. Although everyone has the potential to become an 'Operating Thetan', this state has yet been attained by only a few, although over 3,000 have been declared 'clear'. Such individuals are regarded as considerably superior to ordinary members (and, of course, *a fortiori* to non-members). As is often the case with 'gnostic' sects these advanced states of knowledge and experience require the negotiation of a complex and highly differentiated ladder of courses and qualifications, each of which endows the individual with a certain superiority over those below.

Although in the early stages of progress through this hierarchy auditing is usually conducted by a more advanced practitioner, in the progress towards 'going clear' and the succeeding stages, the procedures are self-audited – i.e. the individual conducts them on himself, having been supplied with the necessary materials and instructions in the form of a duplicated course manual by the organization. The most advanced levels, those of OT7 and OT8, however, are again conducted by another auditor.

Scientology is also administratively strictly hierarchical. Full-time staff members are organized on bureaucratic lines with a chain of command culminating in Hubbard as the final and principle locus of authority. His direct agents are members of the 'Sea Org.', the flotilla of ships which has served as Hubbard's headquarters since his re-entry into the United Kingdom was prohibited. These 'Missions' of the Sea Org. have final jurisdiction on matters of organizational control which they are periodically despatched to adjudicate. Each subsidiary organization has its own Ethics Officers, having the power to arraign other members of the organization on 'ethics' issues which range from incorrect practice of Scientology technique, to expression of doubt or hostility concerning Scientology, and failure to achieve the level of productivity minutely assigned to each organization, each department within it and each employed member of an organization. Appointments and dismissals of all senior personnel are made by Hubbard personally. Nevertheless, in principle at least, the state of Operating Thetan is potentially attainable by all members with the resources to pursue the requisite training and auditing. Hubbard was not the first 'clear' (that is, to have all his engrams eradicated through processing); others were able to achieve this state before him. This has not, however, resulted in any undermining of his authority.[33]

6. *Ethical and ascetic character*

Whilst Scientology embodies a system of ethics[34] – moral rules enjoining behaviour required for right action, happiness, the Good Life, etc. – and even provides an answer to the familiar ethical question 'What must I do to be saved?', this moral code is of highly limited applicability. Its ethics are not a system of general and universal moral rules to be applied in all situations and to all persons. They rather represent an internal system of social control directed at ensuring commitment to Scientological doctrine and practice, and its promotion.[35]

As Dr Wilson has indicated of Gnostic sects generally:

> There are few moral correlates of this ideological position, and those which do exist are typically personal aids to self-fulfilment, for example abstinence in matters of diet, and in use of drugs, tobacco and alcohol.[36]

Smoking, drinking, dancing, television, films, etc. are not in principle eschewed. Drinking and sex are rather frowned upon whilst 'on course', that is, whilst involved in training or auditing, and a film may be banned on the grounds that it is 'restimulative', i.e. liable to restimulate engrammic traumas experienced in past lives (as occurred in the case of Stanley Kubrick's *2001*).[37] Drug-taking and the consumption of alcohol have recently been attacked in Scientology publications[38] for their dulling effect on the mind and their inhabitory effect on 'case-gains' in auditing.

A major contravention of Scientology ethics is any activity which leads to a fall in productivity and profit of Scientology or one of its organizational outlets.[39] Among its 'crimes' are, for example, neglect or omission in safeguarding the copyrights, registered marks, trade marks, registered names of Scientology; holding Scientology materials or policies up to ridicule, contempt or scorn; allying Scientology to a disrelated practice; organizing or allowing a gathering or meeting of staff members or field auditors or the public to protest the orders of a senior. 'High Crimes', punishable by cancellation of certificates, awards, etc. and assignment of a 'Condition of Enemy' are : public disavowal of Scientology or Scientologists in good standing with Scientology organizations; announcing departure from Scientology; and testifying hostility before State or public inquiries into Scientology to suppress it. Punishment for 'ethics' offences ranges from symbolic degradation such as wearing a dirty rag tied round one arm, to total exclusion from all Scientology organizations, training and auditing.

While these may be regarded as components of an ethical system broadly conceived as a set of regulations or norms prescribing approved modes of behaviour, they are almost all designed to protect the organization rather than being of universal applicability in all social situations. What protects and promotes Scientology is good, what attacks or threatens it is evil. What one must do to be saved, therefore, is undertake Scientology processing and training, promote it to one's fullest and offer no criticism of its practices and personnel. Since this is the extent of its ethics, it is clearly not an ethical sect in the sense that it proclaims a rigorous morality radically at variance with that of the wider culture, and itself a predominant element in achieving salvation. Salvation in Scientology is achieved through its techniques, its ethics are designed solely to protect and foster those techniques and the organization controlling them.

Scientology is not only not an ethical sect in the traditional sense, it is also not an ascetic sect. Whilst paying its staff members relatively little, it certainly does not frown on commercial success, which is, indeed, seen as a major criterion of the success of Scientology itself and its subsidiary organizations. Those who undertake professional auditor training are promised a high income – until recently a promise rather better fulfilled by those who worked in a freelance capacity than directly for the organization itself. The altogether non-ascetic nature of Scientology's attitude to wealth and success is illustrated by the following quotation from a letter from the founder's wife, Mary Sue Hubbard, to all Franchised Auditors:

> I want you to make money.
> If anyone of you cannot conceive of an auditor driving around in a gold-plated Cadillac or Rolls, you had better re-orientate yourselves. I like the idea.
> The idea of the poor struggling auditor giving his all at a sacrifice to himself, starving in a garret, is not at all appealing to me, nor acceptable.[40]

It is, further, a boast of Scientology that a number of prosperous individuals and successful firms have employed Scientology techniques profitably in their business.[41]

7. *Totalitarianism*

Scientology is, particularly for its core members, totalitarian. The lives and activities of its staff members are highly regulated by a ramified network of rules and regulations. Any extensive commitment to Scientology necessitates extensive disruption of the member's way of life, through full-time or lengthy part-time involvement in its courses and processing, which except for those with considerable private funds generally requires taking employment with the organization. Despite the fact that such work is ill-paid by conventional standards, it is impossible to pursue many consistent careers – except those such as school teaching which permit one to attend courses during long holidays – without endangering one's job. The organization therefore provides one of the few suitable sources of employment apart from casual labour which permit intensive involvement. Further, there is the added incentive that training is available more cheaply to employees and a certain amount of processing free to those who accept employment contracts with the organization.

Until its (avowed) cessation of the practice of disconnection, Scientologists were obliged to sever connections utterly and irrevocably with those groups, friends, relatives, colleagues, etc. who expressed hostility towards or even any significant degree of scepticism concerning its founder, beliefs and practices. Moreover, total commitment to these beliefs is expected of members. No doubt or questioning of the beliefs or the efficacy of practice is permitted and the ethics system with its quasi-judical proceedings in Committees of Evidence, and frequent Security Checks employing the E-meter as a lie-detector to discover 'suppressive' activity, is designed to locate and eradicate such heresy. The impressive nature of this system of social control is indicated by the frequently voiced fears I met while interviewing apostates, many of several years' standing, that I might be part of this ethics system in pursuit of them.

Those who participate only on the fringes of the movement are, of course, less subject to control. Severest regulation is reserved for the members of the Sea Org., Hubbard's private navy, who are subject to even more stringent Ethics than ordinary members and staff members. Sea Org. personnel sign one billion year contracts to work for Scientology, they surrender their passports on boarding ship, and were at least at one time subject to 'Instant Ethics'. This practice involved throwing the miscreant over the side of the ship (with his hands tied if he could swim),[42] and appears to have been resorted to rather frequently at one stage.

Conclusions

The characteristics of the sect have been much debated.[43] Many of the traditional criteria appear to be contingent features of the circumstances in which sects in Christian cultures emerged. That they be eschatological, a component of the Troeltschian definition, is no longer regarded as an essential feature of the sect. Others, such as asceticism, an ethical orientation, and egalitarianism, seem similarly to be rather a consequence of historical circumstances in which religious protest was legitimated by an appeal to the presumed characteristics of the early church, than part of a universal characterization of sectarianism. The distinction of the sect as a voluntary association dependent upon achieved rather than ascriptive bases of membership no longer appears useful in the contemporary situation of competition amongst religious collectivities, adherence to most of which presupposes a voluntary commitment. The exclusive nature of the sect also requires reinterpretation. Many ideological groups which can fruitfully be regarded as sectarian impose no severe test of merit on entry into the sect – particularly those of the 'conversionist' variety.[44] They nevertheless reserve and employ the right to exclude those regarded as inimical to their interest at some later stage.

Thus the criteria of sectarianism appear finally to centre around the right to exclusion, self-conception as an 'elect' or elite, and totalitarianism. These are all sociological correlates of what might perhaps be taken as the feature common to all sects, which although mentioned in some definitions, has failed to achieve the prominence that it deserves. The sect is a minority group organized around a belief-system regarded by its adherents as a unique and privileged mode of access to the truth or salvation. Such a definition provides a conceptualization applicable to the political groups discussed by O'Toole, Alcoholics Anonymous, deviant health practices, traditional forms of religious sectarianism, and more recent movements such as Scientology which contain components of many of these. It thereby renders possible a cross-fertilization between the sociology of religion and other fields, which has received increasing advocacy in recent years.[45]

NOTES

1. I am grateful to Dr Bryan R. Wilson of All Souls College, Oxford, to Dr Nigel Walker of Nuffield College, Oxford, and to Mr David Gaiman, of the Church of Scientology for comments on earlier drafts on this paper. Mr Gaiman kindly made available a number of documents in an effort to correct my more glaring errors and misinterpretations. I should add that not all their suggestions could be incorporated in the current version and my treatment of this subject would not necessarily meet with the approval of all of them.

2. Ernst Troeltsch, *The Social Teachings of the Christian Churches*, Macmillan, NY 1931; Howard Becker, *Systematic Sociology on the Basis of the Bezeihungslehre and Gebildelehre of Leopold von Wiese*, Wiley, NY 1932; Benton Johnson, 'A critical appraisal of the church-sect typology', *American Sociological Review*, vol. 22, 1957, pp.88-92; 'On Church and Sect', *American Sociological Review*, vol. 28, 1963, pp.539-49; 'Church and Sect Revisited', *Journal for the Scientific Study of Religion*, vol. 10, no. 2, 1971, pp.124-37; J. Milton Yinger, *Religion, Society and the Individual,*

Macmillan NY 1957 and *The Scientific Study of Religion*, Collier-Macmillan 1970; Bryan R. Wilson, *Sects and Society*, Heinemann 1960, 'A typology of Sects', *Sociology of Religion*, ed. Roland Robertson, Penguin Books 1970 and *Religious Sects*, Weidenfeld & Nicolson 1970.

3. Susan Budd, 'The Humanist Societies: the consequences of a diffuse belief system', *Patterns of Sectarianism*, ed. Bryan R. Wilson, Heinemann 1967; Robert K. Jones, 'Sectarian characteristics of Alcoholics Anonymous', *Sociology*, vol. 4, no. 2, 1970, pp.181-95; Roger O'Toole, 'A consideration of "Sect" as an exclusively religious concept: notes on some "underground" traditions in the study of sectarianism', unpublished paper presented at the Annual Meeting of the Society for the Scientific Study of Religion, Chicago, Illinois, October 1971.

4. For earlier discussions of Scientology, see John Jackson, 'Two contemporary cults', *The Advancement of Science*, vol. 23, no. 108, 1966, pp.60-4; John Jackson and Ray Jobling, 'Toward an Analysis of Contemporary Cults', *A Sociological Yearbook of Religion in Britain*, ed. David Martin, SCM Press 1968; Bryan R. Wilson, *Religious Sects*, Weidenfeld & Nicolson 1970.

5. During its Dianetics phase the movement was organized in a rather more cult-like manner. I intend to explore this period in a forthcoming paper, 'From Cult to Sect in Scientology', in which I hope to show the relationship between the concept of the sect that I propose below and that of the cult, employing Dianetics/Scientology as a case study in the dynamics of transition from one to the other.

6. Anaten: A term employed in Scientology to indicate 'a diminution or weakening of the analytical awareness of an individual'. The term is short for Analytical Attenuation. See L. Ron Hubbard, *Scientology Abridged Dictionary*, Publications Organizations, Copenhagen 1965, p.8.

7. Key-In: a term employed in Scientology to indicate 'the moment an earlier upset or painful incident has been restimulated'; ibid, p.21.

8. L. Ron Hubbard, *Dianetics : The Evolution of a Science*, The Publications Organization World Wide, 1950, pp.65-6. Whilst this example relates to Dianetics, the theory of Scientology is based upon similar traumatic events occurring over many 'past-lives'.

9. The final stage of Operating Thetan, OT8, is claimed to have been reached by some members, although many are past the stage of 'clear' and in the early stages of becoming Operating Thetans.

10. As Dr Nigel Walker has pointed out to me, such a sum would not be excessive for a two-three year psychoanalytic training analysis – which normally lasts four years.

11. Mr Gaiman argues that Scientology is geared to expansion rather than to making a profit.

12. L. Ron Hubbard, *Dianetics*, p.1.

13. *The Auditor*, various issues and *Auditor Supplements* 5 and 6.

14. The potential for antinomianism here seems clear. As Wilson has noted: '... conscience ... appears to undergo an unusual transformation in some sectarian movements ... where the concept of elite status is so strongly accepted that the faithful believe that they are a chosen people regardless of their moral behaviour. Being chosen, they might come to see themselves as perfect: thus behaviour that would be sinful in others cannot by definition be sinful for them' (Bryan R. Wilson, *Religious Sects*, p.33).

An antinomian tendency is evident in the description of those assigned a Condition of Enemy or Treason, as 'Fair Game'. 'By FAIR GAME is meant, without right for self, possessions or position, and no Scientologist may be brought before a Committee of Evidence or punished for any action taken against a Suppressive Person or Group during the period that person or group is "fair game" ' (L. Ron Hubbard, *Introduction to Scientology Ethics*, Scientology Publishing Organization, Copenhagen 1968, 1970, as cited by Cyril Vosper in *The Mind Benders*, Neville Spearman 1971, p.141). The current edition of *Introduction to Scientology Ethics*, however, does not employ the term 'fair game'. But see also Sir John Foster, *Enquiry into the Practice and Effects of Scientology*, HMSO 1971, p.129. A *Hubbard Communication Office Policy Letter* also elaborates on the implications of a declaration of 'fair game': 'May be deprived of property or injured by any means by any Scientologist without any discipline of the Scientologists. May be tricked, sued, lied to or destroyed.' (*HCO Policy Letter* of 18 October 1966). A later policy directive, *HCO Policy Letter* of 21 October 1968 from the Hubbard Communication Office, ordered the cessation of the practice of declaring people 'fair game', due to the bad publicity this had caused. It is not clear, however, that the *policy* associated with declaring people 'fair game' was also abandoned as well as the label. See Foster, ibid., pp.127-30. A now rather hostile Scientology apostate, discussing how adherents financed the expensive courses, suggested in an interview with me that the attitude of the organization was: 'It doesn't matter how you get the money, when you come on course we'll clean you up ... we'll pull your guilts ...'

15. An example of its pressure group activity on a political level is the Scientology Mission to the United Nations, in existence throughout 1968–1969. This mission was headed by John McMaster, at that time Scientology's major promotional figure and the 'World's First Real Clear'. The brief of this mission was to 'establish a safe space politically for Scientology ... across Planet Earth' (Interview data).

16. See *Freedom*, 37, March 1972.

17. *HCO Policy Letter* of 22 November 1961.

18. George Malko, *Scientology: The Now Religion*, Dell Publishing Co., NY 1970.

19. In a letter to me from the United States Department of Health, Education and Welfare. Documents made available to me by the Church of Scientology suggest that neither the founding Church of Scientology, nor the Hubbard Association of Scientologists International had any direct involvement in this matter which concerned an organization known as the Distribution Center Inc. It would appear, however, that Mr Hubbard was a 'sponsor' of this latter corporation.

20. The E-meter is a form of electronic psychogalvanometer, similar to the American lie-detector, but employing only the measure of variations in ohmic resistance occurring between the metal electrodes held by the 'pre-clear'. It was invented by Volney G. Mathison in 1950. Hubbard later produced a variation on the original design. In Scientology it is regarded as effective in measuring changes in the mental state of the individual, particularly in indicating that psychically sensitive material is being touched upon in the questioning. It was charged by the FDA in its seizure action that the E-meter was being employed for diagnosis. Machines now carry a disclaimer to the effect that: 'The E-meter is not intended or effective for the diagnosis, treatment or prevention of any disease.' For a discussion of Mathison, the E-meter and Scientology in Canada, see John A. Lee, *Sectarian Healers and Hypnotherapy: A Study for the Committee on the Healing Arts*, Queen's Printer, Toronto 1970.

21. US Department of Health, Education and Welfare, loc. cit.

22. This is referred to in the report of the Foster Enquiry as the first occasion the press in the UK showed interest in Scientology, in late 1960, when the headmistress of a private school in East Grinstead, who was undergoing a course in Scientology, was reported to be taking pupils of hers aged between 7 and 11 through an exercise in which they were asked to imagine that they were dead and turning to dust, as a result of which one small boy was said to have fainted' (Foster, op. cit., p.1).

23. For the Victoria Report, see Kevin Victor Anderson, *Report of the Board of Inquiry into Scientology*, State of Victoria, Government Printer, Melbourne 1965. For the British ban, see *The Times*, 5 June 1968; 29 July 1968; 1 August 1968; etc.

24. See Roy Wallis. 'Ideology, authority, and the development of manipulationist movements', paper to be presented to the International Conference of the Sociology of Religion, The Hague, August 1973.

25. *Freedom*, 32, 1971.

26. *Freedom*, 30, 1970.

27. *Freedom*, 28, 1970.

28. Ibid.

29. *Freedom*, 10, 1969.

30. Joseph Gusfield, *Symbolic Crusade*, University of Illinois Press, Urbana 1963, p.27.

31. Ronald Laing, *The Divided Self*, Penguin Books 1965 and *The Politics of Experience*, Penguin Books 1967; David Cooper, *Psychiatry and Anti-Psychiatry*, Paladin 1970; Thomas Szasz, *The Myth of Mental Illness*, Harper & Row, NY 1961, and *The Manufacture of Madness*, 1970.

32. Max Weber, 'Church & Sect', *Sociology of Religion: A Book of Readings*, ed. Norman Birbaum & Gertrud Lenzer, Prentice-Hall, NJ 1969.

33. This point will be further explored in my forthcoming paper, 'Ideology, authority, and the development of manipulation movements'.

34. On the Ethics of Scientology, as on many other interesting facets of the movement, see Vosper, *The Mind Benders*, Vosper was involved with Scientology for some 14 years.

35. See L. Ron Hubbard, *Introduction to Scientology Ethics*.

36. Bryan R. Wilson, 'An Analysis of sect development', *American Sociological Review*, vol. 24, no. 1, 1959, p.14.

37. Vosper, op. cit., pp.149-50.

38. See *The Auditor*, 71, 1971.

39. This is on the basis of an interesting theory that inefficiency is directly caused by hostility to Scientology: 'In the presence of suppression one makes mistakes ... People making mistakes or doing stupid things is evidence that an SP (Suppressive Person) exists in the vicinity' (*HCO Bulletin*, 12 March 1968).

Conversations with former Scientologists who have worked for the organization suggest that inefficiency in Scientology is endemic, and in large measure a consequence of two factors, firstly overbureaucratization, and secondly an unintended consequence of the Ethics system itself. On the first point, each department and job within the organization is rigidly governed by a (constantly changing) set of rules emanating from Hubbard, who is, of course, floating in the Mediterranean, and not therefore in the best position to handle day-to-day administrative problems. These job specifications have the force of law and cannot be contravened even in situations where they seem to lead inexorably to chaos. Changing the rules or bending them to suit the circumstances would be to 'invalidate the data of Scientology' – a serious violation. Each job and department has a measure of efficiency, its Stat(istic)s – the throughput of letters in the Mailing Department, the number of books sold in the Book Department, the number of 'success points' the student or pre-clear can be persuaded to put into his 'success story' mandatory after completing a series of auditing sessions, in the Success Department, etc. Each individual and department is thus strongly motivated to ensure high statistics for himself/itself (in part also because not only does failure to achieve one's Stats involve an Ethics infringement, but also, since wages are related to productivity, financial loss). A situation prevails once held to characterize the Russian economy under intensive planning, where each factory manager struggled to complete his assigned production quota, regardless of the effect his activities had on the market, suppliers, or other producers. Moreover, due to the severe penalties, subordinates are unwilling to take responsibility for decisions in situations which do not precisely fit the rules, obliging them to make constant reference to their superiors, holding up the job and burdening executives with administrative trivia which draws their time and attention away from their own tasks of general and integrated planning. This has since also become an Ethics offence, known as Dev.T (Developed Unnecessary Traffic).

One typical occasion of inefficiency that comes to mind is that of a 'success show' put on by Scientologists, in which a hall was booked, the performers highly rehearsed, etc., and which could have been an effective promotional activity for the organization, except that no one had been told to prepare and distribute any advertising for the event so that no audience ever appeared to view it. This kind of mistake is no rare occurrence in Scientology.

On the counterproductivity of the Ethics system in organizational affairs, this seems to work as follows: a department has low Stats, a Committee of Evidence is convened to discover and sanction the suppressives involved. The department must appear before this 'Comm.Ev.' taking them off their jobs for extensive periods until someone is scapegoated. By this time their Stats have fallen further due to the time lost, so another Comm.Ev. must be called to find the further or 'real' suppressive. This takes up more time, Stats fall further etc. This inefficiency-amplication syndrome is handled in two ways; either by sending a Sea Org. Mission to get the local organization back on to its feet again by sacking and otherwise removing the inefficient, forgiving the repentant, etc; or more generally by tacitly accepting infringements of the bureaucratic rules until such time as an excuse is needed for expelling someone, when their infringements will suddenly be noticed and dealt with. Ritualism, however, seems an inescapable feature of Scientology organization administration as it is currently structured. See Vosper, op. cit., ch. 12.

40. *HCO Newsletter*, 7 May 1962.

41. See e.g. *The Auditor*, 70, 1971.

42. See photograph in *The Auditor*, 41, 1968. It is the claim of the church that these ethics practices are no longer pursued with the rigour which formerly characterized them. A *Code of Reform* was promulgated in 1968 as a result of widespread public disquiet about such practices. This *Code of Reform* cancelled the policy of disconnection, security checking, the declaration of individuals as fair game, and included a prohibition of 'any confessional materials being written down'.

43. For one interesting recent contribution to this debate, see Allan Eister,

'Toward a radical critique of church-sect typologising', *Journal for the Scientific Study of Religion*, vol. 6, 1967, pp.85-90.

44. Wilson, 'An analysis of sect development'.

45. Peter Berger and Thomas Luckmann, 'Sociology of religion and sociology of knowledge', *Sociology and Social Research*, vol. 47, no. 4, 1963, pp.417-27.

8   The Political Effects of Village Methodism

Robert Moore

The beginning of the eighteenth century saw the beginning of industrialization and urbanization. According to Lecky the class war was about to begin as great masses of workers were drawn to the towns; with traditional social ties dissolved, only the cash nexus held men – especially employers and the employed – together. In this situation there was a religious revival which '... opened a new spring of moral and religious energy among the poor, and at the same time gave a powerful impulse to the philanthropy of the rich.'[1] Lecky was no admirer of Methodism, but he was sure that Methodism had helped to avert revolution.

Drawing on a long tradition of French historiography[2] Halévy asked the question, 'Why did England not have a revolution?' He concluded that one could not find the answer in a study of economic or political institutions. Like Lecky, he concluded that the religious revival of the early eighteenth century was a vital factor.[3] 'The Halévy thesis' has been central to the discussion of the political effects of Methodism since 1913.

Halévy observed that the Methodist revival was not created *ex nihilo*;

> Le réveil évangélique de 1739 ne fut donc pas un commencement absolu, une création *ex nihilo*: il consiste dans une combinaison nouvelle d'éléments préexistants et parfaitement définis.[4]

For Halévy the English nation was (and is) a nation of puritans and the English character serious, reserved and melancholic as compared with the gay, extroverted and irreligious French. The revival of 1739 was a *revival* and not something new, it was a reawakening of important aspects of traditional English culture: 'la vieille inspiration puritaine, qui avait triompher un siècle plus tôt, aux temps de la Republique de Cromwell.'[5] The revival was not a simple response to a political situation. Walpole's scepticism was matched by the decadence of the churches: absenteeism and venality in the established church, political and theological conflict between Dissenters.

> Si la réaction guerrière contre le pacifisme de Walpole s'incarne en William Pitt, la reaction religieuse et morale contre son sceptisme s'incarne en Whitefield et Wesley.[6]

But how did this religious and moral reaction prevent revolution in England?

At the core of Halévy's argument there is to be found a theory about the relationship between the middle class and the working class and a theory about the nature of each class. Of the working class he says:

> Le prolétariat des manufactures et des usines, aggloméré autour des centres industriels, et accessible à la contagion rapide de tout les émotions violentes. Mais c'est une foule ignorante, incapable de prévoir et de deviner elle-même en quel sens se portera son enthusiasms.[7]

If, according to Halévy, the bourgeoisie had been motivated by revolutionary ideas, then, given their position of leadership, the social order might have been overthrown by popular insurrection. But they were neither revolutionary, nor deeply irreligious in outlook. Thus, without revolutionary bourgeois leadership, the proletariat did not revolt. Thus, nearly a century later, non-conformity paralysed revolutionary Chartism by removing from the working class the necessary middle-class leadership and 'deprived of leaders, the populace fell back into a state of incoherence, demoralization and at last apathy'.[8] This, then, is the first point to be drawn from Halévy in answer to our question; the revival revived religious and not revolutionary ideas amongst the leaders of the proletariat.

Secondly, the puritan tradition was embodied in certain kinds of organizations. For Halévy, a notable feature of British society was the tradition of voluntary associations. The right of free association and the puritan tradition belong together. Dissenting groups could only survive on the basis of restraints; the avoidance of confrontations with the state and the restriction of individual freedom necessary for this. These were both necessary disciplines for ensuring survival and they were disciplines revived and reactivated in the eighteenth-century religious revival. Halévy regarded it as somewhat paradoxical that one of the greatest restraints on individual liberty should have been the right of free association. Thirdly, the revival of 1739 and the growth of Methodism amongst the working classes influenced the outlook of indigenous working-class leadership '... The *élite* of the working class [and] the hard-working and capable bourgeois, had been imbued by the evangelical movement with a spirit from which the established order had nothing to fear.'[9]

The lack of revolutionary ideals and the voluntary restriction of individual liberty may have been sufficient to prevent the emergence of a social revolutionary leadership. But there was another factor. The substance of the ideas preached in the revival and embodied in Methodism was specifically non-revolutionary. In a review of Halévy's work Charles Gillispie observed that 'For Halévy the main thing about evangelicalism was not that it was true religion but that it led to individual self-restraint.'[10] Wesley and his followers preached a gospel of individual salvation drawn from the main stream of the puritan tradition already referred to. There were no levelling doctrines, no preaching of the millennium with its promise of tangible and immediate benefits. The Methodists preached salvation by faith, a salvation to be comprehended in the inner experience of a heart 'strangely warmed' and issuing in works of rescue and reclamation among the unregenerate, derelict and dispossessed. According to Halévy, 'They would never be weary of insisting that national regeneration could be achieved only by the regeneration of individuals.'[11]

Self-restraint, individualism and philanthropy, accompanied by a pragmatic approach to problems, found an affinity firstly with liberal economics and secondly with utilitarianism to produce the English character which Halévy found to be so different from the national character of France.

The revival in the eighteenth century had a further long-term effect on political developments. It disciplined the new bourgeoisie, 'restrained the plutocrats who had newly arisen from the masses from vulgar ostentation and debauchery'.[12] Given this restraining influence it was more likely that the poor would accept the position of the rich without developing a critical attitude towards them. At least a factor likely to exacerbate class conflict was reduced. Finally, the revival of religion amongst both the rich and the poor provided some common ground, at the level of beliefs, between them. Thus the cash nexus was not all that held together men of different positions.

It is important to note what we are *not* saying here. We are not suggesting that all the working class and all the upper classes were religious in any sense. Secondly, we are not advancing the notion of an overarching system of values which functioned to integrate society. What is more important, and perhaps only implicit in Halévy's analysis, is to observe the substructure of beliefs and practices which constituted what Alasdair MacIntyre has called the 'secondary virtues'. These virtues consist of 'a pragmatic approach to problems, co-operativeness, fair-play, tolerance, a gift for compromise, and fairness'.[13] These values are secondary because they relate not to the goals that men pursue but to the means by which they pursue goals which are not stated. The secondary virtues formed part of the basis for collaboration and co-operation between social classes in the nineteenth century even though, in fact, the classes were pursuing ends antipathetic to one another.

Gillispie commented that in the nineteenth century 'contemporaries did not find society notably stable in the evangelical, but economically uncertain, decades of the twenties and thirties.'[14] Hobsbawm also noted that there was a good deal of revolutionary feeling down to 1840 but that it was a situation in which the upper classes never lost control.[15] Had other factors been ripe, Hobsbawm concludes, Methodism could not have prevented revolution. He further remarks that Methodism and radicalism advanced together and that in modern times pious men of various faiths have led, or been active in revolutionary movements. These comments seem to do less than justice to the Halévy thesis. Halévy was concerned, as we have tried to show, not with Methodism as a thing in itself which prevented revolution but as a representation of deeper and more universal aspects of English culture and character. Some of Hobsbawm's 'other factors' could not ripen because of the culture in which they developed.

More damaging criticisms of Halévy are contained in other accounts of Methodism. Halévy seemed to see the proletariat as basically inarticulate, rather stupid and capable only of reacting to others. Thus it follows mass emotions, and the ideas of the moment, and it is easily led by the bourgeoisie. He does not ask if religion can have any meaning for the individual proletarian believer, he only asks this question of the elite of the working class. The Hammonds and E. P. Thompson all suggest that religion might have meaning for the believer, whatever his social position. According to the Hammonds the miner or the weaver 'wanted a religion that recognized that the world did not explain itself'.[16] In other words the worker needed beliefs which placed him in a significant world of meanings which transcended everyday life. For the oppressed religion gave, in the words of the Hammonds, 'an assurance that their obscure lives had some significance and moment'.[17] Such notions might be the basis for the development of a radical response to social conditions. But what weakened the workers' revolutionary potential was that Methodists accepted deprivation as a trial of faith and not as an unjust situation to be righted.

Thompson suggests that Methodism met certain psychological needs amongst the oppressed and induced a sense of discipline and dedication into their work. It 'weakened the poor from within' and taught them submission. Methodism was apolitical and counter-revolutionary because it 'brought to a point of hysterical intensity the desire for *personal* salvation'.[18] These are the effects of religion on working men themselves, not the effects of religion mediated by a bourgeois leadership.

The Hammonds and Thompson make more of the paradoxes of Methodism than Halévy. The Hammonds said of the eighteenth century that 'Religion was, in fact, part of the civil constitution of society.' Thus any religious questioning was, in the eyes of the authorities, a questioning of the *status quo*.[19] Methodism was thus associated with sedition; it was in reply to such accusations that the Methodist leadership generated an extensive propaganda on the anti-revolutionary effects of Methodism.[20]

Yet despite the actual and claimed non-revolutionary effects of Methodism, Methodism taught men that they could be free of their immediate circumstances.[21] The Methodist societies were training grounds for democracy; discipline and dedication were valuable characteristics in a trade union leader. The Hammonds saw Methodism as a faith producing men who had political courage of a kind associated with a sense of religious mission. These men also learnt to speak and they learnt to organize in democratic communities of their own creation. These were attributes readily transferable to the political sphere. This consideration perhaps brings the argument full circle, for given men of courage, integrity and ability, what did they stand for? What sort of working-class leadership did Methodism actually create?

None of the writers so far discussed undertook any investigation into the institutionalization of Methodism amongst working men.

The material available to them largely related to Methodism as a national movement engaged in national affairs. Printed sources on local Methodism tend to be hagiographic or (auto)biographies of socially successful Methodist worthies. The writings of Methodist divines survive as part of the national history as do the hymns of those included in the hymn books. We do not know in detail the beliefs of the working-class Methodist-in-the-pew. Thompson suggests that institutionalization of Methodism may have resulted in a modification of 'official' doctrines; the 'pitiless dogmas' were softened by the realities of community life. Thompson also observes that isolated communities can especially make Methodism 'their own' and mould it to their circumstances.[22] Thompson makes an important sociological point; doctrine is likely to be modified both in its transmission to local communities and in the adoption of the transmitted beliefs by the local community.

It would seem to be a matter of some importance to investigate the beliefs of the local Methodist community and to examine the themes arising from the Halévy thesis in the light of the findings. We cannot easily do this for the eighteenth or early nineteenth century. The records we need were not kept, in any form. The late nineteenth century and the turn of the present century is the earliest period from which we can draw suitable evidence based upon the testimony of working-class Methodists. Their recollections can be checked against one another, with the newspapers and against Methodist manuscripts and printed sources. Perhaps most importantly our informants can express beliefs and present their values and outlook to the investigator. But are we not asking a different question, i.e. what effects did Methodism have seventy years ago? Halévy's understanding of Methodism came not from studying the documents of the eighteenth and nineteenth centuries alone, but from experiencing Methodism at first hand also: ' "J'acheve excelle-ment de connaître l'Angleterre en étudiant les Méthodistes", Halévy wrote in beginning the description of [a] Methodist service. "Even today", he was to write in his 1906 articles, "whenever a Methodist preacher brings a popular audience together at a street corner to read the Bible, sing hymns, and pray in common, whenever he induces a 'revival' of mysticism and religious exhaltation", it is "the great movement of 1739 which is being repeated".'[23] We, like Halévy, believe that the experience of a later period of Methodism enhances our understanding of an earlier period. In some respects

Methodism was the same in both periods, though the circumstances were different. Thus it is not an illegitimate undertaking to seek evidence wherever it is available; if Halévy believed his thesis had universal validity, it is an entirely legitimate undertaking to test it in any period.

We might pose a series of questions, derived from the foregoing discussion, which could be asked in an empirical study

1. To what extent and in what ways, was local Methodism non-revolutionary and individualistic?
2. Did Methodism deprive the working class of a revolutionary leadership by creating a 'hard-working and capable' elite?
3. What affinities did Methodism have with other sets of beliefs?
4. Did Methodism discipline the local bourgeoisie?
5. Was Methodism effective in spite of 'other factors'?
6. What are the consequences of Methodism being a community religion rather than a set of beliefs held in the abstract?

In many essays, posing questions on the grand scale is an introduction to a descent into the trivial. The writer discusses what happened to a small (but usually random and meticulously surveyed) sample of the population; or what happened in one village while he was gathering material for a thesis. To answer the questions on the level from which they are derived one would need the amassed findings of many years of research directed towards such questions. No such body of data exists. Thus, while avoiding the banal, we must be content with tentative conclusions drawn from limited studies.

What follows is an exploration of the six questions above by reference to empirical research carried out in an area of mainly Primitive Methodism, focusing on the turn of the present century. The work began from an interest in the role of Methodism as a community religion, and an awareness of the ambiguities of the influence of Methodism on the working class. A group of west Durham mining villages was chosen. They were thought to be typical of the late-nineteenth century pit villages and in the end they seemed to be so, save in one respect, which will be discussed.

The villages grew rapidly from the late 1860s, when the pits were opened. They were mostly built by the local coal owners with bricks from their own brick-flats. The owners were both employers and landlords to the miners. The villages had something of a 'wild west' frontier culture until the early twentieth century; this seems to have been a function of rapid population growth and the attendant social dislocation.

In 1895 the population of the four villages was about 7,600 and in 1901 it was 9,100. Estimates of the numbers of active Methodists vary but on the basis of calculations which tend to underestimate the number of active Methodists the situation was as follows in 1900:

TABLE ONE

Active Methodists at the turn of the century

Methodists	Members	Adherents	Sunday School Children
Primitive	340	1,000	366
Wesleyan	c 150	c 225	not known
Total	c 490	c 1,225	?400

A small Methodist New Connexion Congregation in one village is ignored. These figures suggest that a little over 17% of the population was directly active in the Methodist societies. This percentage actually represents a much higher penetration of the community than about 1 in 6. In 1919, for example, 21% of the population was Methodist on the same basis of calculation; but this meant that nearly 40% of all households in the village included at least one active Methodist. In some cases this was a child only; but the parent of a child actively sent to Sunday School was clearly not totally uninfluenced by Methodism.

At the core of Methodist teaching was the notion of personal regeneration. John 3 and Luke 15, with their stress on rebirth, forgiveness and new life, were popular sources of texts for sermons. Sermons were filled with references to hell-fire and the importance of having one's name in the Book of Life. The extreme sense of urgency in the preaching and the tremendous fervour of the preachers was striking. One miner started to write his autobiography at the end of the nineteenth century; it did not develop beyond a few manuscript pages, but it is compelling evidence of the fervour of the evangelical preachers. In the 1880s he felt he was doing too much preaching;

> Although God greatly blessed my efforts I would like to have been relieved from preaching. It cost me much prayer and sleepless nights...
> I therefore asked God to give me souls as an evidence that I was chosen to the work next time I was planned. I was planned at —— for the first place after and put God to the test. At the night service we had a glorious meeting. Six souls been saved. I resolved that was enough. I durst not doubt my calling again.

The action of personal regeneration was always expressed in a very concrete form; conversion brings salvation from drink and gambling and the associated evils of debt, violence and broken homes. From 1870 to 1914 these ideas were regularly expounded in revivalist campaigns and open-air meetings. Direct comment on social and political issues was rare and came only from preachers who were regarded as eccentric or as trouble-makers.

In the case of the Durham villages studied, Methodists in their seventies and older all commented that the main effect of conversion was that a man gave up drinking.

> (During the missions) the chapels used to be packed, then we used to go around the streets with the portable organ (harmonium). We held midnight meetings outside the public as the drunks came rolling out. Two or three were converted and never went back to drink, died good Christian men. —— was a gambler and drinker; he went to the Minister and signed the Pledge in the middle of the night, and never touched the stuff again, though it was a great temptation passing the public every day. *85-year-old woman.*[24]

> My challenge to him was that drinking was a foolish way to waste his life – there were better things for him ... Homes were wrecked through men being drunkards – their lives and homes were brightened by their conversion, other people could see that this was true ... We kept the village in good order with our Christian work. *Preacher in his late seventies.*

One popular anecdote epitomizes the down-to-earth nature of this outlook: A newly-converted miner was being questioned by his workmates and he found himself at a loss in trying to explain miracles. In desperation he asked them if they remembered the state of his home a few months ago, and did they see it now? If Jesus could turn beer into new furniture and nice clothes for his children, why should he not turn water into wine!

The stress of personal regeneration bred individualism. Faced by immediate social problems in the villages, and by larger national issues, Methodists responded by saying that the world would be put right by putting individual men and women right. There was a tendency not to look beyond men's immediate behaviour to its causes. A highly contrived but popular sermon illustration concerned a boy who did not know enough geography to enable him to fit together a jig-saw puzzle of the world. His father showed him that there was a picture of a man on the back of the puzzle. The boy assembled the man and turned the picture over to achieve a world correctly put together.

Methodism was not the only source of individualism. Temperance organizations worked for individual reclamation in their own way, although they were normally closely associated with Methodist chapels, often sharing premises and personnel. The Co-operative movement also encouraged frugality and thrift;

> It induced (the working class) to think – taught them to be frugal and careful – encouraged them to be temperate – tended to make them better and wiser men – and enabled them to rise to any position in society they chose.[25]

Also contemporary economic thinking and political Liberalism encouraged individualism. (Most of the Methodists would not even consider the policies of the 'drink-supported' Tory party.)

What effects did conversion actually have on men and women in the villages? We find that many men and women were, in fact, saved from lives of drunkenness and poverty. Also men and women living in an unpleasant physical environment and at times violent social environment, found new concepts of human dignity and purpose. The idea of service and a Christian calling was strongly developed amongst the Methodists. In sermons this was usually centred around an exposition of the Parable of the Talents. Furthermore, it was said, even in the face of failure:

> ... one must press on. We do not labour in vain in the Lord. God may be testing our mettle or aiding our Spiritual development ... [that] which ought to characterise all good men [is] ... determined perseverance.[26]

For some men and women fulfilling a calling meant separation from the profane affairs of men, maintaining 'respectability' and pious purity, encapsulated in the life of the chapel. For others it entailed practical service in the community. Between 1890 and 1920, out of twenty-six prominent local Methodists, twenty-one held between them forty-three trade union offices (including seven checkweighmen, three in succession in one village); another twenty-one held twenty-eight posts in political parties or stood as Council lors (fifteen) or JPs (four) and thirteen held office in local Co-operative Societies. This grouping also represents a considerable concentration of community power within Methodism. Other Methodists participated in political and civic activities on a less intense scale.

The reasons for Methodists being elected to official positions in the Durham Miners Association (the miners' union) are almost commonplace in the history of Methodism: (1) Methodists were known to be honest in handling money; (2) their sobriety made them dependable in all situations; (3) they possessed organizing skills which they had developed through chapel activities; (4) they were usually competent public speakers, having gained speaking skills in the Sunday school or as preachers.

From the written records and all first hand accounts the motivation for holding office seemed to lie wholly in the wish to perform useful service and to better the lot of the local miners. There was no overtly 'political' motive in holding office,[27] no desire to bring about social-structural change.

The Methodist miner saw his occupation as a 'calling' and therefore endowed with a transcendent meaning. Important amongst the meanings adhering to the notion of calling was the idea that God had made him a miner in accordance with a divine purpose. It was not an accident of birth or the outworkings of an economic system which made men miners, but God's will. The believer ought, therefore, to accept his social position and attempt to fulfil its obligations to the limits of his ability. It is an essentially non-revolutionary outlook. The colliery owner was also fulfilling his calling and thus authority was made comprehensible and legitimate to the Methodist miner.

The factor which may not be typical was that colliery owners in the villages were Nonconformists (Methodists and a Quaker). Most of the managers were also Methodists, and in one case an ascetic church man. The owners were generous patrons of the local chapels; they also sponsored temperance missionaries and a temperance club. They patronized other village activities as well but not, of course, the Working Men's Clubs. The Quaker owner was also an MP, and in Parliament he advocated licensing reform, the extension of popular education, penal reform and the suppression of the opium trade. Because of the shared nonconformity and the self-evident respectability of the ownership and management the Methodists, and especially the Methodist community leadership, were able to identify themselves, in some measure, with the owners and managers. Meanwhile the respectable Methodists did not fully identify themselves with the 'rougher' miners with whom they worked. They certainly did not share those miners' leisure activities which centred on drinking and gambling.

The Methodists held the owners in great respect. They also held liberal economic views. The notion of calling tended to create a society divided not by power and privilege but on the basis of function. Like some modern sociologists the Methodists believed that society was (or could be) an integrated whole, its maintenance dependent on every individual performing his function within the whole. This view could be backed by analogy with the Pauline image of the church being a body in which members have different functions, all of which are essential to the maintenance of the whole. Thus it was possible for the Methodist miners virtually to regard themselves as partners with the owners in the production of coal. The union leaders stated quite specifically that there was no conflict of interest between miners and coal owners;

> ... the men had no interest in damaging the interests of their employers, because the interests of the employers was the interest of the employed, and the men regarded it as their bounden duty to study their employer's interest.[28]

This was a view of economic relations which the owners reciprocated:

> ... he (the owner) had never admitted, and he hoped he never would admit, that there was any opposing interest between the employer and the employed.[29]

The owners, after initial hostility, encouraged the development of trade unions as means of facilitating the more efficient operation of the market. The owners opposed the unions when the unions attempted to interfere with the operation of the market. Clearly there was room for dispute over what constituted facilitation and interference, but it was a conflict conducted within a broad area of agreement about the nature of economic relations. The owner cited above allowed the union to use colliery premises for meetings 'so that employer and employed might go hand in hand, not only for the benefit of each other but for the benefit of the community at large'.

In one village the owner was a Tory, Anglican brewer, a situation in which the Methodists might not regard their employer so favourably. It was in this village that political radicalism emerged amongst the Methodists. These are tantalizing data, but the one contrast is insufficient to bear the weight of a thesis.

The attitudes we find in the villages were also represented at the regional level amongst the County union leadership. This was Methodist until the 1920s, overwhelmingly so until the First World War.

An important consequence of the sharing of beliefs between miners and owners was the development of a particular view of social stratification. The Methodist viewed society in terms of gradations of respectability based on ethical considerations. There is thus a continuity between owners and Methodist miners. The discontinuities in society were perceived as being within the working class, between Club men and Methodists. The main orientation and loyalty of the Methodist leadership cannot therefore be taken as given: it is problematic from situation to situation. In addition, Methodists hoped to emulate some aspects of the owners' lives. The owners were seen as examples of the results of personal effort. One owner had a classic 'rags to riches' career. It was asked at his funeral, 'From whence did his wealth arise?, and the answer was:

> It was the result of industry – industry combined with frugality, self-denial, economy; sanctified and regulated by the highest principles of genuine religion.[30]

Given these attitudes, it is hardly surprising that in giving evidence to the Royal Commission on Labour in 1891 the Durham miners' leaders refused to countenance any suggestion that the owners might be depressing wages by the use of the sliding scale – in spite of leading questions to this effect by Tom Mann.[31]

Our historical evidence would seem to indicate the ways in which common beliefs united working and owning classes. This unity enabled the owning classes to maintain complete control of the economic and political situation from the time of the beginnings of villages until the twentieth century.

Another consequence of Methodist ethics and individualism was that Methodists were socially mobile. Methodist social ethics did not directly encourage status-seeking, but if one fulfilled one's calling diligently and upward mobility followed there could be no objection to this blessing upon merit. The idea of self-improvement and of the diligent pursuit of a calling did lead to social mobility.

Methodists accepted mining as a manly and useful occupation which could be followed with dignity, but to a degree they devalued it. They hoped their sons would enter professional, white collar or 'clean' jobs; many informants commented that Methodist mothers all secretly hoped that a son would become a Methodist minister. This may be an exaggeration, but a suggestive one. There were also, and increasingly, pragmatic reasons for hoping that one's son would find a job outside mining as it became an increasingly insecure occupation in the twentieth century. The most striking single illustration of the actual social mobility of Methodists is that not one prominent local leader at the turn of the century had a son who went down the pit. Preferred occupations were schoolteaching, medicine, local government and work in shops; a few sons did become Ministers.

Another factor facilitating the upward mobility of Methodists was their ability to all but monopolize such educational opportunity as existed. Parents had aspirations for children and encouraged them to study, the children themselves gained self-confidence through activities in the Sunday school. The Sunday school also taught the value of education for one's spiritual development, it widened scholars' general knowledge and vocabulary and accustomed them to tests and examinations.[32]

Although most of the study material for the Sunday schools was on Bible subjects, some of it might be seen as achievement motivating. The 'Illustrious Dunces' series in the *Juvenile Instructor* is typical; in 1876 the series included 'The Dunce Who Became a Great Writer', 'The Dunce Who Became a Great Engineer', etc. The message of the stories was that one had to try hard in order to succeed.

The Sunday schools also sought to inculcate compliant attitudes towards parents and those in authority. In 1970 children still gave recitations such as 'I'm happy when I'm good' at the Anniversary. Jeannie Walton would have approved; in her discussion of Sunday school work she wrote of a four-year-old convert:

> He became gentle and yielding and full of love, all his old sullen tempers seeming to disappear almost entirely; formerly he was one of the most obstinate and difficult of children.[33]

So far we have found revival and institutionalized religion in the villages to be entirely 'religious' and non-revolutionary. Its effects were ethical rather than political in the first instance. It created a hard working and capable elite amongst the working class. The beliefs also 'disciplined' the local bourgeoisie (it was part of their 'Protestant ethic') and created an area of common beliefs. These beliefs blended with current economic and social thinking to provide a liberal, pragmatic and tolerant basis for the conduct of class relations.

As Methodists filled important positions in local society we need to understand more clearly what being a Methodist meant for the style and content of that leadership.

The trade union leadership accepted the functionalist view of society described above. They believed in reason and reconciliation as means of settling industrial disputes caused – as they saw it – by misunderstandings or temporary imbalances in the market. This outlook they shared with the owners and managers, and it was reinforced by the day to day relations of union leaders and managers, at the place of work; hard bargaining and 'gentleman's agreements'. This state of affairs rested, mainly, on the prosperity of the coal trade; coal was easily won and found a ready market. Fluctuations in the price of coal were reflected in wage fluctuations, all events seemed to accord with the operations of a market system. In the twentieth century coal became harder to win and the miners were expected to pay the price of falling profits and rising costs. They thus faced unending cuts in their standard of living and the situation looked less and less like a market and more like one of exploitation. It was in this situation that the Methodist leadership was put to the test and in which we can best understand the nature of the leadership.

The Methodist union leadership was Liberal and Methodism was identified nationally and locally with Liberalism. The structure of chapels and union lodges served in place of a party organization. This was so much the case that when Labour began to make inroads into the rank and file of the miners in the first decade of the century and captured union lodges, a local Liberal party organization had to be established. The foundation of a Liberal *party* was a mark of Liberalism's weakness, not strength.[34] In 1911 a branch of the Young Liberals was formed in the villages; out of twenty-two committee members eighteen were Primitive Methodists and two Wesleyans. A slightly earlier Liberal Association (of which there are sparse records) had Primitives as President and Secretary (out of four recorded offices).

The Honorary President of the Young Liberals was John Wilson. He had a large personal following in the area, for which he was an MP, he had personal friends amongst the prominent Methodists and he often preached, or spoke at temperance meetings. When he died in 1915 the nomination papers for his successor were signed by at least twenty-four Methodists out of thirty-eight signatories (in the event the bye-election was not held). Thus the leading Methodists firmly adhered to Liberalism when Socialism was gaining strength amongst the miners.

John Wilson and the local Methodists were outspoken opponents of Socialism. Wilson used his monthly circular to counter the Socialist ideas spreading amongst the miners. Wilson and his supporters found the notion of class conflict especially unacceptable:

> We shall be none the weaker if we recognize that we can attain our ideals sooner with less hatred and antagonism, and more reason and compromise ... These are two essentials to make our unions effective for good – discretion and love of conciliation on our part.[35]

In industrial relations this love of conciliation is hard to demonstrate with detailed illustrations from bargaining situations. It can best be shown by comparing the voting record of the miners in the Methodist villages with the rest of the county. The pits in the east of the county were later and much larger than in the west and were never so fully penetrated by Methodism.

We see that the miners' leaders were Methodist and they were Liberals. They did not think in terms of class conflict; they preferred conciliation to economic conflict. We can understand this orientation by reference to Methodist social thinking and current secular social and economic theory, and by reference to the leaders'

TABLE TWO

1909 strike: against reduction of Scottish miners' wages

	For the Strike	Against the Strike	% For
National	518,361	62,980	89
County Durham	25,103	2,786	90
Village A	211	88	70·5†
Village B	211	69	67 †
Village C	365	41	90

Voting records for the lodge in Village D have not survived. Village C was owned by the Anglican.

† Significantly different from county vote at P> ·001

TABLE THREE

Minimum wage strike 1912: ballot to continue with the strike

	For Continuation	Against	% For
County Durham	48,828	24,511	66·6
Village A	219	325	40 †
Village B	141	137	50·5†
Village C	282	103	73 †

† Significantly different from county vote at P>·001

experience of day to day relations with management.

Nonetheless, Methodism did produce political results. A small group of radicals grew up, mainly in one village, around a young schoolteacher. The members were variously engaged in the campaign for women's suffrage, and the peace movement during the 1914-18 war (one died in prison during the war and another soon after his release). Nearly all the survivors were jailed during the 1926 lockout. The group began as a Primitive Methodist Bible Class and the evidence suggests that their awareness of social issues grew through reading the Bible and participating in temperance activities. Their reading of the Old Testament focused on the prophet: 'Those prophets were the first socialists. Theirs was the first passionate plea for the poor, the wretched and the heavy burdened.'[36] In the New Testament, they took the Sermon on the Mount in a more millenarian way than the orthodox Methodists.

The group explicitly rejected traditional Methodist attitudes and opened the local leadership. Firstly, they rejected the individualistic salvation notion and its ethical consequences in Methodist respectability, which they saw as self-righteousness:

> Christians seem to be certain of their own future for heaven and their own superiority to the poor people who are supposed to be in poverty because of their own wickedness.[37]

The writer went on to say that reading Blatchford moved him to pity those '(whom) my early Christian training led me to believe ... suffered through their own faults'. Secondly, they rejected compromise:

> The finger-posts of duty and expediency seldom point in the same

direction. Compromise can never lead to the attainment of the highest ideals.[38]

Thirdly, they questioned the accepted ideas of economic order. For use in a sermon or address the teacher noted a few sentences from Mary Wollstonecraft including:

> ... it is only the property of the Rich that is secure; the man who lives by the sweat of his brow has no asylum from oppression

and later he commented, 'The interests of the coal owner are opposed on many vital points to those of colliers...[39] Fourthly, the group, as Christians, rejected the old-style salvationist doctrines and fundamentalist biblical exegesis. They were followers of the Higher Criticism and avid exponents of Campbell's *The New Theology*. Any one of these four factors would have been sufficient to earn the disfavour of the established Methodists; together they went beyond the bounds to be tolerated and spelt outright rejection of the radicals by the majority. The group was excluded from the use of chapel premises and eventually formed itself into an ILP group.

The intellectual roots of the radicals lay neither in Methodism nor Marxism, but in (1) Seventeenth-century radicalism (Winstanley, the Levellers and the Diggers); (2) Eighteenth-century rationalism (William Godwin, Mary Wollstonecraft, Tom Paine); (3) A transcendentalist tradition (Thoreau, Emerson); (4) Christian Socialism (F. D. Maurice and Edward Carpenter) and Christian anarchism (Tolstoy and the Doukhobors). This list of sources is a very compelling confirmation of the extent to which Methodism was *not* the source of politically radical ideas, even though the organization and activities of Methodism facilitated the emergence of a radical group.

It is ironical to consider that eventually the mass appeal of the Labour movement did not need to be directed to the radicals, but to a wider society more under the influence of traditional Methodism. The radicals were, in the long run, as much a nuisance to Labour as to the Methodists. The Labour party was manned, in the end, by men drawn from the old Liberal tradition, men who could appeal to the respectable and to the more hesitant of the masses. Some of these Labour leaders were actually ex-Liberals who had fought actively against the Labour cause when it was advocated by the radicals. Thus in the emergence of the Labour movement Methodism had a double deradicalizing effect, in providing 'moderate' leaders and an anti-radical electorate.

So far we have only discussed prominent Methodists, the Liberal leaders and the dissident radicals. It is important also to take into account the way in which Methodism was institutionalized in the village for the ordinary believer. An inability to provide an analysis at this level has perhaps been the most serious shortcoming of the works cited in the introduction.

The 'saved' Methodist, or the respectable member of a Methodist family, was separated from full participation in the cultural life of the village. Whilst Methodists and non-Methodists worked together below ground, formed lasting friendships and developed strong solidarities at work, they lived separate lives in the community. The former centred their lives on the chapel, temperance and hymn-singing; the latter on the Club, drinking and gambling. Each way of life was self-sustaining and enclosed from the other. The separation of culture notwithstanding, the chapels provided important social centres for the villagers. The concerts, teas, sales, etc. were entertainments which all the village could attend (and which provided funds for the chapels). For the women of the villages these were probably the only form of gregarious leisure activity available. Within the life of the chapels the regular activities of the choirs, band, fellowships and Sunday schools, and the organization of 'special efforts' for the whole village, provided a series of situations in which people could enjoy warm sociability, friendship and purposive activity. The bonds of shared activity were reinforced by kinship links. Methodists seem to have been endogamous to the extent of marrying within specific Methodist groups (marriages *within* the choir, for example, were common). In any study it is easy to lose track of the complex kinship relationships; any one Methodist seems to be related, however indirectly, to every other Methodist, sometimes in more than one way.

The language used by Methodists to describe the chapel was the language of family and community rather than of formal associations; Methodists said of the chapel, 'I was brought up in it.' Of modern closures, one old Methodist said:

> Why close a chapel if it's not in debt and people are happy there? It's a home to some people, they were brought up in it. Closing a chapel is like taking someone's home away.

All the important stages of family life were marked by activities in the chapel. The joys and sorrows of one Methodist were shared by all Methodists. The chapels themselves were adorned with the gifts and memorials of families who had worshipped in there for three generations; families whose infants were brought to be baptized, whose dead were brought for burial, whose members came to join with other families in marriage. The preacher on Sunday appropriately invited the congregation to join with him in offering up the 'family prayer'.

Thus a Methodist did not belong to an organization only in a formal sense. The Methodist society was an extension of his family, it was his community; most of his significant social relations were with other Methodists. In a formal organization men and women relate to one another in specific ways, in the Methodist society one related to others in a range of situations and roles. The close-knit solidarity of the Methodists was publicly affirmed and reinforced by the choir competitions and the anniversary celebrations.

This further explains the Methodists' avoidance of potentially divisive issues. Compromise, tolerance, a 'live and let live' attitude were essential for the survival of the community. Divisive ideas threatened to spoil the warm fellowship of members and adherents, and to spread out in the form of conflict between and within families. Division was avoided, either by the tacit refusal to take sides or by refusing to allow 'political' issues to penetrate the life of the chapel. This behaviour is also entirely consistent with the view that the church is an organization which reconciles all interests, which has, in other words, a universalistic outlook.

There were both material and ideal differences which might have threatened the Methodists. Material differences were derived largely from the upward mobility of those Methodists who became officials, small men of property or minor professional workers. Ideal differences were likely to arise from developments in theology and from the changing social circumstances of the villages (decline in drunkenness and violence etc.). The 'compromise' position in fact meant that *new* ideas were resisted in the twentieth century. The theology of R. J. Campbell divided preacher against preacher and hence family against family (or family within family). Therefore an attempt was made to re-assert the traditional orthodoxy. Similarly, Socialist ideas threatened the whole basis of the established Methodists' world view, especially their view of the legitimacy of authority and property, on the basis of which they enjoyed good relations with management. The attempt to 'keep politics out of the pulpit' was therefore an attempt to keep Methodist politics Liberal, or as a number of older Methodists suggested during the enquiry, asserting the dominant group's politics against all others.

The majority of Methodists were not directly involved in such debates; they wished only to avoid 'trouble' of any sort in order to maintain friendly social relations within the group. Membership meant a commitment to these relationships and did not entail a high degree of theological or ideological commitment. Methodism was a way of life, not a set of doctrines.

The importance of the communal commitment can be seen by examining the Methodist response to political situations which offered different degrees of division. Our first example entails virtually no division at all. Between 1902 and 1905 the Methodists faced the problems of the Education Act and licensing legislation introduced by the Conservative government. The Education Act was seen as a threat to the survival of Methodism, the licensing legislation as an affront to all the good works of Methodism. The Methodists were all agreed; none supported the doctrines of the Church of England,[39] none drank or owned public houses or had any connection with them. They formed committees to agitate and lobby against the two bills.

It was further agreed that in matters of conscience, as these were, the individual had the right to resist the State. The Primitive minister in fact had his pocket watch distrained and auctioned for non-payment of rates; his non-payment was seen as a legitimate protest against the Education Act. The Methodists in general did not *do* much, but they were agreed and undivided both on the facts of the case and the need for action.

In the First World War a minority of Methodists were active in the peace movement and they refused to register for military service. This was a divisive thing to do. Many Methodist families had husbands, sons and relatives away in the services, some of whom were casualties. The objectors were seen as shirkers by some, but more importantly as men adopting a superior moral stance in a situation where other men were laying down their lives. This was likely to set family against family and create great dissension. In these circumstances the Methodist refused to recognize the right of conscientious objection and the notion of the individual's right to resist the State was much muted. Here the Methodists were resisting a dissident and disruptive minority only.

Two or three of the leading Methodists faced another dilemma. As community leaders, they were placed on military tribunals. They had to sit in judgment on the cases of, amongst others, Methodists seeking exemption for various (usually non-conscientious) reasons. In one case when exemption was refused the applicant was killed at the front; his family left the chapel, blaming the Methodist chairman of the tribunal for the death. The leading Methodists could not avoid the situation of having to judge others. This was potentially most divisive and put the Methodist community under strain.

We have to come forward to the 1920s for our final illustration, but it is a time at which some of the men who became leaders in the late nineteenth century were still in power, or only recently replaced. In the 1926 lockout (in fact from 1921 onwards) the Methodists were threatened ideologically, communally and materially. Conflict of a very open and violent kind replaced traditional industrial relations. Shopkeepers especially were threatened by the stoppage of work, but others too. While the Methodists included a relatively high proportion of officials and businessmen, they also had miners and many mining families among their members. Opposition to industrial action was not possible, indeed it could only have taken the form of advocating capitulation to the owners' attack. The solidarities of work and the traditional communal solidarities of a mining community asserted themselves powerfully. Here we see factors outside Methodism being of perhaps greater importance than religious belief and chapel membership. There were very few Methodists among the blacklegs and few open opponents of the miners.

Collectively, Methodism reasserted the need for conciliation and they advocated good works among the needy. Methodists were active in 'social' work during the dispute and the choirs raised money for relief. But politically they were unable to say anything as they were internally divided, especially economically. They kept silent and asked few questions:

> We often wondered which side people took in 1926. But we tried to be Christians and we agreed to differ ... 'Things said' didn't lead to falling off. At times chapel cemented things together. *Miner's wife, late middle age*

> Individualism was the conditioning factor in the Methodist response to 1926. *Retired local minister*

> Some Methodists thought the General Strike was inopportune. They were not against what lay behind it, but the wrong way of going about it. They thought that constitutional methods were preferable, not strikes and so on. The Methodists thought that not all the possibilities were exhausted.
> *Primitive Methodist minister*

The apparent lack of commitment on the part of the Methodists led to their being accused by both sides of supporting the other. But a curious fact remains. In the villages where the socialist agitation had been most powerful there was some blacklegging; up to a hundred workers in two pits, a handful only in another. The pit with the most conservative leadership, a Liberal of the 'old school', was relatively free of violence and had the fewest blacklegs. From this one example, it would seem as if by 1926 appeals to *traditional* work and community values had a greater chance of maintaining solidarity than appeals to the new Socialist ideas.

Thus to some extent all the commentators in our introduction seem to be right, even though they were at times saying different things. We do not, however, find any grounds for confirming Halévy's view of the working class. They were not foolish and easily led; we found them remarkably resistant to certain ideas and styles of leadership.

Let us return to the issues raised by our six opening questions by way of summarizing the discussion. Revivalist Methodism was non-revolutionary, its beliefs were mainly ethical and formally non-political. Nonetheless, Methodist ethics and individualism found a ready affinity with economic liberalism and political Liberalism. Nonconformity provided a consensus between workers and bourgeoisie and influenced the miners' view of the economic, political and class structure. This also enabled the local bourgeoisie to keep the economic and political situation very firmly in control until the twentieth century. But in situations of great political stress Methodism was not the only historically effective factor.

The influence of Methodism is many-faced. It endowed the hard life of the miner with meaning. It produced a Liberal working-class leadership, which although radical in youth, was conservative in its heyday and hindered the emergence of a Socialist movement. Yet Methodism literally threw out a capable and articulate Socialist leadership while, paradoxically, having produced a political culture in which the Socialists could hardly hope to succeed.

We note that the dominant Methodist attitudes rest in large

measure on a related set of primary assumptions that are seldom made explicit. These include concepts of the fairness of the British constitution ('They thought that constitutional methods were preferable, not strikes...') and of the basic decency and fairmindedness of the owning classes ('... There are two essentials ... discretion and love of conciliation...'). This latter assumption was celebrated in dinners and presentations for the workers every year, in which toasts were drunk to the owners, and the men thanked for their efforts by the managers. Thirdly, Methodist attitudes subsumed the notion that the economy was an objective reality; men had to conform themselves to its demands. Economic conflict was therefore something that men of goodwill could resolve by reasoning together.

The Methodist revival of the 1870s was a revival of the historical puritan spirit: moral uprightness, frugality, self-denial, tolerance and love of reason. This revival came at a time when employers and workers were seeking ways to co-operate with one another for the rational pursuit of their short-term economic interests. The underlying assumption, the basis of MacIntyre's 'secondary virtues', was thus reinforced in a way that was to be significant long after the immediate and 'religious' effects of Methodism had died away.

The development of the peculiarly Methodist outlook on economics and politics depended in part on contingent factors in the economy, which were largely controlled outside County Durham. But it also depended on the way in which Methodism took root among the people. We see it not as a 'movement' but as an extension of, or actually as, an affective community. We need to look not so much at revival, hymn singing and prayers but at Methodism routinized in a community. Whatever other factors may have been unique to the district studied, this would seem to be a universally applicable, and neglected, point. The internal structure of Methodism and the prime meanings of belonging attributed by members assured Methodism's inability to take decisive action, or adopt an unequivocal stance on major economic and political issues which were not directly related to Methodist beliefs or survival.

How does our local study bear upon the assumptions made by Halévy? Whatever social dislocation may have resulted from the creation of a new industrial society, it was plainly insufficient to reduce the miners to a bovine, suggestible mob. Perhaps one of the most remarkable aspects of the miners at the end of the nineteenth century was their resistance to radical political ideas.

Our study has suggested that one cannot assume middle-class leadership of the working class; one must examine the circumstances and extent to which the middle classes are able to lead. Our class of owners and managers were able to lead the working class in the sense that they shared religious, ethical and political beliefs with them. But it is also true to say that they *ruled* the working class because they had, collectively, subjected the working class to crushing political defeats earlier in the century. The middle-class leadership was exercised in small-scale relationships and face-to-face interaction arising from common locality and economic activity – it was not a case of a nationwide class leading the working class at large.

The 'elite' of the working class clearly had an important role as intermediaries between the local middle class and local working class. Here the Halévy argument seems much more convincing. The working class elite were a group tight-knit through kinship and religion; they were closely related through marriage and religion to non-elite members of the community. They embodied the beliefs that the working class shared with the middle class and even when they found themselves in conflict with the owners and managers it was within the framework of shared social and political assumptions. Religion had the important effect, then, of binding the working-class elite to one another, to the rank and file miners, and to the owners and managers. This binding together was performed in the context of respectability, restraint and conciliation. This certainly reduced the possibility of class warfare.

NOTES

In this essay no distinction is drawn between Primitive and Wesleyan Methodists. The area studied was mainly Primitive, but differences between the Methodist denominations was not found to be relevant. In most respects local village differences between churches of one denomination are greater than those between denominations.

1. W. E. H. Lecky, *A History of England in the Eighteenth Century*, Longmans, Green & Co. 1878, vol. II, pp.637-8.
2. See B. Semmel, 'The Halévy Thesis', *Encounter*, July 1971.
3. E. Halévy, *England in 1815* (Vol. 1 of *A History of the English People in the Nineteenth Century*), Ernest Benn 1949, pp.424-5.
4. 'La Naissance du Methodisme en Angleterre', *Revue de Paris* 1906, p.539.
5. Ibid., p.524.

6. Ibid., p.856.

7. Ibid., p.864.

8. E. Halévy, *Victorian Years 1841-1895* (Vol. IV of *A History of the English People in the Nineteenth Century*), Ernest Benn 1951, p.395.

9. Halévy, *England in 1815*, p.371. The comment is echoed by R. F. Wearmouth in his discussion of the nineteenth century: 'These leaders were not revolutionaries... By their integrity and uprightness they demonstrated to the rulers of the land that the country had nothing to fear from the leaders of working men.' See R. F. Wearmouth, *The Social and Political Influence of Methodism in the 20th Century*, Epworth Press 1957, p.245.

10. C. Gillispie, 'The Work of Elie Halévy', *Journal of Modern History*, vol. 22, 1950, pp.232-49, p.244.

11. Halévy, *Victorian Years 1841-1895*, p.396.

12. Gillispie, art. cit., p.239.

13. Alasdair MacIntyre, *Secularization and Moral Change*, OUP 1967, p.24.

14. Gillispie, art. cit., p.243.

15. E. J. Hobsbawn, *Labouring Men*, Weidenfeld & Nicolson 1964, ch. on 'Methodism and the Threat of Revolution'.

16. J. L. and B. Hammond, *The Town Labourer 1760-1832*, Guild Books 1949, vol. II, p.100

17. Ibid.

18. E. P. Thompson, *The Making of the Working Class*, Penguin Books 1968, p.424.

19. Hammond, op. cit. pp.99, 102-4.

20. A propaganda, the need for which was doubtful given that 'the government, at this time of national peril, had no reason to alienate, and every reason to conciliate the Nonconformist'.

21. Bendix has noted a similar paradox whereby the gloomy prognostication of Malthus contained the message that working men were independent, and free to make choices for themselves. See R. Bendix, *Work and Authority in Industry*, Harper and Row 1963, ch. 2, esp. pp.85-6.

22. Thompson, op. cit., p.417.

23. Semmel, art. cit.

24. In common with many others she started these activities at a very early age. One gambling school which met in the woods by another village was broken up when the Sunday school children took their harmonium to them and sang 'Gentle Jesus meek and mild'.

25. *Durham Chronicle*, 25 August 1871. A report of the AGM of the Crook Co-operative Society.

26. A miner's address to Sunday school teachers, about 1885.

27. In a sense, this conclusion is a result of regarding Liberalism as non-political. See below.

28. A local strike leader, reported in the *Durham Chronicle*, 9 May 1879.

29. A Quaker coal owner, reported in the *Durham Chronicle*, 15 January 1875.

30. *Durham Chronicle*, 5 March 1875.

31. See Minutes of Evidence, Group A, vol. I, Qs 347, 348, 614.

32. With the introduction of grammar school scholarships in 1922, the educational attainments of village Methodist children became plain. From 1922-44, 39% of all scholarships were won by regular Sunday school scholars.

33. J. Walton, *Sunday School Teaching: How to Work Successfully*, Wesleyan Methodist Sunday School Union 1876 p.25.

34. See R. Gregory, *The Miners and British Politics 1906-1914*, OUP 1968.

35. *Durham Chronicle*, 4 October 1912. It is interesting to note how the argument in this statement only makes sense if one assumes that the other side to any dispute accepts and abides by the same rules and principles as one's self. Such an assumption was basic to Wilson's thinking. To this extent the statement is a statement of secondary beliefs based on unstated primary assumptions.

36. Private papers of John George Harrison, 1890-1921, citing 'the historian Myers'.

37. Ibid., sermon of 1913.

38. Ibid., notes.

39. Some, who hoped that their children might become teachers, feared they might have to attend church colleges in order to qualify.

9 The Church in the Community: A Study of Patterns of Religious Adherence in a Scottish Burgh

Kenneth J. Panton

Despite the public image of the Scots as a Puritan, God-fearing nation, the nature of their religious commitment has been subject to little in the way of analysis by social scientists. Theological works abound and there are numerous biographies of the bulwarks of the Scottish clergy but the first empirically-based work dealing with the sociology of religion in the country appeared as recently as 1966 in the form of a PhD thesis.[1] The author arbitrarily designated two areas in Edinburgh as working-class and middle-class and used these to analyse different attitudes towards the established church within the two groups, taking into account the subjects' occupations, their parents' beliefs, their education and other class indices. The other major works are those by John Highet.[2] His studies, however, are church-based rather than society-based, focusing on church activities and on members' participation.

This study differs from those of both these authors. Firstly, it is area-based, dealing with different sections of a complete town. Secondly, unlike Robertson's work, it uses data from all of the churches in the community and, thirdly and most importantly, it attempts to relate church membership to other social factors, notably crime, education and amusements, in order to find out what correlations, if any, exist.

Alloa, it was felt, would provide a suitable setting for such a study. A community of 14,000 people situated on the north bank of the River Forth midway between Edinburgh and Glasgow, it is the administrative centre for Clackmannanshire as well as an important industrial town. In addition, its twelve religious groups provide a variety of alternative outlets for religiosity, thus cutting down the number of people who might feel constrained to seek a church suiting their own beliefs outside the town. One other factor weighed in its favour; a preliminary survey revealed that all of the organizations concerned were willing to co-operate in the study and, since the aim was to use church membership as the major indicator of religious attachment and to use central sources rather than questionnaire surveys to obtain the data, this was an important consideration.

Membership was taken as the index principally because it was empirically verifiable. Surveys aimed at individuals might result in respondents giving the answers which they thought were required: there still seems to be an obligatory element in religion which makes many people who are unattached to a church profess interest in religious affairs and others to over-estimate their attendance at worship. Two secondary considerations were also important. Since the fieldwork was to be carried out at the height of the summer, the sample might have been biased if a large proportion of potential respondents were on holiday when they were first called on and numerous return visits would have been extremely time-consuming. The second consideration was simply that, as Glock has emphasized,[3] religion may consist of several strands and because a person attends church more frequently it does not follow that he is more religious (he may consider that attendance is a social obligation, for instance).

On the other hand, the use of membership as an indicator does have its drawbacks, for different churches use different criteria and a standard definition applicable to all religious bodies is impossible to produce. The difficulty is eased somewhat in Alloa because the Presbyterian bodies accept members who publicly confess their faith and the vast majority of churchgoers in the town attend a place of worship which requires such evidence of conviction. Of the other bodies, the very small sects such as the Christian spiritualists do not have 'members' in this sense, but each group was small enough for regular attenders to be known intimately to one another and it was these people who were used in the subsequent analysis. The assessment of sectarian membership, therefore, is not too different from the criterion used to define Presbyterian churchgoers because these churches are able to purge the rolls of those who do not attend communion regularly.

The major difficulty was with the Roman Catholic Church, into which members are born rather than accepted on voluntary confession of faith, although this does, of course, occur. In this case, the method used to circumvent the problem was to consider as members those whom the local priest visited regularly: these were people who, on the whole, attended church quite regularly except for reasons of age or illness. 'Lapsed Catholics' who had not darkened the church doors for several years were not included.

It would have been valuable to compare the membership records obtained from the ministers against some indicator of religiosity measured by questionnaire surveys in an attempt to discover if the findings were markedly different, but time and manpower resources made this impossible.

Within the church groups, the basic unit has been taken as the family rather than the individual, partly because the Roman Catholic clergy preferred to supply its membership data in terms of families rather than individuals, partly because the clergy themselves seemed to regard the family as more important in the normal run of pastoral church affairs, partly because children tend to grow up in the church their parents attend, and partly because it helped overcome the problems of varying family size in different social groups (the Roman Catholic working-class families tend to be larger than their Presbyterian counterparts, for instance). The drawbacks here are twofold – firstly, there may be considerable differences in family size in different parts of the town, whereas it may be the total number of individuals in an area which gives the neighbourhood its distinctiveness through common value systems; secondly, within one family the mother, for example, may attend church whilst father and children do not, though in this case the minister does have access to the home and the family normally accepts his presence.

As with the church data, the information on other social functions was obtained from central sources – bingo clubs, valuation rolls and Town Council officials. The figures on crime were obtained from the offices of the local newspapers because of the difficulty and expense of obtaining charge sheets from the numerous legal departments in Alloa and Edinburgh. These newspapers normally keep copies of all charges which appear before the courts, whether the case receives publicity or not, and these were used in this study. In this way it was hoped that the figures on crime would give an indication of offences committed rather than of cases reported in newspapers.

FIGURE ONE

Key to areas mentioned in the text. For each area, the percentage of families with at least one member on the church rolls is also shown.

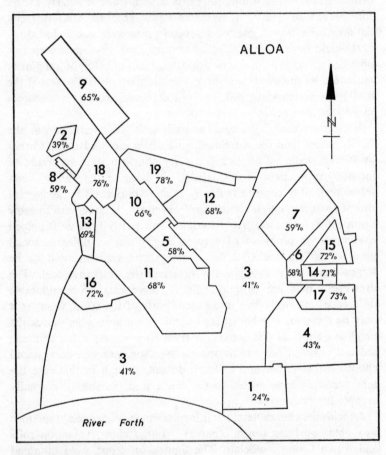

It should be pointed out that social class and perception of social differences include more than the mere aggregations of statistically verifiable trends – it involves something in the minds of people themselves, a sense of 'we-feeling' by which a group identification develops and by which differences from other groups, sometimes very slight, are emphasized. But no one has yet been able to analyse successfully this group feeling. This paper, therefore, will use the factors indicated, attempt to find out whether they correlate or not and try to suggest some explanation for any patterns and trends which become evident.

Because of the lack of Scottish studies, this is above all exploratory: it may be that the results will correlate with findings in England and elsewhere but if Christianity – and religion generally – is a part of culture, altering and being altered by other forces, it is equally possible that the trends in Scotland may differ.

The Town and its Churches

The settlement grew around the fortified residence of the Erskine family who, in 1398, received the barony of Alloa and the Forest of Clackmannan from King Robert III, and by the time the industrial revolution made its impact it had a pool of skills in brewing and distilling, textile production, the working of coal and international commerce. The ease with which the coal was produced and the accumulated skills in these great trades encouraged the establishment of industry and brought employment. In their wake came new house building and the development of educational and other social amenities. The industrial tradition means that the present residents are heavily concentrated in manual occupations although a symbiotic relationship has developed, for the spinning mills of Paton and Baldwin and the knitwear manufacturers of Donbros draw on a workforce which is predominantly female and thus complements the male labour of the breweries (Ind Coope and Maclay), the engineering works (Harland and United Glass) and the now declining coal industry.

Since it is the seat of Clackmannan County Council, Alloa's administrative functions pull the surrounding area into its sphere of influence, a process enhanced by its importance as an entertainment and retail focus which is due to its position as the largest urban centre between Stirling (ten miles west) and Dunfermline (fourteen miles east). Even so, it has a very small complement of professional people and these consist mainly of school teachers (15% of Alloa's population is under fifteen) and the legal, financial and medical experts associated with local government and the provision of public and private welfare services. The industries in the town have now been taken over by larger combines so the major research work is carried out elsewhere and the local factories are regarded largely as training grounds for managerial staff who will move on to higher things in one of the firm's other areas.

The housing is predominantly local authority (68% of the 4,962 houses are the responsibility of the Town Council,[4] 19% are owner-occupied and the remainder rented privately). Many of the housing estates are physically separated from their neighbours by open spaces and where two estates are juxtaposed they are visually different – a trait which, according to some welfare workers in the town, has emphasized the insularity of the groups, helping to produce homogeneity within individual areas but considerable heterogeneity between different parts of the town.

The Alloa clergymen claim that shift-work, the breweries and the heavy engineering industry produce a type of community which creates difficulties for the religious bodies, yet the town maintains twelve churches,[5] including the largest branch of the Church of Scotland outside the four major cities, and nearly 60% of its families have at least one representative on the membership rolls of a church.

TABLE ONE

The membership strength of the churches

Church	Total Membership	Alloa Residents	Residents as % Membership	Alloa Homes Represented	% Alloa Homes Represented
St Mungo's (CS)	2330	1976	85	1106	22·3
Roman Catholic	—	—	—	160	9·3
West (CS)	875	739	85	417	8·4
Moncrieff (UF)	558	430	77	247	5·0
Episcopal	582	425	73	242	4·9
St Andrew's (CS)	375	339	90	197	4·0
Chalmers (CS)	304	249	82	152	3·0
Baptist	145	89	63	68	1·4
Spiritualist	21	13	60	12	
Jehovah's Witnesses	37	10	27	5	0·5
Elim	6	6	100	5	
Christian Brethren	9	3	33	3	
				2914	58·8

CS—Church of Scotland   UF—United Free Church of Scotland

There are four branches of the established church in Alloa, together forming the largest single group of church members but varying greatly in size both between themselves and in relation to other churches, as Table I indicates.

The Church of Scotland as a whole reflects its predominant national position with nearly 38% of Alloa's families represented on its rolls. Robertson calculated that 36% of the country's adults are members of the Church of Scotland, 7% other Protestants and 4% Roman Catholics.[6] He estimated that 58% of Scottish adults are church members, which is considerably higher than even the most optimistic estimates for England and Wales.[7]

St Mungo's, which has by far the biggest congregation, carries considerable weight in local and national ecclesiastical circles – this century alone it has produced three Moderators of the General Assembly. The three smaller congregations were founded by the 'hot-headed evangelists'[8] who hived off from St Mungo's in the eighteenth and nineteenth centuries, forming the free churches. These congregations, like St Mungo's, regarded the whole town as their concern and, when the United Free Church (or, more accurately, most of it) overcame its differences with the Church of Scotland and re-united in 1929, the thorny problem of sub-division of the burgh into parishes appears to have been shelved to avoid more dissension and was never re-considered. Thus each church still sees the whole of Alloa as within its ambit – a factor which has had considerable repercussions, for different sections of society have segregated themselves within the churches.

Table 2 is suggestive of such segregation, showing quite plainly that St Andrew's is best represented in areas of local authority housing whilst Chalmers is proportionately stronger amongst owner-occupiers and St Mungo's is very close to the mean in both cases.

In spite of the differences, however, there seems to be no direct correlation between church membership and house ownership (the correlation coefficient of $+0.07$ indicates a negligible relationship between the two). Neither did members appear to concentrate in the areas nearest to their church.

Moncrieff (UF) Church was one of those which elected to remain outside the union of 1929 and is about equal in strength to the Episcopal Church, which was supported by the gentry and which, despite an especially difficult period in the mid-nineteenth century,

TABLE TWO

Distribution of families on church rolls by housing type

Church	Local Authority	Percentage in Each Group Owner Occupied	Privately Rented
Roman Catholic	82	10	8
St Andrew's (CS)	79	13	8
Baptist	76	19	6
Episcopal	67	21	12
St Mungo's (CS)	67	21	12
Moncrieff (UF)	62	30	9
West (CS)	62	26	13
Chalmers (CS)	51	38	12
Others	54	27	19
All Churches	68	21	11
Distribution of all Alloa housing	68	19	13
% in each group on church rolls	58	66	47

still represents a considerable numerical force in Alloa church life. The Roman Catholic Church is concentrated mainly in areas of local authority housing. One reason for its strength certainly lies in the high birth-rate amongst its members, but Robertson also points out that it gained ground amongst the poorer sections of the community at the time of the industrial revolution, when they became alienated from the established church, which appeared to represent the interests of the mill-owners.[9] Immigration of Irish and continental stock has been so small as to be of negligible effect on membership strength.

The Baptist church was built in 1838 and the present congregation is an ageing community, since the strictures against alcohol and dancing repel adolescents, even those brought up as Baptists. The smaller sects have little impact, individually or cumulatively, on the town.

Areal Variations

1. *Church membership*

Although Paul wrote to his converts, 'Not many of you were wise according to worldly standards, not many were powerful, not many were of noble birth',[10] since the end of the Second World War, with increased interest in the social sciences and the development of statistical methods of analysis, research has tended to suggest that churchgoing is lowest among the manual classes and highest in the middle classes. The Alloa figures, taken in isolation, do show considerable variation in different parts of the town. With the mean membership for the burgh standing at 59%, a map of adherence, taking the housing estate as the basic areal unit, shows a central trough (ten of the twelve churches are situated within this depression) with membership building up to nearly 80% of all homes in the west of the town and falling off suddenly near the edge of the built-up area. In the east and south-east, the change from low to high rates is more sudden, from just over 40% to near the mean value and then to over 70%.

Although these broad trends provide important guides to social areas, it is equally important to investigate the strength of the churches not only in areas of strong variation but also in those of similar overall adherence. Thus, for example, if we consider the detailed affiliations of two of the three areas in eastern Alloa with an overall adherence of over 70% we find considerable differences.

TABLE THREE

The strength of the churches in two areas of similar overall adherence

Church	Area 14	Area 15	Town Mean
St Mungo's (CS)	23·6	22·2	22·6
West (CS)	13·5	7·4	8·4
Roman Catholic	11·2	13·0	9·1
Moncrieff (UF)	10·1	5·6	4·9
Episcopal	7·8	20·4	4·9
St Andrew's (CS)	3·4	1·8	3·9
Chalmers (CS)	1·1	0·0	3·0
Baptist	0·0	1·8	1·3
Others	0·0	0·0	0·5
	70·7	72·2	58·6

St Mungo's predominates in both areas but the other churches vary markedly in strength, notably in the case of the Roman Catholic, the Episcopal, the West Church and the United Free Church. The first area consists entirely of private houses erected at the turn of the century. The second is administered by the local authority and was one of the first to be completed after the Second World War. In social features other than churchgoing, as will be shown later, the two groups, homogeneous internally, differ distinctly from each other. This tendency towards segregation operates throughout the town and is associated with visible differences in the urban landscape – patterns of adherence change abruptly where areas of private and public housing are adjacent.

In part, the tendency is due to the policy of the local authority, which has usually resulted in the grouping of people of similar age and occupation in physically segregated areas. Partly, too, it is a result of redevelopment within the town, for much of the slum property in central Alloa has been demolished and families rehoused in new council estates on the periphery. The group which moves thus does not encounter the problem of readjustment which would have occurred had they found themselves in an area which had already developed an ethos of its own. As a result, established patterns, such as churchgoing, are less easily broken down.

Even so, this segregation within an urban framework is not entirely unsuspected. Emrys Jones, as a result of studies in Belfast, claims that 'human motivation itself tends to conform to a pattern reflecting current social values'[12] and Pahl points out that 'in the British new towns certain areas appear to attract certain types of people, without such areas being very different in terms of rent or architectural qualities ... A greater concern with total life-style for status differentiation and status enhancement is likely to lead to the emphasizing of small differences between one residential area and another ... Segregation appears to be on the increase.'[13] The figures for church membership for the nineteen areas show four zones below the mean, four on or near average and a spearhead of two above a cluster in excess of the mean. If the results accord with current research findings, this string of figures should reflect the town's social structure, with the top two groups forming the social elite and the bottom figure reflecting a community of manual workers with a totally different life-style.

2. *Church membership and bingo*

With the possible exception of television, bingo is Alloa's most popular mass amusement – and the local entertainment industry's biggest money-spinner. Ten years ago there were three cinemas in the town. One has closed completely, a second now depends solely on bingo and the third shows films only at weekends with bingo every other night. In addition, busloads of Alloa people travel outside the town to play regularly at other clubs as far as fifteen miles away. Twenty-four per cent of the 4,962 homes have at least one bingo club member and, as with the churches, women are in the majority.

The De Luxe Bingo Club has 1,714 members, 1,115 (65%) of them female. Nearly two-thirds (65·8%) of these women class themselves as 'housewife' on their membership form. The remainder are mainly workers in the woollen mills, shop assistants and office staff. Only 6·3% have any supervisory or managerial function and, except for nurses, there are no professional women in the club. Of the 599 male members, 589 are manual workers, leaving 7 clerical workers and 3 'others'. Both males and females are thus drawn overwhelmingly from the manual groups in society, with a heavy emphasis in both sexes on the unskilled and semi-skilled sectors.

Similarly, bingo players are segregated within the town itself, concentrating in the south and east. The coefficient of +0·72 shows a high correlation between bingo-playing and tenancy in council houses – five of the nine local authority estates are well above the norm, two are near-average but still higher than any of the areas of private housing and the remaining two, whilst well below average, are still higher than most areas of owner-occupation.

If recent researches are applicable generally and churchgoing does form a continuum from low in the manual occupation groups to high in the highest status areas, and if bingo is most popular amongst the working classes and least common amongst the professions, one might expect the ranking of bingo-playing areas to form the exact reverse of that of church membership. But this is not the case. The areas of highest church membership are not at the bottom of the bingo rank order, on which the lowest values correspond in general with areas in the middle of the cluster which forms in excess of the churchgoing mean.

The correlation coefficient (r = −0·35) shows a definite negative relationship but not as strongly as might be expected. The general tendency is for those areas with a surfeit of church members to have a deficiency of bingo players but four areas are so different from the trend as to merit special consideration. One is the industrial and commercial core of the town (area 3), with its high proportion (53%) of privately rented accommodation. Tenants in these buildings are gradually being rehoused in local authority estates and much accommodation is lying empty, thus leading to underestimation of percentages of both bingo players and church membership.

No such technical explanation can be given for the second area – a zone of high-quality private housing known as Dunmar and erected in 1965 (area 2). It consists of forty-one individually-designed houses sheltered from a major road and from other housing estates by carefully-preserved woodland. The community consists entirely of professional people with a high proportion of householders in the 40–50 age group. The houses are opulently and tastefully furnished: the buyers obviously had little need to skimp and save to buy their own home. Yet this area of high-class housing and high-status residents has one of the lowest percentages of church membership and thus apparently contradicts the continuum thesis.

There are two areas (15 and 17) with very high proportions of both bingo players and church members. Although separated by other residential areas, both consist entirely of local authority houses and their high bingo percentage suggests that the residents fall into the manual sectors. Whereas the strengths of the individual churches varied considerably between Dunmar and the commercial area, here the differences are less but, like Dunmar, they contradict the continuum thesis. If the indications are correct and these are working-class people, their record of church membership is exceptionally high. These areas will stand out again later when other factors are considered: it may therefore be wise to leave any hypotheses on their deviation until all the factors have been considered.

However, for our analysis it is important to find out whether families connected with a church also patronize the bingo clubs. In fact, only 15·9% of churchgoing families also play bingo, compared with 27·7% of non-church households. The differential fluctuates from area to area but, while the percentages reflect the general trend for the area (i.e. where bingo is popular both church and non-church households have high percentages) in fourteen of the nineteen areas non-church households have higher proportions of bingo players and in four of the remaining five areas the proportion of churchgoing bingo players exceeds non-church by a maximum of 2%. The overall trend suggests, therefore, that churchgoing, or factors connected with it, makes the members less likely to attend bingo sessions.

The theory that religiosity is at its lowest among low status groups and highest among high status groups has thus been dented by the findings here. It was also discovered that bingo players tend not to be church members. Before considering the importance of these findings to the general picture, two other factors which may affect the analysis will be considered – education and crime.

3. Church membership and education

The literature of educational sociology is littered with research reports which suggest that the attainment of working-class children is less than that of middle-class children, although the reasons for the differential are subject to dispute.[14] The Alloa figures certainly reflect considerable variations in the pattern of attainment if selection at age eleven is used as a criterion. Overall, there are 44 'passes'[15] per 1,000 homes and 37 failures. These figures, however, conceal a wealth of social differentiation resulting from such factors as age differences in different areas, emphasis on the importance of education, facilities for home study and family size.

Educational attainment correlates with areas of local authority housing in a negative fashion ($r = -0.66$), whereas bingo, it will be remembered, showed an even stronger positive correlation of $+0.72$. It thus seems fair to assume that educational attainment will be greatest where bingo playing is least popular and, in fact, there is a high negative correlation of -0.70 between selection for senior secondary education and the incidence of bingo players. The correlation coefficient between educational attainment and churchgoing, although positive ($r = +0.28$) and showing a small but definite relationship between the two sets of data is, again, smaller than might be expected.

The major deviation in those areas which have below-average

church membership but above-average educational attainment is, once again, the Dunmar estate of private housing. The two other zones in this category are, like Dunmar, the homes of owner-occupiers – one contains families which, by dint of their own efforts, have advanced themselves economically and built their own houses on the hillside overlooking the green, barley-sown carse-lands of the Forth (area 8): in the other lie the homes of some of the older members of the community who have worked hard and bought their own house late in life (area 5).

At the other extreme – high church membership but below-average success at 11+ exams – are the two other areas (15 and 17) which differed from the general trend in the previous section. They now show rates of church membership considerably above average but their educational attainment is below the norm and the incidence of bingo players among the highest in the town.

The other two areas in this category are very different in character. One (area 12) is populated by an ageing community with few young families – a community which consists of owner-occu-piers who saved hard to buy their own houses and now find their upkeep a heavy economic burden. The other (area 18) is very much the opposite, populated by young families living in council houses on an estate opened in 1950. Bingo is nearly five times as popular as in the first area (23% compared with 5%) but church member-ship is also more popular (76% compared with 68%) although both, in this case, are well above the mean.

As with bingo, however, it is still necessary to find out if the degree of success in church homes is greater than that in other homes. Overall, 61% of the children from church homes entered senior secondary schools compared with 43% from non-church homes, a trend which is followed in sixteen of the nineteen areas, although the total pass rate for these areas varies from 15% to 100%. It is interesting that the trend applies not only to areas with above average success but also to those, such as Gaberston (15) and Hawkhill (17), which are populated by working-class families.

4. *Church membership and crime*

Alloa has its fair share of crime. Rarely, however, are offences serious enough to be transferred to the High Court although the same faces appear time after time in the Sheriff Court. The offences considered here are concerned principally with theft, assault and drunken driving – anti-social offences too important to be tried in the small burgh courts, which are concerned mainly with less serious matters such as breach of the peace and drunkenness.

The incidence of crime is, like that of bingo, correlated positively but weakly with the incidence of council houses ($r = +0.23$) but the correlation with bingo-playing ($r = +0.57$) is more striking, as is the similar, but negative, association with educational attainment ($r = -0.50$). There is also a strong negative correlation with church membership ($r = -0.55$) when one considers the areas as a whole but in this case it is impossible to gauge accurately the number of churchgoing families which appeared before the Sheriff because of the difficulty of obtaining more accurate addresses than the mere street in which the accused was resident. The mean figure for the town shows an average of only 20 offences per 1,000 homes but, in fact, only four areas lie beyond the mean and two of these are marginal cases.

By far the most crime-ridden area is that known as the 'Bottom End' (area 1) – a housing scheme built in 1920 to house people from slum properties in the town centre. With 94 offences per 1,000 homes, it also has the lowest rate of church membership, the highest rates of bingo and the poorest educational record – by considerable margins in every case. Its two-storey flatted villas are occupied by unskilled manual workers, often with two or more families sharing the same roof. Yet this area has a group identity and a close sense of inter-dependence and many who move out to more modern accommodation with a greater range of facilities, including more space, come back. There is considerable squalor – alcoholism, illegitimacy, wife-assault, children with lice-ridden hair – but the welfare authorities seem unable to break down the social pattern which has evolved. Often, tenants from this area rehoused elsewhere turn their new homes into a similar condition within a short time.

Thus many people in the neighbouring housing estate (area 4) – the Mar Policies – refuse to have anything to do with the 'Bottom Enders' and prospective Protestant and non-churchgoing tenants have refused houses there because their children would be in the same classrooms as those from the older estate and they fear that they would be drawn into delinquency. But Catholics have no such problem: all Catholic children are educated at one school, and so many Catholics will happily settle here. Housing officials are unwilling to commit themselves on the strength of the tendency but ministers, more in contact with the personal difficulties of their congregation, admit that they are aware of the trend.[16]

It is certainly evident that the Mar Policies are over-represented in Catholic strength (14% of the homes are Roman Catholic – more than one-third of all churchgoing homes – compared with the norm of 9·3%) and, although Catholics are strong throughout south and east Alloa, in the Mar Policies the Church of Rome is the only one of the eight major churches to exceed its town average. In this case, the Catholic church is the strongest in the area, stronger even than St Mungo's, which with only 11·5% of the families on its rolls is only half the strength its overall norm would lead us to expect.

The three areas of low crime and low church membership include, once again, Dunmar – low in church affiliation, high in educational attainment, very low in partiality to bingo and now completely devoid of any criminal record. The Mar Policies, although similar to Dunmar in religious adherence and well below the crime mean, was, unlike the private estate, well above average in bingo and below average in 11+ successes. The remaining area (6) is composed of private houses, built around 1900 and including a high proportion (21%) of rented accommodation. In age structure, it is older than average for the town (there are, for example, 101 secondary school pupils per 1,000 homes compared with an Alloa average of 157).

Integrating the Indices

The previous sections of this study have been essentially descriptive. Where areas have differed from the general trend, some background material on each has been presented but at that point the narrative has stopped. Little explanation has been offered. This policy has been deliberate. It is all too easy, knowing only half a story, to jump to conclusions about the ending. And in theory there is no reason why church membership should be related to the other indices in any consistent manner, especially if Goode[17] is right and religion consists of distinct dimensions appealing differentially to individuals variously located in the social structure, and if social theorists such as Bernstein[18] are right and sub-cultures within society perceive the environment in different ways. The problem is to knit together the collection of correlations, the statements of trends and reports of deviations, so that they indicate whether or not separate groups in different parts of Alloa have different modes of life.

If, as a first step, we reconsider the correlations, it becomes obvious that the strongest relationships are between the secular indices, not between church membership and these indices. This

TABLE FOUR

Summary of correlation coefficients

	Church Membership	11+ Passes	Bingo	Crime	Council Housing
Church Membership	—				
11+ Passes	+0·28	—			
Bingo	−0·35	−0·70	—		
Crime	−0·55	−0·50	+0·57	—	
Council Housing	−0·01	−0·66	+0·72	+0·23	—

could mean that the sacred is set apart from the secular, that it transcends class structures and the individual elements of which class and status concepts are composed. Alternatively, it could mean that the technique of linear correlation does not apply to church membership. This would mean a departure from the ideas of Goode and his associates that 'church attendance correlates quite strongly in a positive direction (with social class)'.[19] On the other hand, it is possible that membership and attendance do not themselves correlate, although it is difficult to find any reason for such a variation. Why, for example, should people less likely to be church members hold beliefs and feelings which motivate church attendance? And, more prosaically, how could the contrast persist in a predominantly Presbyterian area, with its facilities for purging the rolls of members who fail to attend? Those who joined solely for a church wedding or to have their children christened would be removed from the rolls if they failed to turn up afterwards.

If we reconsider the other factors mentioned previously, it will be remembered that the most pronounced bingo-playing areas appeared to be predominantly areas of working-class families (if occupation may be considered to be a suitable criterion). The employment categories, of course, related to bingo players only but there seems to be no reason for doubting that the occupational structure of non-bingo players in the same areas is essentially the same. This belief is bolstered by the high negative correlation ($r = -0.70$) between the area totals for bingo and success at the 11+ examinations, the latter being more pronounced amongst middle-class families. In addition, bingo correlates strongly in a positive direction with council house tenancy, while 11+ successes correlate almost as strongly in the opposite direction and one would expect a larger proportion of working-class families than middle- or upper-class families to rent accommodation from the local authority. Also, crime correlates positively with bingo, negatively with educational attainment and thus seems to be associated with the working-class life-style.

TABLE FIVE

Scores for each area on the basis of standard deviations

Variations from mean in terms of standard deviation

Area	Church	Education	Bingo	Crime	Total Score
1	−2·5	−1·5	+2·0	+3·0	−18
2	−1·5	+1·5	−1·5	−1·0	+5
3	−1·5	−0·5	−0·5	+0·5	−4
4	−1·5	−0·5	+1·0	−0·5	−5
5	−0·5	+1·5	−1·5	+0·5	+4
6	−0·5	+1·5	−1·0	−1·0	+6
7	Mean	−0·5	+0·5	−0·5	−1
8	Mean	+1·5	−1·5	−1·0	+8
9	+0·5	+0·5	−0·5	−1·0	+5
10	+0·5	+1·5	−1·5	−1·0	+9
11	+1·0	+1·0	−1·5	−0·5	+8
12	+1·0	−0·5	−1·5	−1·0	+6
13	+1·0	+1·5	−1·5	−0·5	+9
14	+1·0	+1·5	−1·0	−0·5	+6
15	+1·0	−0·5	+1·0	−1·0	+1
16	+1·0	+1·0	−1·0	−1·0	+8
17	+1·0	−0·5	+1·0	−0·5	0
18	+1·5	−0·5	−0·5	−1·0	+5
19	+1·5	+0·5	−1·0	−1·0	+8

If we consider the mean figure for each of the four major social criteria – church membership, bingo playing, educational achievement and criminality – we can use the standard deviation to judge the extent by which each area deviates from the mean. House ownership is not considered because it has a stronger economic component than do the other four. If, to get an overall picture for area comparison, we sum the deviations in the direction of the middle-class tendencies, each area is awarded a cumulative total in the sixth column of Table 5 (i.e. areas over-represented in the category of educational attainment gain one point for every half-deviation, those under-represented lose a point. In the cases of bingo and crime, points are added for under-representation and subtracted for over-representation.)

The resultant scores vary from −18 to +9 and when fitted on to a straight line graph of church membership show a mixture of positive and negative scores along the line. But inspection of the graph shows that some areas with scores around zero have church membership figures well above the average of 59%, as do some areas with high scores. If the argument defining middle-class traits was correct and if church membership was a continuous line from low in the working class to high at the top of the middle class, the figures would have been lowest at the foot of the graph and highest at the top. The conclusion must, therefore, be that church membership in Alloa does not conform to a linear relationship with class.

It is, however, possible to re-arrange the graph in a non-linear fashion as shown in Figure 2.

Within the town, three churches – the Roman Catholic Church, the Episcopal Church and St Andrew's Church of Scotland – have a reputation as working-class institutions. These churches are over-represented in areas 1, 3, 4, 7, 15, 17, 18 and 19, all of which also happen to be local authority housing estates occupied largely by manual workers. Here the scores run from −18 to +8 and, near the top of the scale, St Mungo's and the West Church – the two largest sectors of the Established Church – increase in importance, as does the United Free Church (a survey by Highet showed that the United Free Church was mostly supported by the working and lower middle-classes).

It would be wrong to classify everyone in areas 1, 3 and 4 as hard-gambling, poorly educated, thieving atheists. There are many who

FIGURE TWO

Postulated relationship between church membership and social class

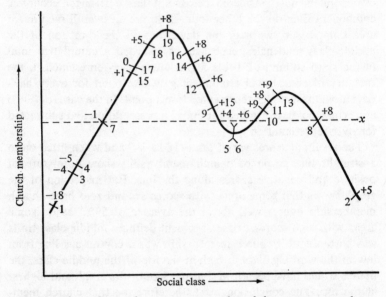

Figures above the graph are area scores, those below are area numbers

work hard and care for their children. Usually, however, this is seen as non-conformity by others in the area and the family is often ostracized. Such families soon become noticed by the local authority and if they ask for a transfer this is normally granted. But their new home has, until recent years, been in Hawkhill (15) and Gaberston (17) and only recently in the Mar Policies (4). The high religiosity of these areas may, to a large extent, be due to those who have climbed out of the Bottom End.

The area at the peak of the curve is occupied by elderly families with long local connections and with a tradition of father and son working together in the breweries, textile mills or mines. Many of the homes now consist of only one elderly widow and this, in part, accounts for the high religiosity since both women and old people are especially prone to association with the church.

The trend towards St Mungo's, the West Church and the United

Free Church is continued and emphasized on the downward arm. The four areas here consist of two areas of private housing built around 1900 (14 and 12), one of mixed private housing of the same era and local authority developments opened in 1930 (16) and a zone consisting solely of public housing (9). In these areas, the predominance of the Roman Catholic Church, the Episcopal Church and St Andrew's has vanished. The private housing is owned by people nearing the end of their working lives, the council area houses many of their offspring. In the private areas, the houses are mainly semi-detached bungalows or two-storey flatted villas. The occupants have working-class backgrounds but have gained posts of responsibility as foremen, inspectors and supervisors. The desire to own one's own home seems to have encouraged thrift – an interviewer soon discovers how important this ownership is to them – but the occupiers are the kind who draw the blinds to prevent the sun from fading the covers on the settee; they find their homes an economic burden but pride in home ownership outweighs such factors.

In the two areas at the base of the trough, the Catholic and Episcopal churches have little strength but the United Free Church and Chalmers Church have become more significant, Chalmers especially being associated with the upper sectors of the middle class. Predominantly private houses, these areas are externally similar to the private sectors in the previous category and rateable values are about the same. But the residents are the offspring of parents whose employment was clerical rather than manual, wage rates are higher and the homes furnished in a more modern and less scanty fashion. In age structure, both sets of areas are similar (less than 100 secondary schoolchildren per 1,000 homes in all cases except the area of council tenants, for example).

The next three areas are composed entirely of private houses. At the turn of the century, areas 10 and 11 were the 'in' places to live and since 1960 area 13 has gained a similar reputation. The houses are detached bungalows or two-storey stone buildings standing in spacious gardens with garages alongside and views north to the Ochil Hills or south to the river. Rateable values (about £100 for a three-bedroomed house) are twice as high as in the previous category and the occupants are drawn from the professions. The streets present an air of affluence with their garages, television aerials and telephone lines to almost every home. Crime is practically unknown.

In these areas, Chalmers is disproportionately strong and St Mungo's above average: the 'working men's churches' are strongly under-represented with the exception of the Episcopal Church in area 13, where the Harland Engineering Company has given grants to enable its technologists to buy their homes. A high proportion of these skilled engineers come from England and adhere to the type of communion in which they were raised. The remaining areas are very similar, and Dunmar has already been described. Thus groups found at particular points on the graph tend to have similar attributes. But the graph is more complex than a straight line and the reasons for the peaks are not explicable directly from the data here. It may simply be that the research work which classified churchgoing as a straight line is not generally applicable, either because of local circumstances or inadequate observation. Or church membership may involve different behaviour patterns from church attendance. Or the reasoning here may be wrong.

It may, however, be important that Robertson found in his sample that 'there is an especially high proportion of regular borderline attenders. This may reflect a genuine tendency to religious activism on the part of individuals poised precariously between clearly manual and clearly middle-class positions.' Robertson also found little evidence of the phenomenon in the literature of the sociology of religion but notes that N. J. Demerath found a similar tendency in his analysis of American church attendance, although the determinants of class position are different from those in Britain in several respects and the findings therefore not directly comparable. But both Scotland and America have exceptionally high church affiliations and this may have some bearing on the situation. Alternatively, different forces acting in different countries may produce the same effect.

The peaks may be connected with 'social climbing' – people straining to assume the values of the group above them. It may be, too, that the strains of living may be greatest, not simply within a particular class, but also in areas of a town where people who fall on a border between class boundaries are concentrated. Where areas acquire status by reputation or visual segregation, those in the class below may emulate these areas in as many ways as possible.

This study is merely a beginning – a suggestion that there may be factors operating which render the linear relationship between church membership and social class inapplicable when the focus is on social areas rather than social groups or individuals. The problem is to discover how social values and patterns of behaviour integrate to produce different life styles in different communities and it would be surprising if this differentiation, considering the potential possibilities of integrating so many social variables, conformed to a straight line.

NOTES

1. D. R. Robertson, 'The Relationship between Church and Social Class in Scotland', PhD. thesis, Edinburgh University 1966.

2. J. Highet, *The Churches in Scotland Today*, Jackson, Son & Co. 1950; 'Scottish Religious Adherence', *British Journal of Sociology*, vol. 4, 1953; *The Scottish Churches*, Skeffington 1960.

3. Charles Y. Glock, 'On the Study of Religious Commitment', *Religious Education Research Supplement 57*, 1962.

4. This figure includes the houses of the Scottish Special Housing Association, for which the local authority acts as factor.

5. Since the research for this paper was completed in the summer of 1969, Chalmers Church and St Andrews Church have amalgamated.

6. Robertson, op. cit.

7. See D. A. Martin, *A Sociology of English Religion*, SCM Press 1967, ch. 2.

8. J. D. Scott, *Life in Britain*, Eyre & Spottiswoode 1956.

9. Robertson, op. cit.

10. I Cor. 1.

11. See, for example, Rodney Stark, 'Class, Radicalism and Religious Involvement in Great Britain', *American Sociological Review*, vol. 29, no. 5, 1964.

12. Emrys Jones, *Social Geography of Belfast*, OUP 1960.

13. R. E. Pahl, 'Trends in Social Geography', in *Frontiers of Geographical Teaching*, ed. Chorley and Haggett, Methuen 1960.

14. For example, J. W. B. Douglas, *The Home and the School*, Mac-Gibbon & Kee 1964.

15. Children, of course, do not pass the 11+ examination. The word is used here as a convenient shorthand. Alloa's education has now been reorganized on comprehensive lines.

16. Lest the impression of mutual antagonism be too great, it should be pointed out that recently a community association has sprung up in an attempt to integrate the residents of the two estates – but the mere appearance of such a body indicates the residents' awareness of a 'them and us' feeling.

17. E. Goode, 'Class Styles of Religious Sociation', *British Journal of Sociology*, vol. 19, 1968.

18. B. Bernstein, 'Language and Social Class', *British Journal of Sociology*, vol. 11, 1960.
19. Goode, art. cit.

The plan on page 186 was drawn by the Cartography Unit, Department of Geography, King's College, London.

10 A Contextual View of Religious Organization

Stephen Yeo

This article derives from a larger study of the changing situation of religious organizations, among many other types of organization, in Reading between about 1850 and 1914. From that case study four principal arguments will be selected. First, some general propositions about approaches and methods in the study of religion in society. Secondly, and following on from those propositions, some descriptions of key features of Reading society in the second half of the nineteenth century until about 1890. Thirdly, the question 'how can religious organizations be better understood in the light of that society?' will be asked. Finally, some of the implications of the forms adopted by religious organizations will be analysed – implications for what else they could do, what functions they would perform, and what would be likely to happen to them in a changing society. The larger study was preoccupied with change. The years 1890 to 1914 were studied in more detail than any other period; they were seen as years of transition between a type of society which had grown up in the town since about 1850 and subsequent phases of twentieth-century social history. The implications of change for religious organizations were described by examining other types of organization alongside them, in the fields of leisure, welfare, education, politics and work. This article will for the most part neglect change, and will neglect other organizations, in the interests of making clear the situation of churches and chapels in a particular type of society which was at its apogee in Reading from 1850 until the 1890s.

The contribution of the social historian to the study of religion must lie in the specificity of his approach. Even if a strictly institutional approach is adopted it should not be a matter of studying a firmly definable constant – 'religion' – whose relationships to society can be listed abstractly and then illustrated from actual situations culled from undifferentiated stretches of time. Such an assumption often accompanies work which proceeds under the title religion *and* society, assuming two separable entities, as though we already had, or as though it was possible to have, a society *without* religion.[1] Religion *in* society perhaps expresses a better perspective, what Lanternari has labelled the 'sociohistorical' approach, 'based on the concept that it is not possible to envision an authentic history of religion outside the broad scope of the culture by which it is encompassed ... A religious phenomenon may be explained only in so far as it is possible to trace its historical origin and development and to analyse it systematically in relation to concrete secular conditions.'[2] Such a perspective may be even more necessary in Britain than elsewhere since Christianity is, in a more diverse way than in some other 'advanced' societies, 'woven into the ... texture of life and settled institutions'.[3]

The necessity for close definition of both place and period follows. While other questions of definition do not magically dissolve following this attachment to historical specificity, they do become more manageable – concerned with 'the particularity of concrete religious situations'. Choices have to be made about whether to concentrate upon beliefs or upon organizations, while recognizing their essential interconnectedness. For the social historian the choice has to be determined partly by the specific place and periods studied (at some times and in some places religious organizations as opposed to diffused beliefs are more important for 'understanding how the fundamental categories through which men apprehend and organize their experience originate, survive and are transformed'[4] than at others) and partly by sources. Getting at beliefs, on anything other than the 'history of ideas' level is extraordinarily difficult, and in some degree impossible for the historian except in peculiarly favourable circumstances. The assumption suitable for my place in my periods of time was that recommended by R. H. Tawney both for 'a primitive people' and 'civilized societies', 'where their treasure is there will their heart be also, and their preferences are revealed by the choices which they make. Their opinions may be learned from their speeches. To know their convictions one must examine their institutions.'[5]

The setting within which those institutions can best be understood is that of the social history of leisure.[6] Religious organizations (mostly churches and chapels obviously, but also other bodies like the Reading Town Mission, two wings of the YMCA, even the Reading Athletic Club in its early days) were voluntary organizations supplying a product for consumption by portions of, or in some cases notionally the whole of the population of the town. The relationships between providers and potential consumers of a leisure product (or anyway a product not usually consumed at work, although Suttons' seed firm provided daily services for their employees before work and the Reading Gas Company hired missionaries from the Town Mission to preach 'between draws' in the 1890s) as those relationships develop over time are thus important. In the period 1850-1914 this part of the setting is complicated by the fact that, increasingly, religious entrepreneurs saw their work in this light: a more self-conscious view of agency became typical, and the problem of adapting the leisure product to meet supposed consumer needs became urgent. The relationship between what people need/want/create 'from below', and what exists/is provided/flourishes 'from above' is a complex one to unravel in a 'mass society'. But if the fate of organizations is primarily *of* their members as opposed to being provided *for* them by others, and the tension between the elements of *of*-ness and *for*-ness within individual organizations over time could be understood, then much about the social history of religion would also have been learned. What is ideally needed is a social history of 'from below' impulses and organizations related to 'from above' impulses and organizations in the broad area of 'religion'. The situation of religious organizations was a historically specific one. The choices they faced, often unconsciously, and the pressures they experienced, often without articulating them, were rooted in a place at a time and rooted in a social system, capitalism, at specific moments of its development. It is societies and social changes that students of religion have to look at, not at the abstracted dynamics of the behaviour of religious organizations. There is no ambition in this article to contribute to that receding horizon which, according to some, will be reached by an accumulation of small studies plus a greater theoretical sophistication, 'the sociology of religion rather than ... the sociology of this or that religion'.[7]

So what about the 'concrete secular conditions' in this case? In the period from mid-century to 1914 Reading exploded from a small town (21,456 in 1851) to a nearly 100,000 strong metropolitan town. The largest percentage rate of growth of population (1871-91) coincided with the growth of the dominant economic institution of the town – Huntley and Palmer's biscuit factory. Employing 400 people in 1862 that factory was employing around 6,000 in 1905. As the *Reading Observer* commented in 1891, 'what Reading would have been without the immense works which comprise the biscuit factory none can imagine'. The reign of the first three main entrepreneurs of the factory, all of them Palmer brothers, was over by 1898. Reading had an earlier social history of some importance – four Anglican churches in use in 1900 and two Nonconformist congregations still in existence at that date being founded in the period of the town's history dominated by the cloth industry and Reading Abbey, i.e. before 1650 – but the focus here will be on the 'biscuitopolis' phase of its history. Rather than characterizing the town between 1850 and the 1890s in the manner of an economic historian interested in indices of growth, the aim will be to describe the type of society flourishing at the time of this growth. To use Gramsci's categories, Reading society will be described immediately before it was greatly affected by 'the imperialist phase of the historical evolution of the bourgeois class', when 'industrial power has become separated from the factory and is concentrated in a trust, in a monopoly, in a bank, in the State bureaucracy'. Our period in Reading saw 'the liberal phase of the historical evolution of the bourgeois class', when 'the proprietor was also the entrepreneur and the industrialist. Industrial power and its source was in the factory.'[8]

Before going into that phase one further preliminary will be helpful. The distinction should be made between ideology and organization, between aspiration and practice, between what the society wished to be believed about itself and what existed on the ground. Even within the aspiration there is a distinction between what might be called rhetoric (bogus aspiration cloaking self-interest in noble phrases) and language (genuine aspiration committedly followed through into practice). What follows is derived from a study of Reading, where the extent to which the ideology had an organizational base in institutions and practices, the extent to which it was a language spoken because it was meant rather than a rhetoric deployed because it was convenient to have it appear that it was meant, was probably greater than in many other places in nineteenth-century capitalism. But the ideas that follow were to varying degrees central to capitalism itself, which, like other systems, generates aspirations and modes of organization whose full development it cannot contain without either itself being transformed or those aspirations and modes of organization being channelled into more convenient forms, transforming themselves in the process. Capitalism cannot embody the best of itself: had Reading society embodied the ideal notions of itself prevalent from around 1850 onwards, but under increasing strain from 1890 onwards, and to some extent realized in institutions and movements during that time, it, and the surrounding society outside Reading, would have been very different from what they turned out to be in the twentieth century. At the macro (capitalism) level the contradictions between ideology and organization, whose intensifying at the micro (Reading) level was a very visible part of the history of the years 1890 to 1914, were always sharper in the period 1850 to the 1890s than they were at the micro (Reading) level. In spite of the fact that market researchers and psephologists love it as the average town Reading was, after all, an exceptional place. While some of the things which will be said below about Reading are true about mid-nineteenth-century capitalism generally, and while all of the things which will be said about it certainly need an understanding of late-nineteenth-century society, what will be said is quintessentially true about Reading. This is because of its take-off into industrial importance after 1850, rather than earlier or later, its domination by a single industry, the domination of that single industry by a single (Quaker) family, the purity of its middle classness as a town ('in no way under any territorial or lordly influence', as W. I. Palmer put it in 1891) and the possibilities inherent in its size – big but not too big still in 1900. But to some extent this is not the point. Whether or not the ideology/aspiration became organization/practice in a sense does not matter for the student of religion in society. It was that it was there at all which mattered for religious institutions, as part of the context which shaped their expectations of themselves, part of the total situation which made them what they were. The history of the expectations religious organizations had of themselves is just important as, and essential for understanding, the history of what they were, what they were doing, and what they were undergoing.

Anyone who has been to a British public school, particularly to one like mine, which was founded in the 1870s, has the advantage of direct experience of some of the ruling ideas informing the life of a town like Reading in the second half of the nineteenth century. The local press, like the school notice-board, was divided on important occasions (such as the last week of the year, or a town dinner with the Mayor presiding – as it were a speech-day) into sections: 'commercial', 'philanthropist', 'religious', 'municipal', 'athletic'. Reports were given on the progress of these areas of 'activity', sometimes explicitly linking them into a common moral framework. Each was important; to be involved personally in more than one was highly desirable; to be committed to at least one in a dedicated and continuous way was an essential attribute of the good citizen, who was a *sine qua non* of the good man. The local Liberal press was not unlike the school magazine, although it also served the function for the whole town which more detailed records of particular organizations served for them – amounting, at its best, to a kind of civic minute-book. Everybody should either be involved in a position of responsibility in one area of town life, or else should be on the way to being so involved. This included the working classes; indeed that it included the working classes was stressed as being a defining feature of the age compared with any other age.[9] Help should be given to those unable or not yet able to be so involved, but help which stimulated an active response not demeaning, pauperizing help. Such help, as in matters of welfare, should be given by local social leaders or by neighbours, in the Samaritan sense, not by experts, professionals or, except in the last resort, by public entities beyond the town such as the State.

For Canon Payne, at the Mayor's breakfast in 1890, 'it was a matter of great gratification to see how many lines were opened up in which the benevolent feelings and tendencies of our townsmen might find some scope for exercise'.[10] None of these 'lines', including the religious, was in a different moral league from the others. All were equally meritorious, but none had merit on its own. The important thing was to relate to at least one thoroughly, and to discern its links with the others. Overdevelopment of one 'line' by an individual, a class, or a town to the extent that it involved neglect or suppression of the others was almost as culpable as ignoring them all. Hence the concern that Reading might become, in the later years of the century, a mere suburb of London – involving the segregation of work from home on a more fundamental scale than was already happening inside the town itself. Hence the concern so frequently expressed as the contradictions grew between 1890 and 1914 that sport or 'amusement' pursued for its own sake or, even worse, pursued for the sake of profit, was on the increase. Sport had wider ends and connections, but these were part of an interlocking system of duties which, vigorously done, would generate a healthy community.[11] Hence, too, the concern that sport could cease to mean participation, for to participate regularly and seriously and not in periodic *festas* as in earlier periods but in continuous well-structured associations was vital.[12] Indeed the fact of participation was at least as important as the formal goals of the organization participated in. Welfare associations, for example, whether Friendly Societies, the Reading Philanthropic Institution, the Reading Soup Kitchen, the Temperance and General Philanthropic Institution, the Charity Organisation Society ... had to meet as well as to perform their external functions. To be too particular about the formal goals would be to diminish the notions of unity within an overall system, of which each separate activity was a part.

Of course there were firm moral certainties and structural constraints within which participation in associations was desirable. It was not a question of participation in order to achieve freedom of the 'do your own thing' variety. Freedom was to be understood in the context of perfect service, and subordination to one's betters. A certain amount of equality in the eyes of God, itself not very often mentioned, did *not* mean any equality of the kind which might need concrete expression in politically transformed institutions or a transformed total society. To continue the school analogy, while prefects were promoted from the ranks and while everyone in the ranks had, theoretically, a chance of becoming a prefect this did *not* mean that prefects would at any future date make masters redundant. The important difference between this version of society and later twentieth-century versions of 'democracy', however, was that the freedom of perfect service and mass moral self-control and common commitment to dominant moral ideas was to be achieved by active participation in which voting, for example, was only a trivial part. The idea of a competitively selected elite whose necessary role was ratified by occasional elections, plus a desirable general apathy, plus a highly developed capitalist leisure industry, was completely foreign to Reading between 1850 and 1890 – although social changes which were to provide the background to the development of such an idea were key parts of the social history of the years 1890 to 1914. Amoral freedom, 'doing your own thing', concentration upon personal or sectional satisfaction at the expense of the community, the development of ideologies which stressed conflict rather than co-operation – these undesirables were to be prevented by continually extending areas for active consent rather than by continually extending areas, like entertainment, for passive acceptance.[13]

Voluntary commitment, both of time and money, was essential. Going to town meetings, initiating even the most public projects (such as a town hall), supporting organizations other than your own (such as denominations to which you did not belong), being at pan-town events (such as the funeral of a biscuit factory almoner, the opening of the new YMCA buildings, the annual event of the Reading Working Men's Regatta), should all be done voluntarily. Almsgiving, the decline of which Beatrice Webb reckoned to be the most striking of all the changes in her lifetime,[14] meant time as much as money. Indeed there was something wrong with vicarious generosity involving no follow-through, just as there was something wrong with easy acceptance of the gift with no consequent *quid pro quo*. The interconnections, and the unity between the different foci of voluntary commitment, were stressed. It was easier to stress them in a town of Reading's size where one man, town clerk after 1866, was said to have with his 'indefatigable energy and public spirit ... touched more or less nearly every effort for the welfare of the town'.[15] The town hall was seen as part of a system, 'an undertaking having for [its] object the social and moral good of the people', the 'crowning work' of a number of related achievements, such as a sewage system, the Mechanics' Institute, the British and National Schools.[16] The Reading Temperance Society, according to William Palmer, was doing above ground what an adequate drainage system was doing below ground. The public library had been preceded by and took over a previous public, but voluntary, library – in the premises of the Reading Temperance Society. The University was, according to its principal ideologue and founder, W. M. Childs, a natural complement to, rather than on a different level from, or a rival to, the Reading Literary and Scientific Society.[17]

Even where organizations did not explicitly see themselves, as did the Reading Philanthropic Institution, as 'epitome(s) of a free community'[18] and as representatives of the best notions of organization and conduct which should be extended to become hegemonic within the whole society, neither did they see themselves as simple providers of entertaining ways of consuming Tuesday evenings. Allied to other organizations they were, they thought, much more than manufacturers of leisure products: the pressure to become just that is a major theme in the social history of organizations, religious and otherwise, between 1890 and 1914.[19] The notion of 'hobbies' safely insulated in a 'leisure' vacuum away from work, away from the business of shaping one's own future, having nothing to do with the way in which a whole society should and could be run was, in aspiration at least, and certainly in the major economic institution of the town, as foreign as the notion of work which had nothing to do with the rest of life, simply an activity which the worker 'sells to another person in order to secure the necessary means of subsistence'.[20] So the biscuit factory was frequently compared to a town in itself, with its events alongside work, its ceremonials, its mutual improvement activities, its clubs and funds.

The focus of commitment was the locality. Efforts were from time to time made to co-ordinate *all* welfare activities, for example, at the local level.[21] Aspirations to create a civic welfare state preceded, and differed in quality from, later aspirations to create 'the welfare state'. The anatomy of the failure of such efforts in the late-nineteenth and early-twentieth centuries may be more significant than their precise nature – but efforts were made. Things could be done at the local level which would seriously offend 'individualism' in its supposed late-nineteenth century dichotomy with 'collectivism' if they were to be done professionally, or by some super-agency such as the state. The statement that 'any aid from the government which superseded local effort was to be deprecated' could be made as much about extension work in the movement towards a university in Reading, as in the more familiar territory for such observations – welfare. 'Men conscious of a power to help their fellows,' as George Palmer said, 'should be willing to take their share in municipal and other government.' 'Other government' included philanthropy, which was part of the ideal of self-government. Indeed municipal and national government were only a small part, and a lesser part, of what 'government' properly meant.[22] The human will was seen as being immensely powerful, and conscious individual choice, rational and responsible, was the only basis upon which a proper politics could grow. Spending money, hours, mental energy in a movement, often divided into many branches, yet seeing its relationship to other agencies: relying upon that type of agency rather than upon the 'change society first' option (and not necessarily thereby merely reformist): stressing individual moral commitment as the most powerful agency for alteration of social circumstances, but expressed through continuously existing associations which did not see themselves mainly as pressure groups acting upon the central government: opening these organizations theoretically to everybody, or at least providing them *for* everybody rather than leaving them as the exclusive property *of* a special constituency – all this was highly characteristic of Reading society in the years c.1850-90.

The phases through which Reading society went both illuminate, and have to be reconstructed from, the phases through which organizations went. 'Concrete secular conditions' necessitate local studies, and yet not discrete local studies, isolated from the wider society. In the space of this paper it will not be possible either to root the description of Reading society 1850-90 more firmly in local examples[23] or to locate that description in the ideology and organization of mid- to late-nineteenth-century capitalism more generally. Reading was an exaggerated example of features prominent in the ideology of English society outside the town of that period, making it peculiarly appropriate as a case study for the late-nineteenth and early-twentieth centuries. It is, however, easy to see that, in a society where the aspirations outlined above were central, religion, in the form of churches and chapels, could have a place. Indeed it is easy to see, at that point in time, that religion would take the form of churches and chapels. Such institutions were natural components of the effort to create continuously existing social organizations *for* others which would eventually become fully *of* those others, but within dominant moral certainties about conduct and organization. A study which concentrated upon an earlier transition than the one between 1890 and 1914, namely the transition to mid-nineteenth-century industrial Reading from eighteenth- and early-nineteenth-century 'Belford Regis'[24] would have much to say about the role of religion and churches/chapels in that transition. They clearly were important in bringing into being as well as in servicing the society just described. But again that is not within the scope of this paper.

How then can religious organizations be better understood in the light of the outline description of Reading society c.1850-c.1890 given above? An exercise which helps is to imagine the society without its churches and chapels. What would be missing in the ecology?

The first answer must be, quantitively, a lot. The size of the presence of churches and chapels, both numerically and physically as buildings in the townscape, should be stressed. Whatever particular denominations thought about their position relative to that of other denominations, the proportion of the potentially-attending population (given age, economic circumstances, working times etc.) for which there *were* seats was much more remarkable than the proportion for which there were not.[25] In this simple sense Reading was an exceptionally 'religious' society. Some 60,000 inhabitants in 1891 had 25,650 seats available in some 40 buildings. Between 1890 and 1914 the Church of England employed at minimum 216 full-time ministers; all 'others' employed at minimum 158 ministers.[26] In some neighbourhoods the buildings could be seen in all directions, with competitors staring from behind their columns or gravestones across narrow streets. As one minister said in 1884: 'It is astonishing how many churches and chapels there are and how many efforts there have been made for the welfare of everyone'.[27] Contrary to later interpretations of decline it could even be claimed that 'the universal growth and expansion of the church of God ... is the leading characteristic of the most glorious and beneficent reign in the history of England'.[28]

Ministers had more of their time not bespoken than did other professional groups. Without them many organizations, events, and meetings in Reading would have been short-staffed. Their role as initiators (e.g. of the movement to found the Royal Berkshire Hospital, the University Extension movement etc.), members of committees, speakers on platforms, attenders at pan-town events was striking. Once the ministers are differentiated it is clear that some of them did nothing of this, some did a lot. Some things none would do – although *one* minister would often play a role in something like the foundation of the Berkshire Agricultural and General

Workers' Union (1892-3) where no others would dare to tread – some things there would be a scramble to support.[29] From the organizations which employed them, and spent much time and effort thinking how to pay them, came many other cadres without whom organized voluntaryism on a level wider than that of churches and chapels would have had even more severe problems. Churches and chapels were the most accessible and local organizations in the system described above. Hence they would be used as bases in pan-town efforts, like organizing events to celebrate a jubilee or coronation, or staffing a Guild of Help. The obituaries of many burgesses who merited notice in the local press described how their local church or chapel was the first organization in which they were active. Activists who first spoke at a church debating society, or whose first entrepreneurial skills were shown in making the Sunday or Adult School flourish, were typical. A key institution like the Trinity Congregational Chapel Alphabetical Society (1874) contained many names later to be prominent in the life of other groups in the town.[30] Institutions other than religious ones (e.g. football clubs, the WEA, the local hospital) are crucial for understanding what, on the level of the immediate urban environment, religion was doing. The halls and meeting rooms of churches were useful plant within the wider system too. Collectively churches and chapels were more important suppliers of such premises than all the others put together – large businesses, the municipality, political parties, large voluntary organizations like the Ancient Order of Foresters, and hybrids like the Reading Co-op. The fate of such halls over the past ten years, as they have become offices for state welfare agencies, headquarters for judo classes and the like, or as they have been pulled down by property developers, has provided unmistakable visual evidence in many towns of the final passing of this earlier phase of social development. The groups for whom the churches' plant had been brought into being – their own agencies – would also be present at, and be part of, the clusters of non-religious groups which came together to do such things as to promote the Association for the Advancement of the Higher Education of the Working Classes (later the WEA), help the annual Temperance Festival, collect and parade for Hospital Sunday, react to flood damage in bad winters in Caversham, man the Guild of Help, and so on.

Institutes, guilds, sporting clubs, Christian endeavour societies.

needlework societies, Adult Schools, libraries, Brotherhoods, Pleasant Weekday Evening societies, youth sections, Women's Owns, temperance societies, missionary associations, coffee taverns – these all clustered around churches and chapels in astonishing profusion. In the terminology of a recent study of social movements they were 'cafeteria' organizations.[31] Attached to the main Baptist chapel in the town were at least forty sub-organizations. There was a curious tendency, as if by some natural law of growth, for these sub-organizations, if they grew to a certain size, to acquire what Charles Booth called their own 'penumbra' of sub-sub-organizations. Such vast apparatuses or 'machines' were a characteristic feature of 'religion' from the 1860s onwards in Reading, as elsewhere.[32]

Churches and chapels were continually, through these agencies, asking their publics to participate in something, or rather in many interconnected things. They evaluated themselves by their success in getting mass response to that request. They would have agreed with W. H. Beveridge's creed 'vigour and abundance of voluntary action outside one's home, individually or in association with other citizens for bettering one's own life and that of one's fellows, are the distinguishing marks of a free society'.[33] At its most extreme the effort was not just characteristic of the period, it was that period's quintessence. There was a common idea that within the activities of any one church/chapel *all* types of sound human activity should be co-ordinated and concentrated, 'as a focus to which gathers all the mental, social and spiritual forces of a district'.[34] No group should escape. There was a danger of 'regarding the social and recreative features (of life) ... as something apart from the distinctively religious'; 'there must be something for all and a place for everyone' at the most neighbourhood level of all, that of the individual church or chapel.[35] The ambitious perspective was that it was at that level, but of course federated to other similar units, that the controls should operate and freedom be obtained through perfect service. The ambition was such that it was perhaps likely to fail, or to feel like failure even when it was succeeding. But failure became even more likely since the ambition flourished at precisely the time when large factors in the wider society beyond the town were working against such efforts – whether they were religious or not.

So the church and chapel were as prolific inventors, diffusers, matrices for new developments within the 'leisure' area, in the period before the major capitalist invasion of that area after the 1880s, as was the public house.[36] Reading rooms, football and other sporting facilities at the most local level, bazaars, and the YMCA, were among their major contributions in Reading. They were not of course entirely promiscuous. Whitley Hall Methodist chapel took the rare decision in 1908 to forgo one successful agency – the Boys Brigade – because of a felt conflict between its para-military goals and their own spiritual ones. What churches and chapels had a natural affinity for and what they did not can in fact reveal something of their particular bias and particular function as religious, as opposed to any other type, of organization in the period. Temperance, for example, in its post-1870 forms was so uniformly acceptable as to break the normal late-nineteenth-century pattern in Reading of churches and chapels losing some of their most dynamic activities to pan-town or supra-town organizations. The Reading Temperance Society actually lost some of its impetus to the lower level churches and chapels at this time. Some forms of educational and welfare activity were entirely acceptable: some forms of political activity, especially those connected to socialism or to the 'woman question' and especially if the interests of the denomination itself were not threatened at the national political level, were entirely unacceptable. This was true of the churches and chapels as organizations, but less true of their paid ministers and some laymen inside them acting as individuals. Religious organiza-tions epitomized and were essential to those aspects of Reading society c.1850-c.1890 which least resembled that which was to fol-low. Yet, at the same time, they showed a bias towards the discrete activities, the concentration upon individuals within an ongoing, rendered-unto-Caesar social order, and the pure leisure consumption which were to become characteristic of the history of social organi-zation in Reading and other places in the twentieth century.

As organizations in a specific society churches and chapels operated within constraints, some of them inherent in their nature or in the nature of society throughout the period, some of them needing a chronology. The assumption that they worked in an a-social vacuum of total freedom was, and still is, a source of many agonizingly expressed feelings of failure amongst activists, but it was of course a false one. Right hands have an awkward habit of being affected by what left hands are doing. In specifying these constraints the problem of representativeness arises. Which religious organizations? How many? What about the ones that were not like the above description? This problem also has dynamic, chronological dimensions which will have to be kept in mind in what follows.

Out of the eighty-three places of worship available for use by the inhabitants of Reading between 1890 and 1914, I was only able to find records for about forty. Some of these records were slight, and supplemented only by odd references in the press. Some were embarrassingly full. There is an inherent bias arising from the sources because, for example, a relatively small sect without a 'penumbra', without any full-time mouthpieces, without any of the characteristics of religious organization which are being stressed here, unless like the Reading Agapemonites it was sufficiently extraordinary to attract press coverage, would be unlikely to leave a good trail for the social historian. Equally, a church which followed through theologically and organizationally the assertion made at the laying of the foundation stone for a new Catholic church in 1905 that 'the church was for God primarily and for the people only secondarily'[37] would not be so easy to cover as, say, the burst of activity following the Wesleyan Twentieth-Century Fund in the town. To add to this bias the study on which this paper is based did underplay the denominational variable. Nevertheless, individual churches and chapels whose nature over time could be observed were tending to get more like the Baptist chapel with its forty siblings already mentioned, even ones with some overt resistance to the trend. There was also a distinct process of denominational assimilation. Primitive Methodist chapels were, for instance, getting to resemble Anglican, Baptist and other units of comparable size, starting with a choir and an organ in the 1860s and ending with 'something for all and a place for everyone' by the 1890s.

The date of ecclesiastical buildings and the district in which they were situated were more closely related to style than was denomination – although in building materials Anglicans continued to favour stone long after they could afford it. Being both expensive and permanent, buildings were themselves a constraint, both while they were being collected for, and after they and their debts had become permanent. In church accounts only the payment of ministers and the provision of schools figured as prominently as buildings among those items which because, so it seemed, they had to be done determined what else, in a world of finite resources, would not be done. To a rank-and-file reader of a church or chapel magazine in late-nineteenth-century Reading it must have appeared as though religion had some intrinsic connection with bricks and mortar.[38] There were deliberate exceptions (such as an interesting group of schismatics who called themselves Congregational Methodists) but there seemed in general to be a law of multiplication of bricks and mortar whereby even groups of worshippers who did not want one acquired 'an edifice standing on a main thoroughfare, imposing, grand and stately'.[39] Then that edifice multiplied into others both on its own site and on others. Then those with thirty-year memories looked back nostalgically to the days before the process started, when the congregation or 'church' in the non-building sense, could consist of other social groups than the ones they had ended up by serving, and could be doing other things than raising money in order to go on raising money for itself.

Raising money for buildings, or for supporting ministers, or for supporting church schools each involved a necessary element of turned-inwardness in the church or chapel concerned. In some cases in Reading that inturning can be watched as it grew. As the missionary group involved in a poor area became 'successful', so the demand grew for an 'iron' or temporary church and then for a permanent, recognizably ecclesiastical building. *Pari passu* the amount of the available budget which could be spent on outside objects decreased. A certain kind of institutional success involved, and felt like, a more important kind of failure. It was simply that, as a church worker saw it in a poor district of Reading in 1904, 'there are a whole lot of people starving for want of fuel and bread ... if less were spent on church machinery and over organization the church would have more to spend on the poor'.[40] Such an inturning process could also happen as a result of well-intentioned outside interventions, as for example when a local business man rescued the Reading No. 1 Corps of the Salvation Army from a series of temporary missionary homes by making it possible for them to build a main street Citadel like other denominations. Running an institution (such as Trinity Congregational chapel) with annual receipts of £2,000-plus inevitably implied that much of what the institution was doing was raising money to service itself. Anything spent outside the chapel was a luxury – like the small amount which went to the poor. Its sibling at Park Institute could only give to the Hospital Sunday Fund in 1913 after it had taken church expenses out of the collections for the day. Yet Park Institute had been especially created to look outwards and to be less ecclesiastical.

Being precise about the *of* and 'from below' elements in these processes, as opposed to the *for* and 'from above' elements over time is difficult. It is easier to cite cases than to generalize, for example, about whether a church in the sense of the one formed by the Zoar Chapel Strict Baptists seven years before they built Zoar, or in the sense of the Reading Hebrew Burial Society formed fourteen years before they built the synagogue, more often preceded a bricks and mortar church before 1850, between 1850 and 1890, or between 1890 and 1914. But schism did become decreasingly typical as a mode of originating churches and chapels in Reading between 1800 and 1914, and local middle-class money coming in large donations at critical moments from small numbers of donors was a much more central part of the coming into being of churches and chapels in the mid-nineteenth century than between 1890 and 1914. Given what was wanted, an 'edifice, imposing grand and stately', and given the poverty of the bulk of the population, whole areas of town and whole occupational groupings could not possibly have such an edifice unless it was provided for them. This was done on a large scale in the mid to late-nineteenth century in Reading, but at the end of that period the providers grew less generous or less accessible and other resorts were tried, most importantly central denominational machinery outside the town, but also in one or two cases, like the Reading Football Club in their different way, investment finance was tried.[41]

The law of accumulation of bricks and mortar afflicted organizations other than churches and chapels, such as the Temperance Society and the YMCA. In the former case it was particularly awkward because the building was planned while there was still the detailed commitment of William Isaac Palmer the biscuit manufacturer around, but had to be finished and paid for without him. Huge profits may now be made by such inner-urban organizations as a result of redevelopment following the £s per square foot imperatives of 1960s-70s commerce but they do not compensate for, indeed they only add to, the distortions in the earlier operation of such bodies through factors about which they did and said nothing but which determined much of their work, like land prices, interest rates, suburban segregation of cities and so on. Being organizations *in* society means being organizations *in a* certain kind of society, whose arrangements are neither inevitable, permanent, ordained by God, nor common to *all* kinds of societies.[42] In the case of that other inward-turning constraint, the costs of ministers, there is evidence (and not just from bodies like the Friends or the Congregational Methodists who did not have them) that it was, from certain points of view, an unnecessary constraint. Neither attendance at worship, nor the extent of the penumbra, suffered in organizations which normally had ministers but which had temporary gaps, or which had far fewer of them than, say, their Anglican neighbours.

Another set of constraints acting upon what churches and chapels could be and what they could do or not do were the consequences of forms of membership, either in the main chapel or in the sub-institutions around it. Joining, or even participating in any continuous way in churches where membership mattered less, involved money. Spare resources were simply not available to a major slice of the population for most of the time.[43] This was an inherent contradiction within this period of Reading capitalism, and to some extent within capitalism itself, in which religious organizations were involved along with many others. Central aspirations of that phase were necessarily to be confined to a small section, not because of the nature of those aspirations, but because of deprivation, relative and in late-nineteenth-century Reading, absolute. For some religious organizations this was a contradiction to which they either adapted, or by which they were not bothered. Exclusion was quite as important a function amongst some churches and chapels as inclusion, and pew rents announced unmistakably the social groups of whom that particular church or chapel was the property. Zoar Strict Baptist Chapel no more wanted everyman and his wife in its membership than did a literary society turned club called the Reading Athenaeum. The overall directions of change over time in this matter of exclusivity were difficult to map in Reading. But it is certainly a mistake to think that pew rents were disappearing in the twenty-five years before 1914. New chapels in all major denominations were being built with them, and some old ones even introduced them at this time. But exclusiveness in the sense of strictness of criteria for membership was decreasing over time in individual chapels, and as a characteristic of churches and chapels as a whole. Certainly the idea of openness and the idea that 'the poor should have an equal chance with the richest of the best seats' was gaining ground, as a yardstick by which religious organizations measured themselves between 1890 and 1914. But the structural and social inevitabilities of closedness remained, as strong in 1914 as in 1850.

The relationship between expectations, organization, and the possibilities and limitations inherent in the nature of the town, the wider society, and the system, is what needs to be periodized. To what extent did churches and chapels want everyone in the town at churches and chapels, or some form of 'religion', in general, or did each want everyone at their particular church or denomination? Probably increasingly the former in Reading. Were religious institutions in the business of attracting 'the public', theoretically everyone in Reading, into their doors or into membership, any more than was the Athenaeum? Probably yes, increasingly so in Reading. What was the relative strength at different dates of churches and chapels of a certain social group, not designed to be generalized from, accepting, even existing in order to ratify the fact that different denominations, different buildings, different ministers, different beliefs and practices, each had their own role to play at their own level, and that none should seek to poach or colonize or ultimately to absorb the others? It was not within the terms of reference of the Athenaeum to absorb or make redundant the YMCA, any more than Heelas (the new 'retail revolution' multiple store in town) expected all the shopping in town to gravitate to them, although the significance of this type of late-nineteenth-century business enterprise lies in its proximity to this aim. What about churches and chapels in this regard? Probably they were getting more like the new retailers in Reading in this period – interested in turnover per inch of shelf-space rather than in the quality of the shopping experience, in presentation of the product, in market 'push' rather than consumer 'pull', in balloon views of the religious scene as a whole rather than seen from below, from the perspective of a single sect or church.

In one week in 1902–3 in the largest Primitive Methodist chapel in town there were seventeen meetings to which a member/attender might go, or of which he or she might be, in many cases, a card-carrying member. Such a penumbra was bound to have consequences, whether intentional or otherwise. Tails do wag dogs, if they are long enough and the dog weak enough. One consequence was a kind of organizational overheating, leading to nervous exhaustion of ministers. 'Nobody who had not worked in a parish could have any idea of the amount of work, strength and time required in simply keeping things going.'[44] Another consequence was that activists whose work turned outwards into the town, say into the labour movement from the Pleasant Sunday Afternoon movement, had to choose between organizational bases: not because of theoretical incompatibility, but because, unless they were deliberately aloof, the natural tendency of work within the church / chapel base was to absorb all available time and energy. Another was either to catalyse the replacement of a cheap, adaptable structure by a permanent, expensive building or to cause the addition to that permanent building of yet more building – halls, schoolrooms and so on. It was often the siblings which led to the new mother-church, rather than the other way round. To make something small easier something very large would be created. Another consequence was to add to the necessity for middle-class patronage imposed by other factors already outlined. It was a trap: it was felt by many siblings to be important that they should rely upon themselves for their expenses. If they did, the subscriptions would have to be high enough to price the people they wanted to reach out of the market: if they did not, if they relied upon non-participating donors, they would be relying upon a particular type of society and would themselves become a particular type of organization.[45] A final result was to add to the connections between religion and *joining*, with all the cultural and economic problems which that concept raised for so great a slice of the population. Joining was another of those features of 'religious' life, like bricks and mortar, which must have seemed to the 'man in the pew' to be part of Christianity itself. One of the jobs of the social historian should surely be to point to such features as being specific to a period and type of society rather than to the creed itself.

The intended consequences of purposeful social action were harder to achieve than the unintended ones. The small number of members/attenders in the agencies of church work who became church members/attenders in the central worshipping aspects of church life was frequently regretted.[46] Whereas congregations in main chapel services were about double the total membership, piecing together fragmentary evidence in Reading suggests that attendance at agency meetings was of the order of half the membership of each agency. There was a felt conflict between institutional and spiritual success in the most 'prosperous' and dynamic chapels. Machinery created to serve its master became the master: what social scientists call 'goal displacement' became a galloping disease. The process of taking up activities in order to strengthen an original aim, but then finding that those activities took on their own sapping momentum in a world of finite resources of commitment, time, and money, had its own logic. Three years after the Methodist chapel already mentioned had refused to sanction a Boys Brigade 'believing as they do that militarism is against the principles of Christ's teaching', and following the relative failure of their alternative – the Boys Life Brigade – the same chapel set a Boys Brigade in motion.[47] The aim of such agencies with their hierarchical structures, militaristic flavour, competitiveness – full of badges, tests, uniforms, drills – may have been to instill discipline in the post-Sunday School age group in order to bring them into the ecclesiastical orbit: their effects were surely quite otherwise, and not unconnected with the two and a quarter million men who volunteered for war before March 1916 – 'the largest volunteer force ever raised in any country', as A. J. P. Taylor noted.

They were also a major part, alongside other agencies like the Christian Endeavour Movement, the Church of England Men's Society, and the Church of England Temperance Society, of the nationalizing of religious and other social organizations in the early-twentieth century. Some, like the Broad Street Congregational PSA, resisted this tendency and tried for a time to remain free from supra-chapel or supra-town structures but, as with denominations with rooted objections to such structures, it did not take long for them to succumb in the nineteenth century. The same thing had happened with Friendly Societies much earlier in the century. The proportion of social initiatives and social organizations coming 'from below', from the locality, certainly decreased compared with those of national or, like Christian Endeavour, international origins and structures. Religious organizations aided and were part of this change. They scarcely resisted it at all.

A further development which they unintentionally, perhaps, abetted through the operation of these vast arrays of agencies was that of the fragmentation of their publics into endless class-specific and age-specific and sex-specific 'targets'. 'The tendency of parochial work', wrote a departing vicar, was 'to increase and multiply in every direction. Each class and sometimes each section, and sometimes each profession wanted something specially done for themselves. They wanted their guilds for girls and also for boys, their Bible classes for factory girls, for servants and for shop assistants ...'[48] Even modes of worship were not expressions of an implicit idea of community, but were held to be appropriate in one form for one section and in another form for another section.[49] Once again the 'from below' and the 'from above' pressures have to be evaluated over time. What was the relative role of structural changes, say in the situation of 'youth' in the late-nineteenth century (educational, familial, economic etc.), compared with manufacturers' orientation of their marketing and sales strategies to this embryonic market through advertisement, and compared with preoccupation with 'youth' as a separate category elsewhere in the society, for instance in ministers' minds? Whatever it was which was primarily responsible for the increasing fragmentation of society into cultural and consuming sub-groupings in the late-nineteenth century it is certain that churches and chapels were either passively observing the process and fitting themselves into it, or were functioning as positive aiders and abetters.

A final consequence of wide penumbras was that their shadow fell upon the whole operation of the church, in the sense that it became difficult to see what was agency and what was central church activity. Means became ends. Halls preceded churches: churches were set up as halls.[50] Bazaars became goods in themselves, not enablers of other goods. Organizations like the Christian Endeavour society for Nonconformists or the CEMS for Anglicans were adopted as agencies by most churches and chapels, in many cases explicitly to counter this observed tendency. Services, like everything else, became methods self-consciously employed, for sections of a 'public', or worse still for the 'masses'. A stepping back from the potential consumer in order to weigh him up, a stepping back from the worshipping life of a church in order to weigh it up in relation not to the felt needs of members but in relation to the supposed needs of potential consumers – this was an increasing characteristic of the organized religion of the period, across denominational boundaries.[51] Both the 'success' of the

institution observed in a local Baptist magazine in December 1898
and the nagging feeling that connected to that success was something less satisfactory were typical: 'Here is an edifice standing on
a main thoroughfare, imposing, grand and stately. The visitor is
struck with its beauty of architecture, whilst the resident regards
it with no small pride as an ornament to the town: the musical
parts of its services are chaste and beautiful; and the pulpit ministra-
tions brilliant and refined; its pews and aisles are thronged with
eager listeners: "Prosperous", you say, "very". But is it?'[52]

NOTES

1. James Obelkevich, 'Religion and Rural Society in South Lindsay,
1825–75', unpublished D.Phil, Columbia 1971, pp.432-3, in dealing with the
question of distinctions between 'religion' and churches, asserts that 'not only
is every society religious: every individual is too. On this assumption, the
question is not whether an individual is religious, but how he is religious'.
For an interesting plea for not separating church and world see Laurence
Bright OP and Simon Clements, *The Committed Church*, Darton, Longman
& Todd 1966, pp.xii-xvi.
2. V. Lanternari, *The Religions of the Oppressed: a study of modern
messianic cults*, tr. L. Sergie, MacGibbon & Kee 1963, pp.vi, 301. For
discussion of how 'a theory that maintains a continuous and systematic
interest in the *interaction* of religion and society seems to be difficult to
develop', see J. Milton Yinger, *Religion, Society and the Individual*, NY
1957, pp.59-60. For a historian who operates with a sensitive notion of that
interaction see J. F. C. Harrison, *Learning and Living: a study in the history
of the English Adult Education movement*, Routledge 1961, pp.155, 172;
see also H. P. Douglass, *How to Study the City Church*, Doubleday 1928,
and H. P. Douglass and E. deS. Brunner, *The Protestant Church as a Social
Institution*, Harper & Row 1935.
3. G. Kitson Clark, *The English Inheritance: an historical essay*, Macmillan 1950, p.171.
4. The last two quotations are from Alasdair MacIntyre, 'A Confusion of
Sects', *New Society*, 9 February 1967 and 'Gods and Sociologists', *Encounter*, March 1970.
5. R. H. Tawney, *Equality*, Allen & Unwin 1931; paper ed. 1964, pp.190-1.
6. For an earlier statement on this see William Pickering, 'Religion –
a Leisuretime Pursuit?', *A Sociological Yearbook of Religion in Britain*, ed.
David Martin, SCM Press 1968, pp.77-93. Also Brian Harrison, *Drink and
the Victorians*, Faber 1971 and 'Religion and Recreation in Nineteenth
Century England', in *Past and Present*, 38, 1967; Stuart Mews, 'Puritanicalism, Sport, and Race: a symbolic crusade of 1911', in *Studies in Church
History*, 8, ed. Canon G. J. Cuming and Derek Baker, CUP 1971.
7. Alasdair MacIntyre, 'A Confusion of Sects'.
8. Antonie Gramsci, *Soviets in Italy*, I.W.C. pamphlet series no. II,
p.7. Huntley and Palmer's became a limited liability company in 1898.

There had been some joint action in the biscuit trade as early as 1877 over the Factories Bill. Towards the end of 1902 there were proposals to set up an Association of Biscuit Manufacturers. In 1903 it had 35 members, but Huntley and Palmers were not involved. In 1910 H. and P. again turned down a proposal made by a firm of brokers to amalgamate the various biscuit makers and turn them into a public company. In 1911 there was another proposal for the big five firms to amalgamate along the lines of the Imperial Tobacco Company. It was only after the war that Associated Biscuit Manufacturers came into being, see *Reading Standard*, 24 March 1923 and *The Chronicle*, 23 March 1923. In the 1890s there were a number of indices of de-localization besides the declaration of a limited liability company, such as G. W. Palmer's permanent leaving of his Reading home for his country seat in 1896, or W. H. Palmer's resignation from the Reading Athletic Club in 1898.

9. *Berkshire Chronicle*, 29 May 1897 (YMCA), *Reading Observer*, 13 November 1897, (Football Club), *Reading Observer*, 4 November 1879 (Town Hall).

10. *Reading Observer*, 1 November 1890.

11. George Palmer told members of the Cricket Club at their 'annual tea and social gathering' in 1891 that they 'should not forget that there were other duties besides cricket. He referred to the Schools of Science and Art, which he would very much like to see appreciated to the full by all young men ...'

12. For national concern about participation in sport see W. T. Stead, *The Revival in the West*, London 1905, and Stuart Mews, 'Puritanicalism, Sport, and Race. a symbolic crusade of 1911', in *Studies in Church History*, 8, ed. Canon G. J. Cuming and Derek Baker, CUP 1971, pp.303-31.

13. Some of the recent attacks upon 1950–60s behaviouralist political science, by going back to mid-nineteenth century theorists of democracy for their critiques, have expounded mid-nineteenth century aspirations in terms which help in the understanding of aspirations central to Reading in this period. For example Lane Davis, 'The Cost of Realism. Contemporary Restatements of Democracy', *A-Political Politics; A Critique of Behaviouralism*, ed. Charles A. McCoy and John Playford, Crowell, NY 1967, p.189, 'The immediate objective of classical democracy has always been to extend the opportunity for individuals to take an equal and an effective part in the management of public affairs. Through this opportunity, it was believed, the horizons of the participating individual would be widened, his knowledge extended, his sympathies made less parochial, his practical intelligence developed. Participation in the management of public affairs would serve as a vital means of intellectual, emotional, and moral education leading towards the full development of the capacities of individual human beings. Participation in politics would provide men with opportunities to take part in making significant decisions and to transcend the narrow bounds of their private affairs. It would build and consolidate a sense of genuine community that would serve as a solid foundation for government. It would provide a strenuous and rewarding field of endeavour by extending opportunities for free activity and self-government beyond the frequently petty sphere of private life into the realm of the public domain which had hitherto been largely beyond the control, or the hope of control, of ordinary men. This opportunity for education in public responsibility is the peculiar and distinguishing contribution which classical democracy makes to the ideal of human dignity and development.'

14. Beatrice Webb, *My Apprenticeship*, Longmans 1926, pp.194-5, n.1.

15. *Reading Observer*, 2 April 1892.

16. *Reading Observer*, 4 November 1879, 7 January 1893.

17. *Reading Standard*, 12 October 1912.

18. *The Nature and Progress of the Reading or Ninth Lodge of the Western Philanthropic Institution for the Relief of the Necessitous and Deserving Poor*, Reading 1843.

19. The ideology of organized voluntaryism in the third quarter of the nineteenth century, and the contradictions that ideology got into when it produced unintended results, such as State action or professionalism, has been well expounded in Melvin Richter, *The Politics of Conscience: T. H. Green and his Age*, Weidenfeld & Nicolson 1964, pp.288-95, 324-36, 374-5.

20. K. Marx, *Wage Labour and Capital*, in Marx/Engels, *Selected Works in one Volume*, London 1960, p.74.

21. They are described in Stephen Yeo, 'Religion in Society: a view from a provincial town in the late-nineteenth and early-twentieth centuries', unpublished D.Phil., University of Sussex 1971, ch. VII.

22. The boundaries between politics and other forms of activity were differently drawn in this period, and less firmly drawn than they have become later in the twentieth century; see Elizabeth Isichei, *Victorian Quakers*, OUP 1970, p.xx and John Vincent, *The Formation of the Liberal Party 1857-68*, Constable 1966.

23. For which see Stephen Yeo, op. cit.

24. The name given by Mary Russell Mitford to her semi-fictional description of early-nineteenth century Reading, *Belford Regis*, London 1835.

25. Already in the introduction to the tables in the 1851 census Horace Mann pointed out that buildings were not, or soon would not be, the problem; *Census of Great Britain 1851, Religious Worship, England and Wales, Report and Tables*, London 1853, p.lxi. Inglis's judgment that the explanation of irreligion in mid-century was normally given in terms of lack of facilities, compared to an explanation in terms of social habit by 1880, perhaps needs qualifying; K. S. Inglis, *Churches and the Working Classes in Victorian England*, Routledge 1963, p.165. The whole perspective of Inglis and that of E. R. Wickham, *Church and People in an Industrial City*, Lutterworth Press 1957, in seeking to explain relative failure rather than relative success, may have led to asking less interesting questions.

26. These figures are calculated from the annual Smith's *Directories* for the town. David Hugh McLeod, 'Membership and Influence of the Churches in Metropolitan London, 1885-1914', unpublished Ph.D. thesis, Cambridge 1971, pp.115-16, has an interesting analysis of the influence of particularly effective ministers in London. He suggests that a good minister could increase the congregation in his own church, but only at the expense of surrounding churches. He calls C. F. G. Masterman's judgment in *The Condition of England*, Methuen 1909, p.204, 'only a very slight exaggeration'. 'You may by special effort of preaching, music or excitement, draw a large and active congregation; but you have done so by emptying the churches of your neighbours. The water is not increased in quantity, but merely decanted from bottle to bottle'.

27. Rev. W. B. Bantry talking to St Lawrence Church Institute in 1884, Tesland, *Extracts from the Reading Mercury ...*, vol. 2.

28. Canon Garry, St Mary's Parish, *Annual Report*, 1894-5.

29. Rev. H. Bassett seconded the main resolution at the meeting of the Berkshire Agricultural and General Workers' Union in the town hall in 1893, *Reading Observer*, 15 July 1893. When a local business man offered Prospect Park to the Corporation their first impulse was to refuse to buy

it. There then came into being an 'Open Spaces Society' to get them to change their mind. On the Executive Committee sat three ministers, and at a town's meeting which they organized seven more sat on the platform.

30. *Trinity Congregational Church Magazine*, September 1905, contained a full history of the Alphabetical Society by O. Ridley. As Ridley wrote, 'the usefulness of the society was increased by the helpfulness of many who have since made a name and place in the public and business life of the town'. A sense of the role chapels and their siblings could play in critical moments in the development of an urban elite may be got from E. P. Hennock, 'The Role of Religious Dissent in the Reform of Municipal Government in Birmingham', unpublished PhD. thesis, Cambridge 1956, and from the chapter on Birmingham in Asa Briggs, *Victorian Cities*, Penguin Books 1968. For the kind of men, on a lower level, for whom participation in church/chapel life was often important at a certain stage of their careers see Josephine Butler, to the *Royal Commission on ... the Contagious Diseases Acts* (1871), quoted in Brian Harrison, *Drink and the Victorians*, Faber 1971, p.26. Describing the working-clas hostility to the Contagious Diseases Acts she said (Q. 12,921), 'I should say the temperance men almost always lead in this matter, – abstainers, steady men, and to a great extent members of chapels and churches ... they are the leaders in good social movements, men who have had to do with political reforms in times past ... they may not be the majority, but they are men of the most weight and zeal in their towns ... and they gather round them all the decent men in the place, when they start a movement they get all the rest to follow, and properly so, because they are men of character'. For an interesting but much later judgment in this context on 'the place of religion in community life', see Arthur J. Vidich and Joseph Bensman, *Small Town in a Mass Society: Class, Power and Religion in a Rural Community*, Anchor Books ed., Doubleday 1960, pp.261-2.

31. Hans Toch, *The Social Psychology of Social Movements*, paperback ed., Methuen 1971, p.17.

32. 'What are ... religious organizations but machinery? Now almost every voice in England is accustomed to speak of these things as if they were precious ends in themselves', Matthew Arnold, *Culture and Anarchy*, 1869.

33. W. H. Beveridge, *Voluntary Action*, Macmillan 1948, p.10.

34. Such ideas were expressed, for example, by the Committee of the Park Institute and Chapel in 1909, or at the opening of the West Memorial Institute attached to the Caversham Baptist Free Church in February 1911. 'The church', pleaded the pastor of King's Road Baptist chapel in 1898, 'to fulfil its true aim should be able to take up each child in youth, manhood, business, family, old age, all through its career, and the church should have, in its life, work for and scope for men, women, children and families of all grades of life'; Rev. Forbes Jackson, *The United Magazine*, February 1898.

35. Rev. L. Harman, *The Parish of St Giles in Reading*, Reading 1946, p.89.

36. For religious adaption to the new mass professionally organized sports of the late-nineteenth century, and for 'the possibility of rivalry between the minister and the promoter – two professional organizers of leisure-time activities', see Stuart Mews, 'Puritanicalism, Sport and Race: a symbolic crusade of 1911', in *Studies in Church History*, CUP 1971, p.311, n.2. This is a later version of the rivalry between church and pub, for which Brian Harrison, *Drink and the Victorians*, Faber 1971, is the best source.

37. *Berkshire Chronicle*, 22 July 1905.

38. The order in which a deputation of members of Wycliffe Baptist Chapel, sent off to Burnley to report on a possible pastor, gave their evaluation when they got back to Reading is perhaps indicative of the way insiders saw the whole: 'they remarked that the buildings were not so large as Wycliffe, but the church membership was greater, all the institutions seemed to be in a flourishing condition and the church seemed to be greatly attached to their pastor. Buildings first, then membership, then the penumbra, then congregational relations with the pastor.' Wycliffe Baptist Chapel, *Minute Book*, April 1907.

39. *The United Magazine*, December 1898.

40. *Berkshire Chronicle*, 2 January 1904. Robert S. Lynd and Helen Merrell Lynd, *Middletown: a study in Contemporary American Culture*, Harcourt, Brace & World, NY 1929, ch. xxi, pp.333-6, have an interesting analysis of how, in spite of a process of denominational assimilation over the period 1890–1925 in Middletown, there was none the less a parallel process of in-turning and increasing denominational rivalry over the same period. They attribute this to 'national denominational organization'. Part V of this work, 'Engaging in Religious Practices', pp.315-413, provides a marvellous contextual view of religious organization.

41. Primitive Methodists, Wesleyans, and Baptists all issued debenture shares as a way of raising money as an alternative to raising a mortgage at high interest rates. For example, Anderson Baptists in Earley copied the Primitives in April 1910 by issuing debentures 'upon the deeds of the bank, offering 4 or $4\frac{1}{2}$% ... which was an inducement to anyone with capital which was at present only realizing $2\frac{1}{2}$%'. In this way their ambition was to raise £500 of the estimated cost of the £1,000 chapel before its opening. Such a resort to capitalist investment techniques failed. By opening day the cost of the church had risen to £1,300 and the amount already raised was a mere £259.

42. W. Rauschenbusch, *Christianity and the Social Crisis*, Macmillan, NY 1907, is good on this.

43. A. L. Bowley and A. R. Burnett-Hurst, *Livelihood and Poverty*, London 1915, revealed that in 1912 more than one person in every four of the working class in Reading was living in a state of poverty.

44. *Berkshire Chronicle*, 2 June 1900.

45. The St Giles Church Lads Brigade, for example, felt it necessary to run a band, a football club, and a cricket club, in order to keep the lads together. In other respects they were self-supporting, and felt it very important to be so. Yet in this case they lamented the fact that 'we must ask our friends to assist us if we are to have (those facilities)', *St Giles Parish Magazine*, 1895.

46. For example, 'nothing more is heard of them', complained the Reading Friends in 1904–5 about the almost 100% wastage of members of their successful Band of Hope after they had left it. The Adult Schools were also 'successful' in Reading but the *Triennial Report* of the Friends in 1897 lamented the fact that few accessions to the church were ever made as a result of its work. For this in the Quaker context see also Elizabeth Isichei, *Victorian Quakers*, OUP 1970, p.133.

47. Whitley Hall, *Management Committee Minutes and Executive of M.C. Minutes* (1907–12). Spring Gardens Society, *Leaders' Meeting Minute Book* (1892–1912).

48. *Berkshire Chronicle*, 2 June 1900.

49. Stephen Yeo, op. cit., pp.177-8; James Oblekevich, 'Religion in Rural Society in South Lindsay, 1825–75', unpublished D.Phil., Columbia 1971,

pp.217, 297, 527, 'the most profound social change of the period, the transformation of a *Gemeinschaft* into a society of classes, transformed religion as well'.

50. Stephen Yeo, op. cit., pp.139,172-3.

51. The best example in Reading is from the Wesleyan Twentieth Century Fund expansion. Whitley Hall and Elm Park Hall were 'erected to meet the needs of the population in our Western and Southern suburbs', *Reading Observer*, 1 June 1907. ' They were living in a new age, when conditions were altered, and the Wesleyan church must meet the conditions ... (the Hall) ... stood for a new form of social religion. Large numbers of people turned to these places as some others turned to their homes ...', *Berkshire Chronicle*, 25 June 1904.

52. *The United Magazine*, December 1898.

1 Bibliography of Work in the Sociology of British Religion, 1972 Supplement

Robert W. Coles and Ronald Iphofen

This bibliography is the fourth supplement to a bibliography produced by David Martin in *A Sociology of English Religion*, SCM Press 1967. The focus of the bibliography is, as before, on the contemporary religious situation in Great Britain, to which historical information is added selectively. We would like to thank readers who have co-operated with us in sending in details of their publications in this field, and appeal once again to researchers to send us details of both research in progress and completed research. The format of the bibliography is as before, except for a new section which is added on Religion and the Media.

1. *General Surveys and Comments on Religion and Society*

Absalom, F., 'The Historical Development of the Study of the Sociology of Religion', *Expository Times*, 82, pp.105-9, January 1971

Blum, F., *Ethics of Industrial Man: An Empirical Study of Religious Awareness and the Experience of Society*, Routledge & Kegan Paul 1970

Clark, D. B., 'The Social Sciences and the Work of the Churches: the Sociological Study of the Parish', *Expository Times*, 82, pp.296-300, July 1971

Danielou, J., 'The Church and the Modern World', *Studies*, 60, pp.117-26, Summer 1971

Glasner, P. E., 'Secularization: its Limitations and Usefulness in Sociology', *Expository Times*, 83, pp.18-23, October 1971

Halmos, P., *The Faith of the Counsellors*, New York, Shocken Books, 2nd ed., 1970

Hansford-Miller, F. H., 'Women and Religion', *Contemporary Review*, 218, pp.184-8, April 1971

Harris, C. C., 'Reform in a Normative Organization', *The Sociological Review*, vol. 17, no. 2, pp.167-85, July 1969

Hill, M., *A Sociology of Religion*, Heinemann 1973

Manschreck, C. L., 'Control and Freedom; the Individual and Society', *Encounter*, 32, pp.183-207, Summer 1971

Marino, C., 'Cross-National Comparisons of Catholic-Protestant Creativity Differences', *British Journal of Social and Clinical Psychology*, vol. 10, part 2, pp.132-7, June 1971

Martin, D., 'Sociology of Religion in the 1960s' (bibliographical essay), *Church Quarterly*, 2, pp.234-41, January 1970

Northcott, C., 'A Decade of Change in the Churches', *Contemporary Review*, 218, pp.292-6, June 1971

Pickering, W. S. F., 'The Social Sciences and the Work of the Churches: Who Goes to Church?', *Expository Times*, 82, pp.260-6, June 1971

Robertson, R., 'A Sociological Portrait: Religion', *New Society*, pp.8-10, 6 January 1972

Rodd, C. S., 'Implications of the Sociological Study of Religion', *Expository Times*, 83, pp.68-73, December 1971

Seebohm, F., 'What Church People Could Do', *Frontier*, 14, pp.200-1, November 1971

Shaw, B. W., 'Religion and Conceptual Models of Behaviour', *British Journal of Social and Clinical Psychology*, vol. 9, part 2, pp.320-7, December 1970

Sissons, P. L., 'The Sociological Definition of Religion', *Expository Times*, 82, pp.132-7, February 1971

Timms, N., 'Religion and Social Work: Diocesan Rescue Societies as a Case Example', *New Blackfriars*, 52, pp.123-32, March 1971

Wearing, A. J. and Brown, L. B., 'The Dimensionality of Religion', *British Journal of Social and Clinical Psychology*, vol. 11, part 2, pp.143-8, June 1972

Whitt, H. P. et al, 'Religion, Economic Development and Lethal Aggression', *American Sociological Review*, vol. 37, no. 2, pp.193-201, April 1972

2. Historical Background

Hill, M., 'Religion and Pornography', *Penthouse*, vol. 6, no. 1, April 1971.

Lyon, J., 'Immediate Reactions to Darwin: The English Catholic Press', first review of "*The Origin of the Species*" ', *Church History*, vol. 41, no. 1, pp.78-93, March 1972

Marcham, A. J., 'A Question of Conscience: the Church and the "Conscience Clause" 1860–70', *Journal of Ecclesiastical History*, 22, pp.237-49, July 1971

Scott, Patrick, 'Richard Cope Morgan, Victorian Religious Publishing, and the Pontifex Factor', *Victorian Periodicals Newsletter*, 16, pp.1-14, Summer 1972

3. Community and Parish Studies

Boal, F. W. and Pooke, M. A., *Religious residential segregation and residential decision making in the Belfast urban area*, Department of Geography, Queens University, Belfast 1971

Paul, L., 'Church and Community in Britain', *Community Development Journal*, 7, pp.59-64, January 1972

Ransford, J. (Parish Policy Research Team), *Survey of the Church's Response to Community Needs in the Area of Moulsecoomb, Brighton*, Sussex University 1971

4. Religion and Education

Dunbar, S., 'Comparative Religion in Education', *Religious Studies*, September 1971, pp.259-64.

Goldstein, D., 'Telling Children about God', *Pointer*, 6. pp.8-9, Winter 1970/1

Mathews, H. F., 'Religious Education: the Way Ahead?', *Expository Times*, 83, pp.132-6, February 1972.

Wright, D. and Cox, E., 'Changes in Moral Belief among Sixth-Form Boys and Girls over a Seven-Year Period in Relation to Religious Belief, Age and Sex Difference', *British Journal of Social and Clinical Psychology*, vol. 10, part 4, pp.332-41, November 1971

5. Religion and Politics

Macy, C., 'The religious factor in Ulster', *Humanist*, 87, pp.5-9, January 1972

Smith, A., 'Church and State in the Irish Republic: the Muddled Present', *Humanist*, 87, pp.11-12, January 1972

6. Sects and Specialized Groups

Beckford, J. A., 'A Sociological Study of Jehovah's Witnesses in Britain', Ph.D Thesis, University of Reading 1972

Campbell-Jones, S. A., 'A Report on English Catholic Nuns', Social Science Research Council, 1971

Davies, D. J., 'The Mormons at Merthyr Tydfil', B.Litt. Thesis, Oxford University 1972

Roberts, D. A., 'The Orange Order in Ireland: a Religious Institution?', *British Journal of Sociology*, vol. 23, no. 3, pp.269-82, September 1971

Wilson, G. D. and Lillie, F. J., 'Social Attitudes of Salvationists and Humanists', *British Journal of Social and Clinical Psychology*, vol. 11, part 3, pp.220-4, September 1972

7. Religion and the Media

Armstrong, H. W., 'Editorial', *Tomorrow's World*, Ambassador College Press, St Albans, January 1972

Bailey, K. V., 'The Part played by School Broadcasting in Religious Education in Britain', *The Educational Forum*, vol. XXI, no. 3, March 1957

Beeson, T., *An Eye for an Ear*, SCM Press 1972

Boyle, A., 'Making of a Philosophy; John Reith at Savoy Hill', *Frontier*, 14, pp.9-15, February 1971

Carre, M. H., 'Saturday Theologians: Religious Articles in *The Times*', *Humanist*, 86, pp.86-7, March 1971

Chandler, E. R., 'Religious Broadcasting Marks its 50th Year', *Christianity Today*, 15, pp.48-9, 12 February 1971

Cooper, B. G., 'Religious Broadcasting in Britain, 1922-39', B.Litt. Thesis, Bodleian Library, Oxford 1961

'Religious Radio, 1921–71', *Christianity Today*, 15, pp.5-6, 1 January 1971
'Grubstaking the Gospel', *Christianity Today*, 16, pp.42-3, 8 October 1971
Day-Lewis, S., 'Sabbath Millions', *Daily Telegraph*, 21 June 1971, pp.10-11
Dinwiddie, M., *Religion by Radio*, Allen & Unwin 1968
'Cue God', *The Economist*, 240, p.28, 3 July 1971.
Gale, G., 'God's own Propaganda', *The Spectator*, p.537, 25 October 1969
Grisewood, H. J. G., *Broadcasting and Society: Comments from a Christian Standpoint*, SCM Press 1949
Heppner, S., 'The Margaret Knight Affair Sixteen Years After', *Humanist*, 86, pp.52-3, February 1971
House, F., 'Some Aspects of Christian Broadcasting', *BBC Quarterly*, Summer 1950
ITA, *Religious Programmes on Independent Television*, 1962
ITA, *Religion in Television*, June 1964
Lamb, K. H. L., 'Religious Broadcasting', BBC lunchtime lecture, 1964-5
McKay, R., *Take Care of the Sense: Reflections on Religious Broadcasting*, SCM Press 1964
Pippert, W. G., 'Passover Passed Over', *Christianity Today*, 15, pp.33-4, 23 April 1971
Pippert, W. G., 'Passover Telecast', *Christianity Today*, 15, p.40. 26 March 1971
Reynolds, S., 'The Devil his Due', *The Guardian*, p.6, 1 April 1968
Silvey, R., *Religious Broadcasting and the Public*, BBC Audience Research Department 1955
Spargur, R., 'Can Churches Break the Prime-Time Barrier?', *Christianity Today*, 14, pp.3-4, 16 January 1970
'The Wronged Box? TV and the Moral Consensus', *Times Literary Supplement*, 6 November 1970, p.1299
Timmins, L., *Vision On: Christian Communication Through the Mass Media*, Epworth Press 1965
Welch, J., 'Religion and the Radio', *BBC Quarterly*, October 1940
Wineke, W. R., 'Problems and Prospects of Evangelical Radio', *Christianity Today*, 15, pp.3-5, 1 January, 1971
Wilkins, L., 'Sharing Power: Issues in Communication', *Church and Society*, 60, pp.61-5, January-February 1970
Wynne, M., 'Did Jesus Talk English?', *Times Educational Supplement*, no. 2263, 3 October 1958

9. Research in Progress

Absalom, J., *Anglo-Catholicism: Ideology and Influence*, Research in Progress, M.Phil., London
Ahern, G. M., *A Study of Anthroposophy*, M.Phil., LSE
Carter, D., *Social and Political Influences of Bristol Church 1828–1914*, Department of History, University of Bristol
Currie, R., *A Statistical Survey of Religion in Britain and Ireland*, Wadham College, Oxford
Dowling, W. C., *The Methodist Ministry Since Union*, Thesis research in progress at LSE
Foster, B., *A Study of Patterns of Christian Commitment*, University of Birmingham
Hams, C. G., *Sociology of Religious Organizations, The Diocese of Bangor*, UCW, Swansea

Hillyer, Ruth, *The Parson's Wife*, M.Phil. in progress at LSE

Hinings, C. R., *The Clun Valley Survey*, Research in Progress at University of Birmingham

Hinings, C. R., *The Organization Structure of Churches*, Department of Sociology, University of Birmingham 1970/71

Hull, J. M., *Aspects of Religious Education with Special Reference to the Problems of Worship*, University of Birmingham

Hunter, John, *The Society of Friends in Birmingham 1815–1918*, PhD in progress at Department of General Studies, The Polytechnic, Wolverhampton

Jarvis, P., *Religious Socialization in the Junior School*, M.Soc.Sc., University of Birmingham

Langstom, Paul, *The Determinants of the Pattern of Methodist Voting in the Unity Scheme at Circuit Level*, University of Keele

McCleod, D. H., *Membership and Influences of the Churches in Metropolitan London 1885–1914*, PhD, Cambridge 1971

Patterson, Sheila, *A Study of Migration to England*, Research in progress, Institute of Race Relations

Peel, John, *Hull Family Survey; Re-Study after Five Years*, Department of Social Studies, Teesside Polytechnic

Robinson, T., *The Formation of the Church of England Board of Social Responsibility*, University of Sheffield

Roiser, M., *Measurement of attitudes with special regard to religious attitudes*, PhD, Thesis in progress, Department of Psychology, University of Bristol

Wollaston, B., *Church Arrangements in New Towns*, MA, London (projected)

Wright, D., *Different Personality Types of Religious Believer and Non-Believer*, Department of Psychology, University of Leicester